Mass Media and the politics of change

mass media and the politics of change

Jerry L. Yeric
University of North Texas

F. E. Peacock Publishers, Inc.
Itasca, Illinois

Copyright © 2001

F. E. Peacock Publishers, Inc.

All rights reserved

Printed in the U.S.A.

Library of Congress Catalog Card No. 00 130329
ISBN 0-87581-434-4

10 9 8 7 6 5 4 3 2 1
05 04 03 02 01

Dedicated to Peg

contents

preface

The revolution occurring in the media is drastically *changing* the way Americans live and how they view the world of politics. The public's general interest in the media and politics reached new heights in the late 1960s and early 1970s with the increased role of television in American political life. However, one only needs to examine a standard American government text of this period to find scant attention given to the media. Currently, however, these texts devote entire chapters to the subject. As the nation has become more dependent on a changing mass media for its political cues, and as the media have been transformed through mergers, acquisitions, and new technologies, the need to understand the media and their relationship to government is not only necessary—it is *critical*. The media are the conduits of power in modern American politics. In order to appreciate the relationship between the mass media and politics one must first place this relationship in perspective. This is essential in any study, but it is particularly true in any effort to examine the magnitude of change between the media and politics. Why have the media become the center of political discourse? To comprehend today's mass media and politics, we must first understand the evolution of both the media and the political process and how each affect the other. We have explored these paths and have created new ones for the reader to follow as they seek the answers to the relationship between the media and politics.

The author is deeply indebted to those who pursued the media's role through the years and the insight they have provided, and accepts complete responsibility for the interpretation and presentation of their works. The study of the media is truly an interdisciplinary adventure. Important contributions to the understanding of the media's significance are found in psychology, sociology, journalism, communications, history, and political science. I remain indebted to those who have read and provided important comments and suggestions on the manuscript either in its entirety, or in parts. I wish to express my sincere gratitude to Professor Robert Savage, Department of Political Science at the University of Arkansas, for his thoughtful comments and suggestions, and to Professor C. Richard Hofstetter of the Department of Political Science at San Diego State University, not only for his comments and suggestions on sections but also for his initial work on the media that has been an inspiration to pursue this project. Also I thank my colleagues Dr. Karl Ho and Dr. Austin Kang of the University of North Texas, who provided important technical advice. Finally, I express my gratitude to my students, who continue to raise important questions concerning the media and politics and have made this an enjoyable and rewarding enterprise.

The staff at F.E. Peacock Publishers has been outstanding in its help throughout this project. My association with F.E. Peacock Publishers has been both professional and personal for which I am deeply indebted. Ted Peacock and Dick Welna have maintained their commitment and support, while allowing free rein. Dick Welna has been instrumental to this endeavor and has helped guide it to completion. Both believe strongly in the importance of the political and social sciences in the understanding of events and the world around us. Diane Culhane not only provided invaluable editing and comments, but also persisted in asking important and challenging questions throughout the process. Through Diane's continued probing for answers to the world of politics, I gained insight and a friend. Kim Vander Steen has helped move this project to its completion. This book has been made more enjoyable due to the support of my family and their interest in it—for which I am deeply grateful.

Jerry L. Yeric

CHAPTER 1

The Emerging Role of the Media

The American political landscape is undergoing a profound transformation, and the most important factor in that transformation is the changing role of the mass media. Where once the political parties dispensed their messages through party-owned or -dominated newspapers, today's media are independent and diverse, and the parties now depend upon them. Where once the political parties were the primary source of one's political information, today the media perform that function. Where once the parties provided a philosophical base, today their positions are segmented and frayed, built on sound bites and video bites. And where candidates were once selected by the political parties in "smoke-filled rooms," they now depend on media image-makers to present them to the public.

William J. Crotty and Gary C. Jacobson observed two decades ago, as this transformation was well under way, "Television is the new political God. It has supplanted the political party as the main conduit between the candidate and voter. It is the principal influence on the voter in a campaign and his chief source of information. It is a medium of information that he is most dependent on and the one he trusts most implicitly. However, it is both an expensive and unpredictable master."[1] That observation is still accurate today. What has changed is the media's level of involvement in the political process. The study of the mass media and politics today presents a complex puzzle. Common sense tells us that the media are primary forces in politics, yet scholars have vacillated when it comes to defining the media's role in the world of politics. This book explores this puzzle. We are concerned here with the way the media have altered American politics. The key to solving the puzzle lies not only in examining the media's current roles, but also in noting the transformations that have occurred in the relationship between the media and the political system through the years.

The mass media have been instrumental in our nation's development. We need only reflect on the forging of the Constitution and the subsequent

1

struggles over its ratification to see the prominent role of the media in the formative years of our political system. It was through the newspapers of that day that spirited debates about the evolving document were waged and compromises finally reached.

Today the media are targets of questions concerning their relationship to the behavior of individuals, groups, and society in general. There are those who believe that the media have a virtual grip not only on political life but also on society as a whole, and dictate the course of the nation. Others, while not dismissing the media's importance, are less willing to accept the premise that the media control the political process and society. Instead, they argue that individuals' psychological predispositions refine, change, and even block the media's intended message. Between these two extremes are many more nuanced views regarding the media and their role in American politics. The connection between the media and the political process in America is the focus of this book.

Those attempting to better understand the social, political, historical, and economic systems of a nation often focus on change. This concept is particularly useful in the examination of the relationship that exists between politics and the mass media. As Wibur Schramm and William E. Porter have observed:

> The media have been involved in every significant social change since they came into existence—intellectual revolutions; industrial revolutions; and revolutions of tastes, aspirations and values. They have taught us a basic process: Because humans are above all information-processing animals, a major change in the state of information, a major involvement of communication, always accompanies any major social change.[2]

This nation's history is filled with events that demonstrate this close connection. However, it has not been until recently that the changing role of the media received as much attention from scholars and pundits as more recognizable events. Powerful events that altered the course of the nation and changed the very fabric of society have included the Revolutionary War, the Civil War, World Wars I and II, the Great Depression, the Korean and Vietnam Wars, and the civil rights movement. These events were highly visible and easily identifiable and therefore needed less media interpretation. However, other important events have not been so easily identified, and their importance is often underestimated by the public. The development of teletype, the rail system, mass production, automation, and the computer were all transforming events that had enormous impacts on the nation. Most of these developments were not perceived at the time of their introduction as likely to affect the nation as strongly as they ultimately did.

This book is about one such transforming event—political change in the American political process brought about by a confluence of smaller changes that have substantially altered a 200-year-old political system. Clearly our political system has been undergoing continual change, but at no period in history has this change been as rapid or as intense as it is today. At the center of this change have been the mass media.

More specifically, this book is about changes in the relationship between two powerful forces—the political process and the media. In recent years citizens have expressed concern over what they believe to be a new relationship between the two. Numerous authors have described the movement away from traditional political institutions to a greater reliance on the media. Some, like Kevin Phillips, argue that in the post–Industrial Revolution period, effective communication has increasingly replaced political organizations as the key to the political process, an event Phillips calls the "communications revolution." The concept of power is fundamental to an understanding of any political system. If major changes are occurring in political-media relations, then the political system will reflect such changes. The focus of this inquiry is on the changing roles of *both* the media and the political system. The contention is not that the media are the sole cause of all change, for a reading of American history would quickly dispel such a thought, but rather that the relationship between these two worlds has intensified and many of the traditional political functions have been either abandoned by political institutions or usurped by the media. In today's political world candidates must possess characteristics that make them "media" attractive. Questions of issues and substance have been replaced by how well candidates are perceived through the media.

As both Arizona Senator John McCain and former New Jersey Senator Bill Bradley challenged their parties' leading candidates in the 2000 primaries, the media quickly presented the campaigns in terms of how well the candidates were performing in various polls. The defection of Pat Buchanan from the Republican Party was presented in the terms of what it meant to the Republican Party's nominating process and how it would affect the general election. The media's decreasing emphasis on holding candidates accountable has led some journalists to contend that the media have been reduced to serving as bystanders or accomplices in the artful manipulation of politics by professionals hired to handle the candidates and their images.

The increasing influence of one medium—television—has brought about repeated charges of media interference in the political process. Recent presidential elections provide prime examples of television's growing role in the selection and governing process. A candidate who is perceived as "warm" and "charming" and who "comes across the best" on television has an advantage in modern politics. Image has replaced substance. "Personality" has always played a role in politics, but prior to the 1960s candidates were selected primarily by political parties and their supporters. Today candidate selection is more direct, with most candidates being nominated by delegates selected in primaries. As a consequence, the public has become more dependent on the media as its primary source for information and the media increasingly emphasize "style" over substance. For example, in the early stages of the 2000 presidential campaign the media did not cover differences in the positions of Texas Governor George W. Bush and Vice President Al Gore on issues such as abortion rights, environmental policies, patients' rights, and school vouchers.[3] Instead, the media focused on polls that indicated Governor Bush was ahead of the vice president.

It is fashionable to blame the media when the political process falters or fails, and to dismiss them when the process is working smoothly. This view of the relationship serves neither those in the media nor those in the political world. More important, it obscures the real working relationships that have always existed between the two. In the earliest days of the republic, political parties formed around strong personalities and created newspapers that reflected their philosophies and positions. Those early newspapers reached a small, well-educated population and conveyed the positions of the political factions that owned them. Only rarely did opposing positions appear. Today the focus has shifted from a "party-centered" political system to a media-driven, "candidate-centered" system. Candidates no longer need to have a long party affiliation, but need only to claim a party's name. For example, in 1990 David E. Duke, a former Ku Klux Klan leader, became the Republican Party's nominee for the United States Senate in Louisiana as the result of a primary election. In a highly unusual move, the leaders of the national Republican Party disowned Duke, and he was unsuccessful in his bid for the Senate.

To understand the relationship between American political institutions and the media, one can examine it from a variety of perspectives. We have chosen to examine the media's role in fundamental aspects of the political process for two reasons. First, this approach follows a long and easily recognized organization of the study of American politics. Second, those interested in politics invariably ask what role the media play in American politics.

changes in the Relationship Between the media and the political system

A quick reflection on government, its duty and its importance to daily life juxtaposed against how it is presented to the public helps explain the confusion, distrust, and cynicism commonly found in the public. For instance, Congress was designed to reflect society and to represent those in the various parts of the nation. Today if one were to gauge society by "talk shows" and news programs, one would judge it angry and hostile. Anyone who watched Congress in action during the impeachment and trial of President Clinton would have found evidence to confirm that impression. Anger and hostility have become pervasive in American society, including its political life. Following the fifteen deaths at Columbine High School in Littleton, Colorado, there was renewed national concern over hostility in society, ranging from juvenile violence to general safety issues. The media became the focus of a great deal of this attention, with violence in movies, television, music, and computer games the center of attention from both the public and elected officials. A Gallup poll conducted in June 1999 found six out of ten Americans viewed violence in these areas as an extreme or serious problem.[4] In the aftermath of Littleton, President Clinton convened the leaders of the entertainment industries and urged them to reduce the amount of violence they depicted. *The Jerry Springer Show*, for example, toned down its program and Hollywood executives placed greater emphasis on family-oriented material.

The impeachment of President Clinton also provides a view of our political system, the behavior of public officials, and the media's insatiable craving for the sensational, for the dramatic, and for conflict. The American public perceived impeachment very differently from Congress or the media. As the president maintained high job approval ratings, the public disapproved of the House and Senate's manner of handling the issue, urged their senators to vote against removal, and blamed the Republican Party for the impeachment.[5] The media's reporting on the impeachment focused on who was winning and losing, not on the public's reaction.

Why was there such a disconnection between the public, the government, and the media? The answer lies, in part, in change. There are three major transformations that are currently affecting the political process to a degree unprecedented in our history. Changes in the political process itself range from the decline of political parties in the selection process to methods used by candidates to attract votes to voters' methods of ascertaining information important to their decisions. There are changes in the way all information is obtained and controlled. The media have an opportunity to enhance the public's understanding of the world of politics. Finally, there are changes in technology that are closely related to the changes mentioned above.

In this book we shall examine changes in the relationship between the political system and the media, and the impeachment of President Clinton helps illustrate those changes. For instance, people are receiving their information about politics from sources never before thought to be informative or authoritative, such as late night talk shows, MTV, and other forms of media that are either new or not previously associated with the political process. A 1996 Pew Research Center poll found that one quarter of those surveyed claimed they learned about the 1996 presidential campaign from Jay Leno or David Letterman. This figure jumped to 40 percent for individuals 30 years old and under. Another 15 percent claimed MTV was a source of campaign information.[6] Aside from the lack of substance these programs provide viewers, they demonstrate a high degree of irreverence toward both candidates and the positions they seek. According to the Center for Media Studies, Jay Leno, David Letterman, Bill Maher, and Conan O'Brien told 1,712 jokes about President Clinton in 1998.[7] Those involved in politics are acutely aware of the power of such programs. Paul Begala, a former White

House aide, was frequently asked to appear on the Don Imus radio talk show. Imus regularly skewers President Clinton on his show, but Begala said, "I get more feedback from being on Imus than from any other media appearance—'Crossfire', 'Meet the Press', 'Nightline', 'Today'."[8] This trend toward merchandising politics as entertainment has been steadily growing over the past two decades. Mergers, competition, and the reduction of resources for news have all accelerated the trend. The entertainment culture became part of presidential campaign politics in 1992, when candidate Clinton played his sax for Arsenio Hall, schmoozed with Larry King, and chatted with students on MTV. Since then, programs like Larry King have become common vehicles for individuals announcing their intention to seek public office, not the party organization or the press conference.

Assessing the changes

In Chapter 2 we explore the rich and colorful history of the mass media in American politics. Understanding how the media have evolved, from the writing of the Constitution to the current media merger frenzy, provides an important base for evaluating changes in the media and the political system. To understand today's relationship between the political system and the mass media, as well as to dismiss some myths concerning the media, we need a clear understanding of the past, and Chapter 2 serves this function. Chapter 3 addresses the issue of the mass media's link with democracy. If democracy is to operate effectively, citizens must have information, and the media's presentation of politics and society is critical. The evolution of the media from dependence on political factions for their economic survival to political parties' and candidates' dependence on the media for their survival is in itself one of the more significant transitions in the American political landscape. How individuals obtain their information and the media's social, psychological, and physiological effects on them are explored here.

Chapter 4 focuses on the ways scholars have attempted to measure the media's impact on individuals and the political system. All studies of the media have an explicit or implicit approach to how the media operate. During the initial years of radio it was widely believed that radio programs directly influenced listeners, and this assumption affected how scholars approached the study of the media. It was reinforced by the impact of the October 30, 1938, broadcast of H.G. Wells's *The War of the Worlds*. Although the script of the broadcast mimicked the format of radio news of the time, the announcer, Orson Welles, clearly stated at the beginning of the performance that the program was fiction. The subsequent program consisted of dance music from a New York hotel interrupted by ever-more-frequent, ever-more-devastating news bulletins about explosions on Mars, a space vehicle landing in New Jersey, and ensuing death and destruction. The resulting panic was reported in papers across the country. The broadcast disrupted households, interrupted religious services, created traffic jams, and clogged communication systems. Hadley Cantril's *The Invasion from Mars*, a classic in mass communication research, was based on work by a group of researchers at Princeton University organized to assess the influence of radio on listeners in the United States.[9] It is essential that those interested in understanding the media are aware of these early studies and the assumptions on which they rest, as well as obstacles to measuring the media's influence on individuals and institutions.

Chapter 5 examines the freedoms of and regulations on the media. Media regulations are rooted in the political process, and directly affect the media's freedoms. The growth of television and the Internet have produced increasing strains on the relationship between freedom of expression and society's right to protect its members from unwanted and harmful intrusions. The tensions between freedom and regulation have always existed, and many disputes end in the courts. For example, the Rev. Jerry Falwell sued *Hustler* magazine publisher Larry Flynt in a highly publicized case for libel and invasion of privacy and a separate but related claim—infliction of emotional distress. The case was precipitated by the inside cover of the November 1983 issue of *Hustler*, which was a crude parody of a Campari Liqueur ad with the headline "Jerry Falwell talks about his first time." At the bottom, in small type, was a disclaimer: "Ad parody—not to be taken seriously." The case eventually was heard by the Supreme Court. In its decision, written by Chief Justice Rehnquist, the Court denied Falwell his claim, stating, "[I]n the world of debate about public affairs, many things done with motives that are less than admirable are protected by the First Amendment."[10] The Court declared that even "outrageous" satire can be deserving of protection.

Chapter 6 explores the backgrounds of those who present information to the public. Do their demographic characteristics and political orientations reflect society as a whole? Is there a bias in the news? And what impact do the media elite—owners and corporations—have on what is presented?

Chapters 1 through 6 focus on the media. Subsequent chapters address the consequences of the media's role in political change. Beginning with Chapter 7, the effect of the media on political behavior is investigated. The increasing importance of media ads and their cost to the political process both financially and socially are examined. The strong connection between campaign funding and the media, particular television, has become an increasing public concern. Efforts to restrict contributions have failed. For example, during the first six months of 1999, eight months before the first primary in New Hampshire, Governor Bush had raised a record $36.5 million, Vice President Gore, $18.5 million, and Gore's only opponent at the time, former Senator Bill Bradley, $11.5 million. Campaign funds have been increasingly used for media ads, with over 60 percent of 1996 presidential campaign expenditures going to this purpose.

Candidates flood key states, regions, and populations with media ads in an effort to win support.

The changing role of the political campaign as a result of the modern media is then explored. The impact of political talk radio in the elections of the 1990s and the ways the media now cover campaigns are addressed. Finally, the media's increased reliance on public opinion to create and report on political events is examined. The increased use of polls initiated by the media and the subsequent reporting of their findings raise many questions about the depth of political reporting. Surveys indicate that 60 percent of news media professionals believe polls are right most of the time, with a majority indicating polls have a positive impact on society.[11]

There is an increasing gap between those making executive business decisions and those in the newsroom. While there are many dimensions to this gap, the most significant involves each group's perception of the world. Some of the gap is accounted for by differences in gender, race, age, and income, but there are also differences in political orientation. Political reporters generally have a different political orientation than those who own the media.

Chapters 8 through 10 address the relationship between the media and the institutions of our national government. Chapter 8 focuses on the presidency and addresses changes in style and coverage as a result of media changes. One effect of the increased role of the media on the presidency is the decreased number of presidential news conferences. Modern presidents have a variety of other media outlets at their disposal, and these allow the presidents to set the agenda. Presidents have at their disposal radio and television talk shows, the Internet, faxes, and e-mail. Congress is the focus of Chapter 9. Here we examine the media's role in changing old "folkways" and in developing new ones. The media, particularly C-SPAN, have altered not only how Congress is reported, but also how candidates are elected and behave as elected officials. Our political system has moved away from "party-centered" politics, where political parties were the keys to success, to a "candidate-oriented" system that places greater emphasis on personality. We also examine how Congress is presented in the media.

The least-known branch of government, the judicial, is examined in Chapter 10 through an analysis of how the media cover the courts and particularly how cameras are used in the courtroom. The media's expanded coverage of court proceedings has increased the public's knowledge of this branch. The creation of Court TV and increased network coverage of highly visible cases have been instrumental in this process. However, by focusing on emotional appeal, the media risk misrepresenting the legal process. In addition, the lines between information and entertainment are often blurred. For example, such popular television shows as *The People's Court, Judge Judy, Judge Joe Brown,* and *Judge Mills Lane* are primarily entertainment programming. In Chapter 11 we investigate the changing role of the media in coverage of the military in the post–Cold War era. As the United State's role in the world has changed, so too has the media's reporting.

The sophisticated consumer

All communications require that those receiving information apply a measure of skepticism, not merely accept the information as flawless. We have seen that the first newspapers were propaganda instruments of political factions and did not attempt to report objectively. As the number and accessibility of media outlets have increased, the issue of objective reporting has become increasingly important. The Internet is a wonderful place to gain a wide and diverse range of information on nearly any subject, but is the information received through cyberspace accurate? And how do we recognize false and inaccurate information? Such questions are not unique to the Internet, but have always concerned those interested in the media's role in society and the political process. Scholars have often demonstrated when bias occurs. However, there is another form of media behavior that has received far less attention—misrepresentation. Misrepresentation can be either deliberate or unintentional. Deliberate misrepresentation occurs when those reporting knowingly deceive those receiving the information. Such misrepresentation is usually obvious. Unintentional misrepresentation requires a sophisticated audience to detect it.

For example, during the early months of the 2000 presidential campaign, members of the media reported that Governor Bush was able to work constructively with Democrats. And indeed many Democrats did support his proposals during the 1999 session of the Texas legislature. What reporters failed to point out was that Texas Democrats are generally conservative, so the difference between Democrats and Republicans in Texas are often miniscule. Indeed, many current Texas Republicans once held office as Democrats. Finally, the governor of Texas is only the third most powerful statewide elected official, so his or her actions are not extensively covered by the media. Subtle yes, but important to an understanding of the complete picture of Texas politics. Another example is the media's reporting on prayer in public schools. Most often it is reported that the Supreme Court is opposed to prayer in schools, but in fact the Court is opposed to *state-sponsored*, vocal prayer or Bible reading.[12]

Summary

In the preceding pages we addressed the question public officials, scholars, and reporters, as well as interested citizens, are increasingly asking—How do the media affect politics? To assess the role of the media, one must first place them into some context, for it is only then that one begins to see and understand their increased role in the American political system. The media and the political system have a long history of mutual dependence. New technologies have historically been closely related to social changes, but never more so than today. The pace and method of information transmission, from the Internet to faxes and e-mail, have altered the balance between the media and political institutions once more. Instantly accessible information has both positive and negative effects. The positive occur when citizens can see their government at work or learn more about important events. The negative side is the flood of information that is increasing reliance on opinion and speculation at the cost of accuracy. Some observers believe that the power has shifted from neutral reporters to sources whose agendas are well hidden.[13] Now more than ever consumers need to be sophisticated in their consumption of information, for if they are not, the nature of democracy will be profoundly altered.

endnotes

[1] William J. Crotty and Gary C. Jacobson, *American Parties in Decline* (Boston: Little, Brown and Company, 1980), 68.

[2] Wilbur Schramm and William E. Porter, *Men, Women, Messages, and Media* (New York: Harper & Row Publishers, 1982), 15.

[3] Susan Feeney, "On the Same Page," *Dallas Morning News*, June 28, 1999:1.

[4] Gallup Poll, June 11–13, 1999.

[5] *New York Times*/CBS News Poll, January 30–February 1, 1999, *New York Times*, February 3, 1999:1.

[6] Howard Kurtz, "Getting the News from Jokes about the News," *Dallas Morning News*, January 29, 1999:2C.

[7] 1998 Year in Review, *Media Monitor*, 13(January/February 1999):10.

[8] Kurtz, *op. cit.*

[9] Hadley Cantril, *The Invasion from Mars: A Study in the Psychology of Panic* (Princeton, N.J.: Princeton University Press, 1940).

[10] *Hustler Magazine, Inc.* v. *Falwell*, 485 U.S. 46, *Med. L. Rptr.* 2281 (1988).

[11] "The Core Principles of Journalism," *The Pew Research Center for the People & the Press*, March 31, 1991.

[12] *Wallace* v. *Jaffree*, 472 U.S. 38, 105 S. Ct. 2479, 86 L. Ed.2d 29 (1985).

[13] Bill Kovach and Tom Rosenstiel, *Warp Speed* (New York: The Century Foundation Press, 1999).

CHAPTER 2

The Evolution of the Mass Media in America

With few exceptions, social scientists have only recently begun to focus their attention on the media and their role in the political process.[1] This area is currently receiving increased coverage in American government texts, professional journals devoted to the study of the role of the mass media in American politics, public opinion polls, and the media's own attention to the relationship, as evidenced by the growing number of media critics and books written by journalists on the topic. This fascination with the role of the media in the political process is focused in five areas. The first includes the relationship between the media and individuals. Excellent studies exploring the effects of the media on voting, other forms of participation, socialization, nominations, and campaigns abound.[2] The second is the institutional nature of the media. Studies have focused on organization, production and coverage, and manipulation that stem from the institution's context of the period.[3] Questions arise relating to the structure of society and such individual characteristics as educational level, economic situation, and values—*internal factors* that help shape the relationship between the mass media and the political process. *External factors*, such as wars, international tensions, and the general world order, are also important in the relationship. The third area is the balance between the media and political institutions, or the dependence of each on the other.[4] The fourth is the effect of new technologies, particularly the way technological advances have changed the media's coverage of politics, causing a shift in the balance between the two. The final area includes structural changes that have occurred within the institutions themselves. The two greatest are the weakening of political parties and the growth of media conglomerates.

Obviously, these areas are highly interrelated and attempting to unravel them is difficult. However, understanding them can help clarify the five periods of major change in the media's relationship to the political process in America. Indeed, since our nation's inception in 1776, one theme has remained constant in this relationship—change.

This chapter traces the evolution of the media and the political system and the five periods that saw major shifts in the relationship between these two institutions.

The partisan press: 1775–1830

The period between 1775 and 1830 was dominated by the partisan press. While external social forces were the focus of concern during the struggle for independence, after the colonies gained independence from Great Britain attention shifted to governing. Internationally, the new nation was faced with the task of developing relationships with other nations. The struggle for control of the new nation became an important concern for those in positions of political leadership. Their first task was to establish foundations for the nation. To do this, leaders needed to mobilize support for a new political process in a society characterized by no formal rules of governance or tradition, low levels of participation and education, and an absence of mass media.

By the end of the Revolutionary War, political power existed primarily in the form of persuasion, and the press was the primary channel for expression of this power. It is not surprising that the emerging press of this period was highly partisan and highly centralized. The nation's independence had been established, and the power to ensure the government's legitimacy. This new persuasive power was expressed through the press. As Richard Merritt explains, it must be borne in mind that "seventeenth-century American colonies existed in a state of semi-isolation, separated from one another in many cases by stretches of uninhabited wildness and more generally by inadequate systems of intercolonial transportation and communication."[5]

The new press was economically dependent on the political factions of the period. It was through the skillful use of the press that the new nation was able to successfully address key elements in the governing process—power, integration, legitimacy, and unity. The long and tumultuous relationship between the press and political institutions was forged on the anvil of the successful struggle for independence.

The structural changes brought about by the ratification of the Constitution were no less important than the development of conflicting political factions. The conflicts resulted from different philosophical positions honed during the constitutional debates by the strong personalities of those involved. At this time, however, there remained no adequate method of communicating these positions to large segments of the population. Instead, political discourse on the Constitution was restricted to the elite, while most citizens were not engaged.

Printers, who had been held in low esteem before the revolution and had suffered economically, enjoyed a new prestige during the constitutional ratification process. However, this increased prestige was not accompanied by an equal rise in economic status. Papers were unable to survive independently. Consequently, the relationship between the press and politics became symbiotic, offering both members of the media and politicians mutual benefits and seductions.

While the post-revolutionary press made distinct gains in prestige, the two most significant developments during this period were the transformation from a strictly commercial press to one that relied heavily on politics and the increasing and chronic financial weakness of the political press.[6]

An emerging political structure evolved from the rigors of writing and ratifying the Constitution. This process was accomplished in the absence of an established media structure. The press of the period, however, was instrumental in communicating different political messages, mobilizing support for candidates and their ideas, and providing a broad rubric for the emerging partisanship.[7] As Richard Rubin explains, "The press in the early days of the nation became the connection with the mass population, not political parties, or organizations. . . . It was the press that became the focal point for the first mass political parties."[8] The press in the developing nation was more than just a means of free expression—it was the *critical link* in the political process.

One of the government's first concerns was the lack of a "political" newspaper in New York City, the nation's capital. There were a number of commercial papers, but the city was without strong and reliable political newspapers that reflected the two major political factions—the Federalists and the anti-Federalists. A number of Federalists, led by Alexander Hamilton, worked to correct the situation. A Bostonian Federalist named John Fenno was hired in 1787 to edit a new paper called *The Gazette of the United States.* Fenno, a former school teacher, had begun to develop a reputation as a journalist with his heavily partisan Federalist views. Financial support and frequent editorials written by Alexander Hamilton, John Quincy Adams, and other Federalists aided the *Gazette.* Under Fenno, the *Gazette* became the voice of the Federalists. It served as the forum for the debate over the proper role of the president in foreign affairs when Hamilton, writing under the pseudonym "Pacificus," argued that the Constitution entrusted the conduct of foreign relations to the executive branch "subject only to the *exceptions* and *qualifications* which are expressed in the instrument."[9] Madison replied as "Helvidius" that Congress was the policymaking arm of the national government and possessed full authority over foreign affairs except for that *specifically* granted to the president.[10] Thus, while the paper was highly partisan, it facilitated important discussions of current issues and in some cases granted opponents of the Federalists an opportunity to state their positions.

Federalists and their supporters throughout the country used the *Gazette* to help promote the Federalist philosophy. The paper served as an influential means of communicating the official position of the Federalist government. It was so important that when the seat of government was moved to Philadelphia, Fenno and the paper also moved. Yet the paper was in desperate need of financial support because of the high cost of printing and the limited audience. It could not sell enough copies to offset its costs and so Hamilton arranged for official patronage for the *Gazette* through the printing of orders of the national government and its legislation from the Treasury and Senate. These orders, which were called "by authority" because their publication was authorized by the federal government, gave some financial relief to the paper. But even with this economic aid, Fenno and the paper faced imminent insolvency in 1793, a mere four years after publication began. A loan from Hamilton and other Federalists helped sustain the paper. At the same time other Federalists, most notably John Jay and Rufus King, granted a loan to Noah Webster, a respected journalist who had strong Federalist views, to begin publishing the *American Minerva* in New York in December 1793. The paper proved to be a good one for its time, largely due to the writings of Webster himself. The *American Minerva* under Webster's active leadership ceased publication in 1797. During its short life it served an important political function in mobilizing opposition to defeat the Jay Treaty.

As the first Washington administration completed its first year, conflict within the administration was sharpening as the two major antagonists, Hamilton and Jefferson, waged political and personal attacks. Republicans, who supported Jefferson, sensed the impact the Federalists, particularly Hamilton, were having through the *Gazette*. They decided to create a rival paper to counter the writings of the *Gazette* and to express the position of the Republicans. With the aid of Madison, a close friend of Jefferson, the Republicans secured the services of Philip Freneau, a classmate of Madison's at Princeton. Freneau had acquired a reputation in the literary and journalist community for his patriotic verse and satires during the Revolutionary War. These writings had earned him the title of "the poet of the Revolution." To make the offer financially feasible, Jefferson offered Freneau a position as a translator in the State Department. This job required very little time and paid $250 a year. Freneau eventually accepted the offer, moved to the capital, and founded the *National Gazette*, a semiweekly, in October 1791.

Now each faction had a political leader and a means to communicate its positions and attack those of its opponents. As Frank Mott notes, "Freneau, who perceived himself as a crusader against the Federalist domination, stridently attacked Hamilton, Adams and eventually Washington. These attacks helped to polarize groupings and organize conflict among the nation's top leadership and to an increasingly attentive public."[11] Mott argues that Freneau, more than anyone else, through his wit and sense of adventure as editor of the *National Gazette*, in two years made American political journalism "a kind of Donnybrook Fair of broken heads and skinned knuckles."[12]

The impact of the rival newspapers on the political process was threefold. It widened the breach between Hamilton and Jefferson, it helped mobilize the

Republican Party into an effective opposition party, and it aided in the dissolution of the Federalist Party. Jefferson wrote in 1793 that the *Gazette* "has saved our Constitution which was galloping fast into monarchy and has been checked by no one means so powerful as by the paper."[13] While the *National Gazette* under Freneau's direction had a profound impact on the political environment, it discontinued operations after two years. While there were a number of causes that contributed to the paper's death, such as Jefferson's leaving the cabinet, the primary cause was the same as that of its chief rival—finances. Political newspapers lacked the circulation or advertising to be financially successful. Another paper that advocated the Republican positions was the *General Advertiser,* known more widely as the *Aurora.* Its editor was Benjamin Franklin's grandson, Benjamin Franklin Bache, but it too was short-lived, lasting from only 1793 to 1798.

Two distinct views of the press had emerged by the end of the 18th century. The Federalist majority in Congress perceived newspapers as instruments of potential social unrest and civil strife, while the Republican minority viewed them as powerful weapons against the incumbent majority. By the 1780s the interdependence of political interests and the press was clearly established, and for the next three decades the newspapers remained highly partisan and were frequently run not by journalists but by politicians. This period has been referred to as the "Dark Ages" of journalism.[14] Mott calls it a time when "few papers were ably edited; they reflected the crassness of the American society of the time. Scurrility, assaults, corruption, blatancy were common place. Journalism had grown too fast."[15]

Nonetheless, this also was a time of enormous growth in American journalism. The early press occupied a unique position by the end of the first decade of the 19th century. Both government officials and citizens regarded papers as potentially powerful, even though they remained economically weak and dependent on parties or government for subsidies of one kind or another. The independent spirit that swept across the nation was also found among the early editors. While press freedom was acknowledged as important, press independence was not. The papers were free to cover a wide range of topics, unlike their English counterparts, but they lacked the economic means to do so. The editors were politicians first and editors second.[16]

Beginning in 1800, the *National Intelligencer* developed national influence, served a succession of Republican presidents, and reported on congressional debates. Congress rewarded its editors, Joseph Bales and William Seaton, by appointing them the official printers of the Senate and House. During this same period a major technological advance occurred that affected the press. The Napier printing press, the first steam-driven cylinder press, was imported from England. The *New York Daily Advertiser* began to use this new technology in 1825. This new method of printing would be particularly important in the next period.

The initial relationship between the media and political interests was one of enormous political and social change. During this time a new nation was born, political cleavages emerged, and a relationship between the press and political institutions began to develop. In the next period the press's reliance on political patronage began to wane rapidly as the press moved toward independence.

media Development: 1830–1890

The period following the establishment of the new nation brought major changes in the relationship between the media and political institutions. Socially the nation was growing, and accompanying this growth were major internal forces, including an expanding middle class and the continued struggle over the proper role of government. The Civil War and its aftermath were the most significant events of the period.

The period began with a highly partisan press that focused on a small segment of the population. As described earlier, the press had helped mobilize mass support for the emerging political parties, thus increasing national unity. With the aid of politicians, the press had been transformed from a commercial institution to a highly political one. The cost of this transformation was threefold. First, the press had become dependent on politicians and government for its economic survival. Without government contracts and loans from political groups, papers could not have survived. Second, the journalistic quality of the early papers had been subordinated to political goals. Finally, politicians had become dependent upon the press for channeling their messages to the public. A mutual dependence had been established, but its form and character would undergo profound change in the next period.

The dependent relationship between politicians and the press that characterized the early period was inextricably altered on September 3, 1833, with the publication of nation's first "penny press," the *New York Sun*. In the 1830s the newspapers began to reflect "not the affairs of an elite in a small trading society, but the activities of an increasingly varied, urban, and middle-class society of trade, transportation, and manufacturing."[17] More important, the penny press perceived ordinary events as news, while earlier papers had focused on political debate and dialogue.

This new orientation of the press was based on economics. Lowering the price of the newspaper from six cents to a penny and selling single copies instead of subscriptions altered the economics of publishing a newspaper. In addition, these papers developed social sources of news and did not depend on political sources. To have mass appeal, the penny press concentrated on timely, familiar subject matter and frequently treated politics indifferently, if at all.

By 1835 there were three penny press newspapers in New York with a combined circulation of 44,000. The newspapers sought advertising of all varieties. Commercial and professional advertisements increased, but most controversial was the expansion of medical advertisements. The traditional dailies attacked the penny press as lacking moral judgment in accepting such ads without question. In 1841, for example, the *New York Sun* and the *New York Herald* were singled out for running advertisements for a leading abortionist in New York City, Madame Restell.[18] But the penny press took a laissez-faire approach to advertisements, for they provided a major source of revenue that, in turn, granted political independence.

The penny press also invented the modern concept of news. The papers regularly printed foreign as well as national and local news. Court reports and police records were part of the news content, and the coverage of politics dramatically changed. Instead of the highly partisan statements common in the earlier period, the penny press reported on presidential addresses, trials, and other government actions without partisan commentary. The press had become independent of politics in both economics and content. Horace Greeley, in establishing the *New York Tribune* in 1841, claimed to be founding a "journal removed . . . from servile partisanship on the one hand and from gagged mincing neutrality on the other."[19]

In the 1840s and 1850s American journalism continued the penny press tradition. The *Boston Herald* in 1847 attempted to bring balance and independence to its political coverage by hiring George Tyler, a Whig, as its morning editor and William Easton, a Democrat, as its afternoon editor.[20] While this arrangement did not last, it illustrates the attempts to establish independence. In 1856 President Buchanan discontinued the use of a Washington paper for a personal and party organ. Four years later the Government Printing Office was established, ending the practice of patronage through printing government work "by authority," a critical tool of the partisan press. It should be remembered that shortly before the end of the 18th century a public information act had been passed that required the secretary of state to select one newspaper in each state to publish federal laws. However, if a state did not have a single paper capable of statewide distribution, the secretary of state, *at his discretion*, could choose up to three newspapers in each state to publish new federal legislation. Since the papers were printing the material by the authority granted them by the national government, this designation was an important source of income, prestige, and patronage. Papers that were viewed as important in Jefferson's presidential campaign received valuable contracts. Secretary of State James Madison used his power to build the foundation for a national political party. This government support received less attention after the Madison administration. The practice of awarding papers special permission to print government material and paying them was a de facto nationalization of a political information network between local and national politicians.

The Civil War intensified the need for accurate information, but it did not change the basic nature of the press. While circulation was increased through extra editions and the number of reporters increased, the competition among papers continued, as did their independence from political control. By this time an identifiable press corps had settled in Washington. It included a colorful group of talented, opinionated, self-styled "bohemians," and numbered in its ranks were crusaders, lobbyists, politicos, and novelists. Reporters were almost all white, male, middle class, and college educated. A Washington "newspapers row" developed where papers alternately competed and collaborated with one another.[21] The *New York Herald* had as many as forty reporters covering the war. Newspapers accepted military censorship and sometimes even paid their reporters by the word for news about the war.[22] The war changed the newspapers' view of society. Prior to the war most liberal views, such as those promoting temperance, public education, free soil, and universal suffrage, were freely expressed in the press, but these were among the first casualties of the war.

Important social and technological changes were occurring at the same time. Technological developments that directly affected the press included the cylinder press in 1814, the stream-driven press in 1825, the telegraph in 1844, paper derived from pulp rather than rags in 1886, and Marconi's wireless in 1896. While each had an impact, the telegraph produced the most profound changes in reporting. It provided a means for newspapers to transmit stories to rural America. As the railroads expanded, the miles of telegraph lines increased fourfold in the last decade of the 19th century, and newspapers found new markets for their products. The Associated Press of New York was established in 1848 and expanded in the 1880s. The association found it could sell its news to local areas, thus providing a service that was both practical and economical for it, as well as for the papers that bought the service over the telegraph. To win and maintain customers, the wire service needed stories that were politically neutral, for they were disseminated to all parts of the nation.

Increased literacy was another factor that created demand for news. The audience for newspapers expanded with the introduction of public education in 1830 and increased literacy. While it is difficult to directly relate the newspaper sales to the growth in literacy, there was obviously a connection.

Finally, some maintain that the evolution of the press was a natural process. Walter Lippmann argued that all nations' presses pass through four stages of development. The first is a monopoly controlled by the government. The second is a press controlled by political parties. In the third stage political dominance is replaced by commercial interests. The final stage occurs when working for the press develops into a profession.[23]

Regardless of the reasons, the American press underwent significant changes during this period. It was increasingly bipartisan,[24] decentralized, and corporate in structure. The struggle had shifted from representing particular political positions to competing for readers.

Several factors changed the nature of the press during this period. Economic support for newspapers increased through larger circulation and more advertisers. Distribution came to rely on street sales, rather than subscriptions. The news was redefined, and newspapers moved toward aggressive street reporting, with reporters assigned to such beats as crime, finance, sports, religion, and foreign affairs. Competition forced newspapers to collect and report news swiftly. Finally, such figures as Stephen Crane, Frank Norris, Dorothy Dix, and Mark Twain achieved prominence through their writings.

The combination of social and technological developments moved the press away from partisan politics and toward a more corporate structure. In the process, the power of political parties and the media was enhanced. Political machines replaced the media as the critical factor in mobilizing political support, and the media redirected their attentions from politics toward entertainment and sensationalism. As the media consolidated their economic base, this stage was completed.

The uneasy Alliance: 1890–1930

Several major social forces had an indelible impact on the American landscape in the late 19th and early 20th centuries. First was the change from an agrarian to an industrial nation. This was accompanied by a major shift in residential patterns, as the population became increasingly urban. The many ramifications of these changes have been well documented. External forces were influential during this period as well. World War I and the changing role of the United States both in the war itself and in the postwar years placed new demands on the political system.

The press was also changing. By the 1880s the penny press had made advertising an accepted part of newspaper publishing. About the same time journalists became organized and recognized as professionals, and in 1883 they established their own professional journal, *The Journalist*. But the most dramatic change was the press's association with the "Age of Reform." Between 1890 and 1915, the news was redefined. Journalists, like other professionals of the period, became obsessed with "facts" as part of their more general interest in the "scientific method." Society became the journalist's laboratory, and "scientific observation" of reality was the goal of a new generation of reporters. Many journalists had formal training in the sciences, including Lincoln Steffens, a reporter for the *Evening Post* who had done graduate work in Wilhelm Wundt's famous psychology laboratory, and Ray Stannard Baker, who had taken special interest in science courses at Michigan State Agricultural College. Other influences on the reporters of this period came from the works of Herbert Spencer (1820–1903), Charles Darwin (1809–1882), John Tyndall (1820–1893), and Aldous Huxley (1894–1963).

While the scientific orientation was central to these reporters' approach to writing, it was the social conditions that provided the substance. The reform period produced journalists who believed in a "scientific method" of reporting the facts, as the facts were what people wanted. The period produced an uneasy alliance between two groups that believed "facts" could reveal the truth—journalists and urban reformers. Paul Nord believes they "saw themselves, in part, as scientists uncovering the economic and political facts of individual life more boldly, more clearly, and more realistically than anyone had done before."[25] The reformers were caught in a paradoxical situation—they feared journalists yet needed their support. Reformers "feared the power of the irresponsible 'yellow press' to beguile the masses with fakes, libels, and sensationalism. Yet they believed in democracy, they trusted public opinion, and clamored for facts, and more facts."[26] The *St. Louis Post-Dispatch* summed up the attitude of the press when it noted in 1893, "The influence of the newspaper on public opinion is measured by the information it inputs to men capable of doing their own thinking."[27] The reformers recognized that newspapers could have different kinds of influence. They could persuade or fool through argument or bombast, or they could more subtly shape their readers' whole frame of reference by providing them with material—facts and perspectives with which they could eventually shape their own "social reality."[28]

Thus, while reformers were skeptical of the press, they also perceived it as a means to influence the public. The press could mobilize groups, channel information, and increase conflict over public goals, all of which were vital to the reformers' objectives of urban reform. In *The Semi-Sovereign People*, E.E. Schattschneider argued that "all forms of political organization have a bias in favor of the exploitation of some kinds of conflict and the suppression of others because organization is the mobilization of bias. Some issues are organized into politics while others are organized out."[29] The reformers wanted to use the press to mobilize the mass public into an active voice for social, political, and economic change, and they perceived the press as a means of reshaping the power alignments in urban America. Reformers and reporters were linked by a common approach and the belief that the masses could distinguish right from wrong and act for change *if* given the facts.

By the turn of the century the press was performing a function comparable to a century earlier—mobilizing public support for certain positions. The difference was that this time it was free from partisan political direction. Magazines also appealed to the masses during these years, as they too turned their attention away from elite readership to mass appeal. Magazine journalists dramatized the need for reform by writing exposés of what was unsavory in business, government, and daily life. While this change began in the late 1890s with the *Harper's Weekly* crusade against the Tweed ring, it was not until the turn of the century that the muckrakers launched broad mass appeals. The leading magazine of the time, *McClure's*, published Ida Tarbell's famous series on Standard Oil. *McClure's* sent Lincoln Steffens to focus on municipal government, and the result was a series of articles on municipal corruption. Ray Stannard Baker contributed articles belaboring unions for wrongdoing during a coal strike. The peak of the muckraker era was 1906, when ten muckraking journals had a combined circulation of nearly 3 million. In addition, books such as Jacob Riis's *How the Other Half Lives* and Upton Sinclair's *The Jungle* were widely read.

Although the alliance between reformers and reporters was an uneasy one, it helped achieve many municipal reforms. Unlike the press in the early days of the republic, this press was a watchdog of government and led to direct changes in the relationship between government and the citizenry in some cities. Reformers and reporters believed grassroots democracy and home rule were crucial to municipal reform, and they also believed that "facts" would overcome corruption and lead to good government.

The emergence of magazines as important channels of information to the upper and middle classes was also established. At the turn of the century six popular magazines—*McClure's, Cosmopolitan, Munsey's, Ladies' Home Journal, Collier's,* and the *Saturday Evening Post*—had circulations running into the hundreds of thousands. Their political significance lay in the fact that they joined the crusade against big business and corruption and on behalf of social justice. Many of the magazine writers were also newspaper journalists who frequently wrote stories for both. Over time, the magazines not only became affordable to larger segments of the population, but also became forums for the discussion of many political and social issues of the day.

The Electronic Era: 1920–1980

The 20th century brought about a profound transformation in the relationship between the media and the political system. President Theodore Roosevelt's activist approach to the presidency extended to his relations with the media. Roosevelt viewed the presidency as a "bully pulpit" that could be used to gain support from the public and to influence others in government. He sought and gained access to the press of the early 20th century to forge a more personal relationship with the American public. He is believed to have held the first presidential press conference.

Within a few years the president's ability to use the press changed dramatically with the advent of radio. Radio changed the style and altered the substance of American politics. It represented a major departure in the relationship between the media and politicians. As described above, the print media by the 20th century were independent, decentralized, and fiercely competitive. However, in November 1920 the print media lost their monopoly on mass communications. The new medium, radio, entered the political arena when station KDKA in Pittsburgh broadcast the presidential election returns. While KDKA was one of only a handful of stations in 1920, this event signaled the beginning of a new generation in mass communications.

The public's rapid acceptance of this medium was illustrated by two factors. Within two years the demand for radios had exceeded the availability and the number of radio stations had grown from a dozen to nearly

600.[30] The formative years of radio, 1920 to 1926, were marked by all the virtues and defects of a new enterprise. A rush to develop the new market brought with it rapid expansion, ingenious improvisation, and reckless and frequently unscrupulous competition in which the interests of the public were often subordinated to personal gain.[31]

The new medium struggled to establish itself in terms of regulation and financing. As with the early press, radio's financial base was uncertain. None of its pioneers foresaw broadcasting's becoming solvent, let alone profitable, and as a result they perceived the medium in terms of public service, not private enterprise. On reflection, this seems incredible, given the fact that newspapers were setting circulation records. Yet David Sarnoff, who put together the first network of radio stations (NBC) in 1926, conceived of the network as a nonprofit enterprise, a corporation without earning power, financed by annual contributions.[32] A year later a second network, CBS, was formed, and radio was well on its way to altering the social and political life of America.

Warren G. Harding was the first president to use the radio, but it was Calvin Coolidge who became its first effective communicator. The conservative Coolidge used radio to build public support for his administration.[33] While the Republicans made a successful transition to the new medium, the Democrats' initial venture was a disaster. In 1924 the Democrats broadcast their presidential nominating convention, where delegates were deeply divided over personalities (Al Smith and William McAdoo) and issues, including the Ku Klux Klan. The public's reaction to the Democratic convention was not positive. Because of deep divisions, 103 ballots were needed to select a nominee. A casualty of the broadcast medium was one of the most famous stump speakers in American history, William Jennings Bryan, for he came across poorly on the new medium. At the same time radio was credited with giving a boost to a new orator— Franklin D. Roosevelt.

After seven years of failure to govern itself, the broadcast industry *requested* the government to regulate its stations, licensing, and frequencies. This resulted in the passage of the 1927 Radio Act, which established the Federal Radio Commission (FRC). By 1932 the radio had become a major political force not only at the national level, but also in many states. Congress passed the Federal Communications Act in 1934 to refine the role of the FRC. Among other changes, the new act established a new commission, increased its size from five to seven members, stipulated that chairmen had to be appointed by the president, and broadened the scope of the commission to include the telephone and telegraph. By 1948 radio had developed into a significant form of political communication.

Although radio remains an important medium in politics, it had a major impact on politics for only a short time, essentially one generation of voters. During its short dominance, radio was responsible for fostering the growth of government broadcast regulation, as well as for altering the nature of successful political personalities and changing methods of campaigning. It grew from a medium opposed to advertisements to one that was heavily dependent on advertising. One national political figure is clearly identified with radio—Franklin D. Roosevelt. Both his personality and the circumstances of the Depression and World War II contributed to his close association with radio. Roosevelt perceived the press as hostile and disdained columnists as a whole. He used radio to bypass the traditional media, to present his personality and his programs to his constituents during a period of profound social and economic turbulence.

During the period of radio's growth, newspapers found increased competition from magazines and both newspapers and magazines had to compete with radio. Thus, what began as an uneasy alliance between political forces and the media ended with different segments of the media competing with each other.

Profound social and political changes marked this era. The nation began the period in the midst of the Great Depression. New political alliances formed that would endure for decades. The dominance of the Democratic Party, under the leadership of Franklin D. Roosevelt, was a political force that was not seen again at the national level until the 1950s. Powerful international developments included World War II, the Korean and Vietnam Wars, and the growing power of the Soviet Union. World War II had an impact on the balance between political institutions and the media, for the media were vital in communicating news events and mobilizing support for the Roosevelt administration's domestic and foreign policies. Roosevelt, a popular president with excellent radio communication skills, used the radio to perfection.

Also during these years the information sector of society came to employ more people than any other.[34] The industrial sector was most dominant during the 1940s and 1950s, and then began to be superseded by the information and service sectors in the 1960s. The political structure that had served the country well for over one hundred years was also undergoing change. Direct primaries, increased suffrage, the new rules of politics, and aging political organizations all helped weaken the once powerful political parties. Competition among the media also strained that sector. The number of daily newspapers declined and readership decreased, while television viewership increased for a time.

The development of television paralleled that of radio. The first long-distance telecast occurred in 1927, and a year later New York Governor Alfred Smith accepted his party's nomination facing television cameras on the steps of the state capitol in Albany. The audience was very limited but the technology developed rapidly. In 1940 the Republican Party telecast its national convention to an audience estimated at 40,000 to 100,000 people in Philadelphia and New York. With World War II came the need to focus on radio technology more than television because of its direct application to sonar and radar, which were critical in World War II, and it was not until after the war that television was pursued with the intensity of the prewar years.

In 1948 the Federal Communications Commission (FCC) authorized the construction of 160 television stations but also froze construction at this level until 1952, the same year television created its first political personalities. Tennessee Democratic Senator Estes Kefauver, chairman of the Senate Crime Investigation Committee, used television to promote himself and his committee by broadcasting the committee's hearings from New Orleans. The telecast was not the senator's idea, but that of station WDSU. The station's attempt to increase viewership represented an early example of the impact of commercial considerations on television programming. The televised hearings made Kefauver a common household name.

Another early television political figure was Wisconsin's Republican Senator Joseph McCarthy, whose Committee on Un-American Activities gained notoriety in the early 1950s. McCarthy's unsubstantiated, televised attacks on individuals who appeared before his committee brought him recognition as well. However, neither senator was able to translate their new fame into long-term political gain. Kefauver failed to capture his party's presidential nomination in 1952 or 1956, and the Senate eventually censored McCarthy for his behavior.

By the 1960s television was changing the relationship between the media and political institutions. From 1947 to 1960 the number of homes with televisions jumped from 1 percent to 87 percent.[35] Another transformation in American politics was once again occurring, but this time at an unprecedented pace. Where it had taken newspapers nearly a century before their full political significance was felt, radio had reached its peak influence in thirty years and television in less than fifteen. Where newspapers were once the primary form of mass persuasion, now there were many. Where legitimacy was firmly grounded once established, and where once the media depended on the political system for their survival, the political system was now again dependent on the media. The relationship between the media and political forces had come full circle.

The corporate media: 1980 to the present

The most important ownership feature of American media is that they are controlled by the private sector. Unlike in other nations, there are no government-sponsored and -operated media in the United States. The tradition of private ownership stems in part from the view that diverse and independent media provide a safeguard in a democracy. Through the years ownership patterns have ranged from individuals to large corporations. Today media owners include business, labor, religious, and ethnic groups, and this diversity arguably promotes variety in programming and support for a wide range of public policies. But the patterns of media ownership today also jeopardize the free flow of ideas.

There has been a growing trend toward mergers in the communications industry, especially over the past two decades. In 1998 there were 427 mergers in the communication and broadcasting industries, and the collective value of the resulting corporations was $226.8 billion.[36] This figure is one fourth the total value of the top ten mergers in 1998. There are three primary forces driving these mergers. First, once two companies merge, others feel pressure to follow to compete. Second, the media represent one of the fastest-growing sectors in the economy. One way to keep pace with economic growth is to merge with other companies and increase market size. Finally, there has been a steady deregulation of the media. Other corporate mergers may lead to increased market power, oligopolistic pricing, and restrictive trade practices, but media mergers can change a country's values, ideas, and politics, perhaps even character.

Potentially the most significant, the proposed merger between America on Line (AOL) and Time Warner, provides irrefutable evidence that the line between the "old media" and the "new media" no longer exists. This merger signals the rapidly changing nature of the mass media and American politics. The joining of the nation's oldest newsmagazine, *Time* (1923), with the contemporary Internet provider AOL (1985) will drastically change the political communication process and the way people receive information. It will force those who believe that the Internet is the last frontier of media competition to rethink their position. Furthermore, the wide variety of entertainment programming that will be available may make it more difficult to interest the public in political and public policy news. Finally, the merger will make it increasingly difficult for the consumer to distinguish between news reporting and entertainment.

There are four primary patterns of media ownership today: independent, multiple, cross-media, and conglomerate. We shall examine each below.

Independent Ownership

Independent owners of the mass media predominated in the late 19th and early 20th centuries. Independent papers were run by individuals or corporations that ran single ventures and nothing else. Benjamin Day, John Gordon Bennett, William Randolph Hearst, and John Pulitzer are all names associated with the independent newspapers, although not always in a positive manner. Independence began to decline in the 1960s. In the late 1940s over 80 percent of the nation's daily newspapers were under independent ownership, but by 1989, 80 percent were owned by corporate chains.[37] By 1997 ten companies controlled most of the daily flow of information (newspapers, television and radio stations, and magazines) in the United States, down from fifty in 1984.[38] The few independent newspapers that remain are decreasing in number and do not represent a significant proportion of outlets today. This same pattern is found in other forms of media.

Multiple Ownership

One replacement of independent ownership has been multiple ownership, in which individuals or corporations own several outlets of the same type, such as radio or television stations, cable channels, or newspapers. The 1990s saw a marked decline in the number of newspapers and independent radio and television stations. This has been viewed by many as a sign of a weakening democracy because diverse viewpoints have increasingly been reduced by group ownership, but the trend is expected to continue.

Cross-Media Ownership

When an individual or corporation owns multiple *types* of media, such as newspapers and television stations or newspapers and radio stations, the pattern is referred to as crossownership. Cross-media ownership is one of the largest areas of media restructuring in America. The Gannett Company, for instance, owned ninety-three daily newspapers, fifteen television stations, and nineteen radio stations after it merged with the Multimedia Company in 1995. Westinghouse Electric, which acquired CBS in 1995, a year later acquired Infinity Broadcasting and its 160 radio stations for $3.9 billion. In the fall of 1999 Viacom purchased CBS for $37.3 billion, representing the largest media acquisition at the time and creating the largest media company after Time Warner.

A danger occurs when one owner controls a significant proportion of media in the same location. Media monopolies have been prohibited since the mid-1970s except when they were already in existence. In August 1999 the FCC ruled that media companies could own more than one local television station in the nation's fifty largest markets. One consequence of the FCC's action was that newspaper organizations began pressuring the FCC and Congress to ease the cross-ownership rule. The Viacom/CBS merger set off a new round of discussions, since the new company exceeded by 6 percent the limit on stations per area set by the FCC at the time of the merger.[39]

Table 2.1 shows the number of Westinghouse and Infinity stations (prior to the Viacom purchase in 1999) and the audience share by city in 1996. This acquisition not only provided Westinghouse with an average of 30 percent of the radio market in these cities, but also brought in three of radio's biggest names, Don Imus, Howard Stern, and Charles Osgood. With this purchase Westinghouse owned 160 radio stations with estimated revenues of over $4 billion. The ten cities include one fifth of the nation's population.

Conglomerate Ownership

Perhaps the most disturbing pattern of media ownership is the conglomerate, in which individuals or corporations own media enterprises *along* with

Table 2.1
Westinghouse / Infinity Radio Holdings

MARKET	NUMBER OF STATIONS	SHARE (%)
Los Angeles	6	26
New York	7	36
Chicago	10	32
Dallas/Fort Worth	10	38
San Francisco	8	19
Washington	4	21
Philadelphia	6	44
Houston	5	20
Boston	6	39
Detroit	6	30

Source: "The New Empire of the Air," *U.S. News & World Report,* July 1, 1996:12. Copyright, July 1, 1996, *U.S. News & World Report.*

other types of business. Leo Bogart notes that these mergers represent "only the tip of the iceberg. An increasingly tangled web of alliances, partnerships, and other connections embrace all players in the new global communications. Companies engage in joint ventures that permit them to pool capital, spread risk, share information, acquire talent and expertise, and explore future markets."[40] The communications industry has several attractions. It is a growth industry, it represents a global market, and it provides a means of disseminating positive information.

There is growing evidence that the conflict of interest that accompanies conglomerate ownership leads to less news content and less diverse programming. The problem associated with cross-ownership goes beyond the sheer numbers of stations owned—it involves applying different values and expectations to traditional forms of political communication. The owner of the *Kansas City Star* in the 1880s believed that a daily newspaper was "a necessity to every intelligent person, who desires to keep posted on the current events of the day."[41] Contrast this statement with that of the chairman of Walt Disney Company upon acquiring Capital Cities/ABC.[42] Michael Eisner announced the acquisition as "a once-in-a lifetime opportunity to create an outstanding entertainment and media company."[43] He added, "It is about

table 2.2
Disney Holdings

BROADCASTING	PUBLICATIONS	MOVIE COMPANIES	TV DISTRIBUTORS	CABLE PROPERTIES	MUSIC	THEME PARKS	SPORTS AND OTHERS
ABC Television	Seven daily newspapers	Walt Disney Pictures	Buena Vista Television	The Disney Channel	Hollywood Records	Disneyland	Anaheim Angels Baseball
ABC Radio Network	*Discover* Magazine	Touchstone Pictures	Touchstone Television	A&E Television	Wonderland Records	Walt Disney World	Mighty Ducks Hockey
Individual shows	*Los Angeles* Magazine	Hollywood Pictures	Walt Disney Television	Lifetime Television			Celebration (real estate)
Home Improvement	*Women's Wear Daily*	Caravan Pictures		ESPN			Reedy Creek Energy Services
Ellen	*Institutional Investor*	Miramax Pictures					Vista Insurance Services
Regis and Kathie Lee	Hyperion Press						
Siskel and Ebert							
KABC and several local TV stations							

Source: Betsy Streisand, "It's a Diverse World After All," *U.S. News & World Report*, July 14, 1997:46. Copyright, July 14, 1996, *U.S. News & World Report*.

increasing revenues."[44] To increase revenue, Disney reduced many of the news staffs acquired in the purchase. Table 2.2 lists the diverse holdings of the Disney Corporation. Clearly its primary focus is not news and information, but entertainment.

Conglomerates—Disney ABC, Viacom CBS, General Electric NBC, and Time Warner Turner—own the major television networks. The question for those studying the relationship between the media and political interests is, does this concentration of ownership distort or corrupt Americans' perception of the world? Does General Electric and Viacom's heavy involvement in other areas bias their networks' reporting on issues? Does the Disney ownership of ABC increase television viewers' exposure to Disney products and movies?

There is increasing evidence that the lines that divide the various units are increasingly blurred. For example, ABC broadcast a special on the making of the Disney film *The Hunchback of Notre Dame* that happened to coincide with its release. In addition, several ABC stations covered as news a gala celebration that Disney threw for the movie in New Orleans. In another example, on March 21, 1999, the ABC Sunday news program "This Week with Sam Donaldson and Cokie Roberts" closed with a discussion of the upcoming Oscars, with Donaldson predicting victory for *Shakespeare in Love*, a film produced by the parent company of ABC, Disney.

In this era of mega-media companies, what people *are not* hearing or seeing is as important as what they are.

A New Era in the Relationship Between the Media and political Interests

The social, political, and economic climate of the past two decades has produced a new era in the relationship between the conglomerate media and political interests. Three major factors have been responsible for this new era. The first are economic conditions. The end of the Cold War forced new alignments in corporate America, which were achieved through aggressive mergers and acquisitions throughout the economy. These profoundly changed the communications industry. The second have been changes in the regulation of the media. From the Reagan administration's relaxation of the FCC rules involving multiple ownership, reporting, and licensing to the Clinton administration's passage of the Telecommunication acts, the media landscape has been profoundly altered. The acts made license withdrawal more difficult, directed the FCC to stop comparing the merits of new applicants with existing license holders, and created a new and powerful source of soft money for political campaigns in the process. Both factors provided an incentive to large corporations to acquire and expand their holdings in the communication industry. Finally, rapid new technologies, such as communication satellites, cable television,

VCRs, computers, and fax machines, have not only altered the way information is obtained but opened new markets and investment opportunities. These factors have made the past two decades a period of incredible change in the role of the media in American politics.

In contrast to the period 1775–1830, when the centralization of news was a product of politics, today politics is a product of the media. The political process has become dependent on the media to a degree unprecedented in history. For example, the media have become very active in the political process itself. Newspapers have become more active out of increased pressure from broadcasting. The American Newspaper Publishers Association actively worked to kill the Swift–Tauke bill, which would have allowed the "Baby Bells" (e.g., Bell Atlantic, Bell South, and Southwestern Bell) to compete with newspapers for classified advertising and other informational services that have traditionally been a major source of revenue for newspapers.

Control over the news has shifted from professional journalists to corporate executives. After its purchase of NBC in 1986, General Electric made its chairman, John Welch, head of the network. The following year Welch complained about how NBC News was reporting the stock market collapse and insisted that newspersons stop using phases like "Black Monday," "alarming plunge," and "precipitous drop" in describing the event.[45] A month later Welch's replacement, Robert C. Wright, announced that General Electric had decided to form an NBC political action committee, and that members of the network's management were expected to contribute generously, since NBC's future depended heavily on political developments in Washington. Wright explained, "Employees that earn their living and support their families from the profits of our business must recognize a need to invest some portion of their earnings to ensure that the company is well represented in Washington, and that its important issues are clearly placed before Congress. . . . Employees who elect not to participate in a giving program of this type should question their own dedication to the company and their expectations."[46] The corporate operations clashed with the orientation of the veteran news personnel. The conglomerate media have led to the dismantling of the news organizations in the networks in favor of the entertainment divisions.

Today ten corporations control most of the information flow in America: News Corporation, Viacom, Disney/Capital Cities, Time Warner, Sony, TCI, Seagram, Gannett, and General Electric. As a result, these companies shape and limit news coverage to meet their economic needs, rather than the public's need to know. These new guardians of the communications industry have a different outlook from their predecessors, as the statements of their executives illustrate.

The media conglomerates have become the new base of political power in American politics, replacing the traditional political parties, interest groups, and voters. Today's politicians are dependent on the media to an unprecedented extent. The impact of the media is twofold: in their ability to affect perceptions of candidates and issues, and in their ability to affect the political process through large financial donations. According to Common Cause, during the 1997–1998 election cycle 161 entertainment/media and telecommunications industries provided over $5 million in soft money to the Democratic and Republican parties. They were the largest providers of soft money, accounting for 16 percent of all soft money in the election cycle.

As the media become increasingly involved financially, the relationship between the media and political interests remains a two-way street. Politicians still use the media to their advantage, rushing to sites of such disasters as earthquakes, floods, bombings, or shootings. The media also use politicians by covering their emotional confrontations with members of the public or the media and dramatic events in their pasts, such as John McCain's war experiences. Increasing profits is the media's main objective, and has been increasingly so since the 1980s.

Another common influence on relations between the media and political interests in the 1990s was the role of new technology. In the 1800s the cylinder press and the telegraph reshaped the media's focus and content. The new technology of the 1990s included the increased use of satellites, minicams, and cable.

In the 1800s the political parties were well defined, their role clearly delineated, and loyalty strongly entrenched. Today political parties are ill defined, their role diminished, and their public support eroded. Regardless of the changes, the one constant is that both the media and political interests need and use the other.

cyberpolitics

In 1969 the U.S. Department of Defense created the Advanced Research Projects Agency Network, or ARPANET, with the goal of establishing a survivable communication network for all organizations involved in defense-related research. In 1983, with the help of National Science Foundation (NSF) grants, university researchers expanded this rudimentary network into the Computerized Service Network. Five years later, again with assistance from the NSF, a new high-speed area network to be used in education and research facilities in the United States and worldwide—the Internet—was born. In 1993 the first Web browser, Mosaic, was released.

The growth of the Internet use has been explosive, but two factors frequently limit its use in politics. The first is cost. Internet users consist predominantly of people with high incomes, high levels of education, and high-status occupations. Second, most people do not use the Internet to gather political information. At this time interpersonal communications and other forms of mass media remain the primary channels of political information. In their study of Internet usage in the 1998 election, Dulio, Goff, and Thurber concluded, "The election of 1998 was the first time a high percentage of campaigns developed Web sites, and the first time a number of important campaigns began to experiment with soliciting on-line contributions."[47] They also found that the Internet was being used in ways that were similar to traditional campaigning.

However, as the Internet becomes more accessible, politicians and political parties are beginning to realize its potential benefits. Many Web sites allow visitors to voice their opinions on issues. In 1999 President Clinton became the first president to participate in a live Internet chat. Bill Bradley, in his bid for the Democratic nomination in 2000, became the first presidential candidate to raise more than $1 million over the Internet. Bradley was also the first candidate to use an Internet ad campaign. For only $25,000, he placed banner ads on two free e-mail providers, *www.juno.com* and *www.hotmail.com*. The ads contained a picture of the candidate and alternated between two messages, "Tired of politics as usual?" and "I am. See what I'm going to do about it?" A direct link to Bradley's Web site also appeared in the ads. The Arizona Democratic Party was the first to experiment with on-line voting in its 2000 primary, and the Republican National Committee began selling Internet access on *GOPnet.com*, competing with other established Internet portals, such as Yahoo and America Online.

The Internet is used in the political process in four ways. First, it is used to promote politicians' policies and positions. Second, citizens use it to search for information, including political information. Both uses are increasing as the cost decreases and politicians and the public become more sophisticated users. The congressional Web site logged 3,736,902 visits the day the Starr report was released over the Internet, compared with a normal daily average of 236,409. Other Web sites were also heavily used to access the report.[48] Third, the Internet is used to identify potential donors on the basis of established criteria. Finally, political parties and candidates are accessing databases available on the Internet to ascertain voters' residence, replacing the door-to-door canvassing employed by political organizations prior to the Internet.

The 1994 congressional elections returned control of Congress to the Republican Party after forty years. Even more significantly, in 1994 the Internet became an important means for communicating political discontent and developing political organizations. For example, Richard Hartman, who was enraged by what he perceived as pork (excessive and unrelated spending) in the crime bill passed by Congress, began tapping out his opinions in a computer bulletin board on the Internet. He received numerous supportive responses and was encouraged to run against Speaker of the House of Representatives Thomas Foley of Washington's 5th Congressional District. Hartman then formed a PAC called "Reform Congress: The De-Foley-Ate Project." He publicized it on the Internet and talk radio shows and raised $26,000 in small checks. As Lawrence Grossman explains, "The money paid for ads and an anti-Foley car parade. . . . Mr. Hartman then created a steering committee of 12 persons from around the country, 10 of whom he . . . had never met or even *spoken* with. They coordinated their activities on the

Internet, which had an estimated eight million regular users and was growing at a 15 percent rate each month."[49] Congressman Foley was defeated in his re-election bid and the era of cyberpolitics had arrived, raising many questions concerning the nature and shape of democracy. One question involved representation, more specifically, how the public can hold local elected officials accountable for their actions when they can finance their campaigns with funds raised from people they do not represent.

During the 1996 presidential election campaign, candidates, political parties, and numerous interest groups produced Web pages that disseminated information to millions of users of the Internet. On election night the traffic on the MSNBC site was five times the normal level as people sought immediate results. CNN estimated that its Allpolitics site had 50 million "hits" or visits that night. Many newspapers had writers following the campaign and reporting on the election as it was portrayed on the Internet. The *Dallas Morning News*, for instance, had Jeffery Weiss cover the online political campaign of 1996. Clearly, a new era in politics had begun, and the exact nature of the effects remains unknown.[50]

The growth of the Internet has been examined in a series of polls conducted by the Pew Center, which found that 41 percent of adults used the Internet in 1998, compared with 23 percent in 1996. Online news consumption rose from 4 percent in 1996 to 26 percent, with an estimated 74 million users, in 1998. These figures continue to increase; in 1999 the Pew Center found that half of all Americans had access to the Internet.

The Internet is still used primarily by those of higher socioeconomic status. The disparity in online access by socioeconomic status is creating an information gap between those who have access to certain resources and those who do not. Furthermore, the Internet requires that users have the intelligence and training to navigate its rich and complex environment. As an information source, the Internet places considerably greater demands on users than does television.[51] The change that this technology brings to the political process will not be fully understood until it reaches the masses, and then greater individual effort will be required to be politically well informed because individuals will need to make choices about what they will or will not research on the Internet.

summary

This chapter has traced the evolving relationship between political institutions and the media, and noted periods of major change. Between 1775 and 1830 political institutions dominated the media through the financial control of newspapers and their content. Between 1830 and 1890 the development of the cylinder press, the telegraph, and pulp paper and an increase in literacy rates helped usher in an era in which parties did not control the papers but became more dependent on them. In the same period the content and format of papers evolved to appeal to larger mass audiences. In the next, "reform" era, 1890–1930, journalists and political reformers used one another to promote good government. Since 1930 technological inventions have again altered the nation's method of obtaining political information. Broadcast media, first in the form of radio and later television, dynamically changed the nature of American politics and the media.

Major changes today are occurring in technology and ownership. Deregulation of ownership, which began in the 1970s, is altering the reporting of politics. Mergers have become increasingly profitable, and media mergers represent some of the largest. The combination of today's emphasis on personality over substance with a decrease in major alternative news is reshaping American politics. Finally, new technology is again providing new political tools, although their impact is still evolving.

All these changes have transformed American politics and the media. Only with a clear understanding of the past can we understand the changing relationship between the media and the political process.

Endnotes

[1] Much early research focused on the psychological effects of the media—newspapers, radio, and later television. The work most identified with the beginning of modern media studies is *The People's Choice*, by Paul Lazarsfeld, Bernard Berelson, and Hazel Gaudet, published by Columbia University Press in 1944. However, there were earlier works, such as George Lundberg, "The Newspaper and Public Opinion," *Social Forces*, 4(1926):709–715, Hadley Cantril and Gordon Allport, *The Psychology of Radio* (New York: Harper and Brothers, 1935), Paul Lazarsfeld, *Radio and the Printed Page* (New York: Duell, Sloan, and Pearce, 1940), Frank L. Mott, "Newspapers in Presidential Campaigns," *Public Opinion Quarterly*, 13(1944):348–367, and Joseph T. Klapper, *The Effects of Mass Media* (New York: Bureau of Applied Social Research, Columbia University, 1949).

[2] Some examples of this area are Bernard Cohen, *The Press, the Public and Foreign Policy* (Princeton, N.J.: Princeton University Press, 1963), Kurt Lang and Gladys Engel Lang, *Politics and Television* (Chicago: Quadrangle Press, 1968), Jay Blumber and Denis McQuail, *Television in Politics* (Chicago: The University of Chicago Press, 1969), Thomas Patterson and Robert McClure, *The Unseeing Eye* (New York: Putnam, 1976), Michael Schudson, *Discovering the News* (New York: Basic Books, 1978), Dan Nimmo and Robert Savage, *Candidates and Their Images* (Pacific Palisades, Calif: Goodyear, 1976), Austin Ranney, *Channels of Power: The Impact of Television on American Politics* (New York: Basic Books, 1983), Michael Robinson and Margaret Sheehan, *Over the Wire and on TV* (New York: Russell Sage Foundation, 1983), Doris Graber, *Processing the News* (New York: Longman, 1984), Daniel Hallin, *Sound Bite News: Television Coverage of Elections, 1968–1988* (Media Studies Project Occasional Paper, Woodrow Wilson International Center for Scholars, 1990), Kathleen Jamieson Hall, *Dirty Politics, Deception, Democracy* (New York: Oxford University Press, 1992) and *Packaging the Presidency: A History and Criticism of Presidential Campaign Advertising* (New York: Oxford University Press, 1992), Thomas Patterson, *Out of Order* (New York: Alfred Knopf, 1993), S. Robert Lichter and

Richard E. Noyes, *Good Intentions Make Bad News* (Lanham, Md.: Rowman & Littlefield, 1995), and Marion Just, Ann Crigler, Dan Alger, Timothy Cook, Montague Kern, and Darrell West, *Crosstalk* (Chicago: University of Chicago Press, 1996).

[3]Judith Efron, *The News Twisters* (Los Angeles: Nash, 1971), Edward Jay Epstein, *News From Nowhere: Television and the News* (New York: Random House, 1973), C. Richard Hofstetter, *Bias in the News* (Columbus: Ohio State University Press, 1976), David L. Altheide, *Creating Reality: How TV Distorts the Events* (Russell Sage Foundation, 1976), Donald Shaw and Maxwell Mc-Combs, *The Emergence of American Political Issues: The Agenda Setting Function of the Press* (St. Paul, Minn.: West Publishing Co., 1977), and Herbert J. Gans, *Deciding What's News: A Study of CBS Evening News, NBC Nightly News, and Newsweek and Time* (New York: Vintage, 1980).

[4]David Paletz and Robert Entman, *Media Power Politics* (New York: The Free Press, 1981), John Tebbel and Sarah Miles Watts, *The Press and the Presidency: From George Washington to Ronald Reagan* (New York: Oxford University Press, 1985); Robert Entman, *Democracy Without Citizens* (New York: Oxford University Press, 1989); Timothy E. Cook, *Making Laws and Making News: Media Strategies in the U.S. House of Representatives* (Washington, D.C.: Brookings Institute, 1989).

[5]Richard Merritt. *Symbols of American Community 1735–1775* (New Haven, Conn.: Yale University Press, 1966).

[6]Richard Rubin. *Press, Party, and Presidency* (New York: W.W. Norton and Co., 1981), 8.

[7]*Ibid.*

[8]*Ibid.,*19.

[9]*Ibid.,*13.

[10]Frank Mott, *American Journalism: A History of Newspapers in the United States Through 260 Years: 1690–1950* (New York: Macmillan Co., 1950), 124.

[11]*Ibid.*, 13.

[12]*Ibid.*, 124.

[13]P.L. Ford, ed., *Writings of Thomas Jefferson* (New York: G. P. Putnam's and Son, 1914), 231.

[14]Rubin, *op. cit.*

[15]Mott, *op. cit.*, 123.

[16]Rubin, *op. cit.*

[17]Michael Schudson. *Discovering The News: A Social History of American Newspapers* (New York: Basic Books, 1978), 22–23.

[18]*Ibid.*

[19]Horace Greeley, *Recollection of a Busy Life* (New York: J.B. Ford, 1869), 137.

[20]Schudson, *op. cit.*

[21]Donald Ritchie, *Press Gallery: Congress and the Washington Correspondent* (Cambridge, Mass.: Harvard University Press, 1991), 3.

[22]*Ibid.*, 89.

[23]Walter Lippmann, "Two Revolutions in the American Press," *Yale Review*, 21(1931):440–448.

[24]With the exception of the Populist campaign of 1896, when the Populists centralized their press and reintroduced partisan politics as the primary focus of their papers.

[25]Paul Nord, "The Politics of Agenda Setting in the Late 19th Century," *Journalism Quarterly*, 50(1981):565–573.

[26]*Ibid.*

[27]"George Gould's Inquiry," *St. Louis Post-Dispatch*, April 20, 1893: 1.

[28]*Ibid.*

[29]E.E. Schattschneider, *The Semi-Sovereign People* (New York: Holt, Rinehart, & Winston, 1960), 61.

[30]Charles Siepmann, *Radio and Society* (New York: Oxford University Press, 1950).

[31]*Ibid.*

[32]*Ibid.*

[33]Edward Chester, *Radio, Television and Politics* (New York: Sheed and Ward, 1968).

[34]Wilson Dizard, *The Coming Information Age* (New York: Longman Publishers, 1986).

[35]Robert Bower, *Television and Politics* (New York: Holt, Rinehart, & Winston, 1973).

[36]Hulihan Lokey, *Mergerstat* (Chicago: W.T. Grimm & Co., 1998).

[37]Ben Bagdikian, *Media Monopoly*, 4th ed. (Boston: Beacon Press, 1992), 4.

[38]Ben Bagdikian, *Media Monopoly*, 5th ed. (Boston: Beacon Press, 1997).

[39]At the time the limit was 35 percent of the market share and the Viacom/CBS merger represented 41 percent.

[40]Leo Bogart, "The Imperial Movement: What Does It All Mean?" *Media Studies Journal*, 10(Summer/Autumn 1996):15–27.

[41]Trevor R. Brown, "A Calling at Risk," in David Weaver and G. Cleveland Wilhoit, eds., *The American Journalist in the 1990s: U.S. News People at the End of an Era* (Mahwah, N.J.: Lawrence Erlbaum Associates, 1996), 243.

[42]In an odd twist of fate, the *Kansas City Star* was part of the Disney acquisition.

[43]Brown, *op. cit.*

[44]*Ibid.*

[45]Lawrence K. Grossman, *The Electronic Republic: Reshaping Democracy in the Information Age* (New York: Viking Press, 1995), 84.

[46]*Ibid.*

[47]David A. Dulio, Donald L. Goff, and James A. Thurber, "Untangled Web: Internet Use During the 1998 Election," *PS*, 32(March 1999):57.

[48]Jennifer Files and Kendall Anderson, "Curious Caught Up in the Web," *Dallas Morning News*, September 12, 1998:23A.

[49]Grossman, *op. cit.*, 47.

[50]Jeffery Weiss, "Cyberpolitics," *Dallas Morning News*, February 3, 1996:22a.

[51]Erik P. Bucy, "Social Access to the Internet," unpublished manuscript.

CHAPTER 3

The Media's Link to Democracy

The media's development has been interwoven in complex ways with the advancement of all societies. John Thompson has called this process of social change "modernity," and the central element is the media.[1] Thompson explains, "If we wish to understand the nature of modernity— that is, of the institutional characteristics of modern societies and the life conditions created by them—then we must give a central role to the development of communications media and their impact."[2] As explained in Chapter 2, such developments as the telegraph, broadcasting, communication satellites, and the Internet have caused significant changes in the media, political institutions, and society.

The Origins of Democracy

The word "democracy" first began to appear in Greek writings on politics in the 5th century B.C. It is a compound of two Greek words: *demos*, meaning "the people," and *kratos*, meaning "authority," or *kratein*, meaning "to rule." Thus, democracy means rule by, or authority in, the people.[3]

Democracy in its earliest form developed during the Age of Pericles in the Athenian city-state, a community most Greeks of the period regarded as popularly governed. The government was composed of all male citizens over the age of 20.[4] The closest to the ideal democratic model in America is the New England town meeting, where small groups of citizens gather to discuss and decide public issues. The main element in a democracy is the exchange of information, debate, and discussion that ultimately lead to decisions. Participation by all the people in decision making is possible only in small areas and small groups. As communities and nations grew, total citizen participation became unworkable and was replaced by the concept of "representative" or "mediated democracy."

Mediated Democracy

"The people" rule in a large society by electing individuals who then represent the larger group. Thus, elections perform two vital functions. First, they are a method of selecting those who will represent the larger group of citizens. Second, they serve as a means to hold representatives accountable for the actions they take on behalf of the citizens.

But how do citizens know what their representatives have done? This is where the media perform a critical function, for they report to the people on the actions of their representatives. Democracy is *mediated* by the mass media because citizens rely on them for information. The media channel information to citizens so that they can enter into informed discussion, debate, and ultimately decision making. As the nation has grown, so too has the role of the media. As noted earlier, as new forms of media have been introduced, greater numbers of citizens have gained access and the time between a representative's action and the constituency's knowledge of this action has decreased. Today's citizens can know almost instantly about representatives' actions. The size of the nation also contributes to citizens' reliance on the media to represent reality. Benjamin Page has noted that if each American took two minutes of speaking time to discuss an issue (such as the death penalty), the discussion would take 500 million minutes, 347,222 days, or 950 years.[5]

Today's citizen must depend on the media for information. Consequently, the importance of the role of the media in the political process has increased dramatically, and has created other problems for representative democracy in the media age. As Dan Nimmo and James Combs point out, "...for most persons, political realities are mediated through mass and group communications, a process that results in the creation, transmission, and adoption of political fantasies as realistic views of what takes place."[6] Democratic societies are governed through debate and discussion, bargaining and negotiation, and ultimately compromise. Among the most important political actors in representative democracy are the media, for they are the channels of political communication, the conduits of political persuasion. This is why it is essential to understand their evolving role in the democratic process. However, mediated communication is only part of the larger social context in a representative democracy, for the media also reflect that context.

Basic Elements of a Democracy

There is no set number of elements that a government must have before it is classified as democratic. Depending on the writer, the criteria vary considerably. However, most scholars on the subject, regardless of their orientation, agree that the following four elements must be present to ensure a representative democracy. The first, and one of the oldest, is *popular sovereignty*. This means that the entire population is involved in decisions, if not directly, then through their representatives. Lord Bryce wrote, "The word democracy has been used even since the time of Herodotus to denote that the form of government in which the ruling power of the State is legally vested, not in any particular class or classes, but in the members of the community as a whole."[7] Thus, the citizens are the ultimate source of power.

The second element is *political equality*. Each member of the community must have the same opportunity as his or her fellow citizens to participate in the decision-making process. If any citizen or group has more power (through such devices as special officeholding requirements or voting requirements), a privileged class results and there is no democracy. Robert MacIver notes that political equality means not merely voting ("one man, one vote"), but depending on the "assessing of alternatives with a view to translating one of them into action."[8] Democracy does not exist in the absence of choice.

The third essential element is *popular consultation*. In a democratic government the people must be consulted about the policies they wish those in power to pursue. The officeholders, having learned of the people's desire, should then proceed to do whatever the people want them to do.

The final and most controversial element is *majority rule*. Decisions concerning such policies as health care reform, as well as decisions involving who should represent the citizens, are to be settled by the majority. This is the method a democracy uses when two or more alternatives are being considered. And since alternatives are essential to democracy, the method of choosing among them is vitally important to the process.

Majority rule is controversial because it does not address the wishes of the minority, and if a democratic society is not sensitive to those in the minority and they are left unprotected, the society will eventually break down. The United States has attempted to provide for the protection of minority rights through the formal means found in the Constitution, including the right to assemble and to petition government and freedom of speech. Post–Civil War amendments that were directed toward former slaves also addressed this issue, as did the Nineteenth Amendment, which gave women the right to vote. Minority protections have been extended through court decisions and such legislative actions as the Americans with Disabilities Act. As a result, American minorities have various protections not found in other democracies, such as Great Britain or France. Since the majority is ever-changing, depending on the issue and time, minorities must be given some protection, if for no other reason than that today's minority often becomes tomorrow's majority. In the area of civil rights, it was once believed that only qualified men ought to vote, but in 1920, with the passage of the Nineteenth Amendment, women were enfranchised and today women make up more than half of all voters.

Each of these elements of democracy—popular sovereignty, political equality, popular consultation, and majority rule—relies on the transmission of information to citizens so they can make rational, meaningful decisions. In modern democracies public deliberation is mediated through professional communicators, rather than individual citizens or even small groups. The media's role has always been critical to the democratic process, as we saw in Chapter 2. Full access to information is essential to democracy. Political theorist Giovanni Sartori has written, "Electoral power per se is the mechanical guarantee of democracy, but the substantive guarantee is given by the conditions under which the citizen gets information and is exposed to the pressures of opinion leaders."[9] Or as Carl Friedrich argues, "The emergence of constitutional government, and in particular the crystallization of the systems of popular representation as we know them, are inextricably interwoven with the growth of the modern press. Without it constitutional government is unimaginable."[10]

While these four elements represent the "essentials" of a representative democracy, they also represent ideals, for they are not always attained. Within the real world of politics the struggle to achieve these ideals is carried out, and the media are an increasingly critical component in the process. Because the mass media are so important to democratic government, we need to examine some of the more subtle ways they affect the governing process.

The media and political socialization

Political socialization provides the fundamental link between the political system and its citizens. Political systems cannot operate effectively without the general support of their citizens. This is true of all political systems, but particularly of democracies. Democratic governments depend on their citizens to abide by the laws and support them through such acts as paying taxes and voting. Political socialization is the way citizens learn and develop attitudes about the political world. It is the process that forms the individual's attitudes, beliefs, values, and opinions about politics, and it is a continuous process, although most of the learning occurs in childhood.

Understanding this process is important to understanding how individuals develop their political attitudes and beliefs. There are several approaches to the process, but political scientists and social psychologists have most often relied on learning theory to study it. Richard Dawson and colleagues distinguish between two general forms of political socialization: *indirect* (or latent) learning and *direct* (or manifest) learning.[11] Indirect learning involves the acquisition of nonpolitical attitudes that later shape the individual's political attitudes, and direct learning involves the acquisition of content that is specifically political.

Indirect learning takes place in two steps. First is the learning of nonpolitical attitudes, and second is the transposition of these attitudes onto political subjects, thereby forming political attitudes. For example, children who develop a positive attitude toward their teachers, nonpolitical authority figures, will, when they later become aware of political figures such as the president, transfer this positive attitude to them. This will not occur if certain factors intervene in the process. For example, if a child's parents hold highly negative attitudes toward the president and other politicians, the child may not transfer his or her positive feelings about teachers to the president, but rather the negative feelings he or she perceived at home. Either way, the role of political socialization is enormous, and early socialization lays the foundation for later political orientations.

Our political system is vast, complex, and often confusing, and may seem quite distant to the average citizen. Most citizens today do not have the time or energy to sort through the information they need to fully understand the complex issues facing their government, as citizens did in the Age of Pericles. Citizens today tend to rely on a kind of mental shorthand, a simplified set of ideas, to interpret and respond to political developments.

The political socialization process provides citizens with several ways to develop this mental shorthand. First, it is through this process that citizens acquire a general knowledge of the political system (information about the structure of government, political institutions such as the courts, Congress, and the presidency). Second, the process provides a means of learning about specific issues such as health care, AIDS, or budget deficits. Third, it helps citizens develop a general philosophy of government, such as liberal or conservative. Fourth, and fundamentally important to democracy, the process teaches the concepts of participation and civic duty. Fifth, it helps citizens develop a general attitude toward the political system itself—supportive or alienated. David Sears and Nicholas Valentino, in their study of pre-adult socialization (10- to 17-year-olds), found that presidential campaigns produced "substantial pre-adult gains in the attitude domains most salient for the campaign, as reflected in greater affective expression, information, and attitude crystallization."[12] Their findings suggest that periodic political events catalyze pre-adult socialization, generating predispositions that persist into later life stages.[13] Sixth, political socialization provides an orientation toward authority figures in terms of trust or distrust. Finally, and most abstract, is the development of an attitude toward the political "rules of the game," which can range from compliance to rebellion.

The importance of the political socialization process to the stability of government and the effectiveness of democracy cannot be overstated because representative democracy depends on the process for survival. The process has provided for smooth transitions in the nation's history as the country became more complex and government more remote. Richard Merelman has suggested that this process has greater importance today for stability of government than ever before because the traditional means of controlling people—physical force and economic pressure—have either failed or been declared illegitimate.[14]

What is the media's role in the process? Political scientist Paul Beck has offered a model that is particularly helpful in studying the agents of political socialization. He points out that, to be an influential agent, an individual or institution needs *exposure, communication*, and *receptivity*.[15] To be influenced by the media, an individual must be exposed to the media, receive communications from the media, and be receptive to those communications. These three conditions are altered by one's stages in the life cycle. An older person may respond to messages differently than he or she would have when younger.

Socialization studies prior to the 1970s largely ignored the mass media, focusing instead on the influence of parents, schools, churches, and peers. Early research on the media's role in the political socialization process concluded that people who pay more attention to the media are usually better informed politically,[16] that the media do not have a direct impact on people's attitudes,[17] and that media exposure reinforces political orientations.[18] Yet even as these findings were being reported, others studies were concluding that the media have a significant impact on the political socialization of children. For instance, a 1973 study of Kentucky high school seniors in economically depressed rural areas found that most of the students' political information was obtained from television.[19] In a 1970 study, researchers assessed mass media usage, political knowledge, and campaign activity among adolescents in five Wisconsin cities.[20] They concluded that public affairs and political knowledge over time "should be considered as an independent (or intervening) variable in the political socialization process, not merely as one of many dependent variables."[21] Neil Hollander in his study of adolescents' views of the Vietnam War concluded, "The major substantive finding . . . is the importance of mass media as a source of learning about an important political object, war. This finding casts considerable doubt on the present utility of much of the previous research on the sources of political socialization, and indicates that researchers have, perhaps, been passing over the major source of political learning. *The new 'parent' is the mass media*."[22]

The mass media are receiving greater emphasis in today's literature. Doris Graber notes that the "bulk of information that young people acquire about the nature of their political world comes from the mass media."[23] There are at least four reasons for the new emphasis on the media. First is the rapid growth of television. Today the role of the media in politics cannot be ignored because of television's central role in the socialization process and politics. Citizens spend more time viewing television than ever before, and politics has invaded all areas of programming. In the 1992 presidential campaign Arkansas Governor Clinton's appearance on MTV introduced presidential politics to a generation that had previously had little direct exposure to presidential candidates.

Second is the effort to more accurately measure media effects. Early socialization studies generally discounted all media influence unless it consisted of direct contact outside the classroom between the child and the media. As research designs became more sophisticated, the assumption of direct contact with the media was modified and indirect media effects through parents and teachers were included. Current researchers believe that much of what a child learns about the political system is a result of what parents or teachers learn and then pass on to the child. This is particularly true in the case of television. Third is the weakening of the traditional American family caused by the proliferation of single-parent families and two-career households, which create fewer socializing opportunities for parents. The amount of time parents spend with their children has declined markedly over the years, producing greater reliance on television for entertainment and information for both parents and children.

Finally, new technologies have provided for more programming directed toward the youth audience. George Gerbner and colleagues, in their study of the media and family images, conclude, "The mass media have come to absorb many socializing functions of the family."[24] The mass media expose individuals to images of power, success, and dominance in society and provide individuals with models of behavior. Current studies of the media's impact in the socialization process generally conclude that the media have become the single most important agents in early childhood—a finding quite different from those in the studies of the 1960s and 1970s.[25]

Adult Socialization

Political socialization has its greatest impact on the young. However, because the process is continual, it has implications for all citizens. Public opinion polls indicate that the media furnish most new orientations and opinions acquired by adults throughout their lives. This is a belief that communication scholars have long held. Therefore, as Doris Graber points out, "The mass media must be credited . . . with a sizable share of continuing adult political socialization and *re-socialization*. Examples of re-socialization—the restructuring of established basic attitudes—are shifts in sexual morality and racial attitudes that the American public has undergone since mid-century and the changing views on relations with mainland China and Russia."[26]

Once basic orientations are developed in early life, they usually remain stable, and later learning largely refines and augments them. The attitudes, values, and norms learned in early life serve as filters, or screens, for later experiences. An individual who has been socialized to have a strong positive orientation toward the Republican Party will normally use this orientation to filter messages about politicians—positively toward Republicans and negatively toward Democrats. An individual who has been socialized to view government and its programs as negatives, believing the less government the better, will be less likely to be active in any political party. Individuals who face major changes in lifestyle may revise their political positions. For example, individuals who were socialized to believe government should not be involved in their daily lives might be resocialized as they age and require medical services or other government assistance. If they did not change their position, they would likely use the media to obtain the information they needed to support their existing position.

How does the socialization process relate to the success of the democratic system? It is through socialization that citizens obtain basic values, beliefs, and attitudes about democracy, but they also become familiar with the symbols of that democracy, such as the flag, the eagle, and Uncle Sam. The media have performed an increasingly important role in this process as new technologies have decreased the distance (in both time and space) between citizens and the actions of those who govern them. Still, media messages are interpreted, and the particular interpretation given a message depends on the individual's socialization. There are other effects associated with the media that are related to socialization and democracy, including the media's effects on the social, psychological, and physiological development of the individual.

social effects of the mass media

While the media perform a vital role in the democratic process, their influence on the individual citizen depends on his or her position in society. Some segments of society have benefited more than others from the media's representation of events. Early newspapers in the United States had their greatest impact on the small literate population. However, their impact was not restricted to those who could afford a newspaper and had the ability to read, for traveling town readers and public debates spread the news of the printed press.

The reach of radio, too, was initially restricted, as only a small portion of society could afford this medium. Television did not become pervasive in America until the late 1950s and early 1960s. Between 1949 and 1959 ownership of television sets grew from 6 percent of Americans to 90 percent.[27] Today, as print publications, radio, and television are all widely used forms of mass communication and integral parts of the political process, the Internet is effecting another major transition. Like its predecessors, the Internet initially had a limited, elite audience. In 1995 only 14 percent of the general public said they went online at home or at work, and that figure climbed to 22 percent in 1996. Only 4 percent use the Internet to obtain information about current affairs.[28] The average Internet user in 1996 was male (58 percent), 36 years old, with a household income of $62,000.[29] This profile is changing rapidly as the cost of computers declines and computer literacy increases. In 1996, 60 percent of the Internet users had been using the medium less than one year. In the 1996 presidential campaign both President Clinton and Senator Dole had extensive Web sites. Today government Web sites make it easier for citizens to obtain information from and communicate with various public officials. In 1996 only the Internet and C-SPAN provided gavel-to-gavel coverage of political party conventions, as network television abandoned that role. The pattern of transition from one medium to another is clear. In the initial phase only a small portion of the population has access to the new medium, followed by increasingly shorter periods before the majority have such access. Television is the most recent medium to have a widespread acceptance.

Many have argued that as society becomes larger and more complex, the mass media are creating a homogenized culture as they appeal to the widest possible audiences. Of course, this homogenization is relative. Different social groups have always existed in America and these groups frequently have their own specialized media.

Nevertheless, for most Americans the media world is the *real* world, whether it is news, politics, entertainment, or advertising. Something is believed only *after* the media have reported it. The media's effect on various social groups is important because the media are vital channels of political information. Understanding the media's impact on different groups greatly aids our understanding of politics.

In an attempt to examine the relationship between the media and social class, Bradley Greenberg and Brenda Dervin examined the use of the media by the urban poor and the general population.[30] They hypothesized that there would be considerable differences in the types of media usage between persons in the two groups, that those with low income would rely more on television and less on the print media. They also hypothesized that persons with low income would exhibit similar patterns of media usage, regardless of race, and that these patterns would differ from those of the general population. To test these two hypotheses, the authors interviewed residents of low-income areas and the general population in Lansing, Michigan.

Figure 3.1 shows their findings as they related to the first hypothesis. The poor are more homogeneous than the general population in their viewing

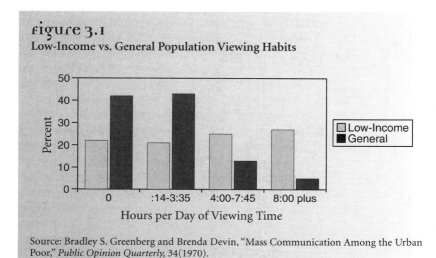

figure 3.1
Low-Income vs. General Population Viewing Habits

Source: Bradley S. Greenberg and Brenda Devin, "Mass Communication Among the Urban Poor," *Public Opinion Quarterly,* 34(1970).

habits. As the number of viewing hours per day increased among the poor, the number of viewing hours among the general population sharply declined. The researchers also found the poor were more homogeneous than the general population in their viewing habits. Their findings also confirmed the second hypothesis—that class, not race, was the crucial factor in media usage.

Figure 3.2 shows the amount of television viewing by poor white and black populations. While there is some variation, the general patterns are similar. When asked which medium—television, radio, or newspapers—they preferred for world news, low-income respondents claimed television 69 percent, compared with the general population's 38 percent. However, when low-income whites and low-income blacks were asked which medium they preferred, the results were identical—69 percent preferred television. The study confirmed both working hypotheses and found that media use was associated with socioeconomic status and not race. The broader implication of this finding is that the media may not have the same effect across society.

A related issue concerns the content of media programming, for if television is a centralized system of "storytelling," what stories does it tell? The issue of television's content continues to be the focus of concern among the public, politicians, and scholars alike. Issues of violence, language, morals, and ideology are debated in political campaigns, and are central to discussions of "proper" television programming.

George Gerbner and others at the University of Pennsylvania's Annenberg School of Communication undertook a rigorous study to determine the long-term effects of social patterns portrayed in television programs on the culture.[31] One section of the study was devoted to what the researchers termed "message systems analysis." They identified patterns of program

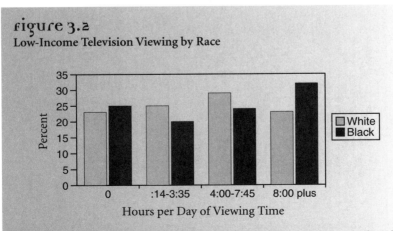

figure 3.2
Low-Income Television Viewing by Race

Source: Bradley S. Greenberg and Brenda Devin, "Mass Communication Among the Urban Poor," *Public Opinion Quarterly*, 34(1970).

content, related them to the demographic characteristics of society, and found that middle- and upper-income groups were more heavily represented in television programs than in the actual population. For example, (1) 25 percent of television characters were blue-collar, "service" class compared to 67 percent of the actual population. (2) Senior citizens were drastically underrepresented on television compared to their numbers in the population. (3) There were three times as many male roles as women.[32]

Subsequent works have supported these findings. Robert Lichter and colleagues identified the social backgrounds, personal traits, and activities of over 7,000 characters from a sampling of television programs aired between 1955 and 1985. Themes, morals, and social commentary were also analyzed for 620 program episodes.[33] The authors' findings confirmed earlier studies that found male roles greatly outnumbering female, with men portraying nearly 90 percent of all professional roles during the period of their study.[34] The authors also found that women were depicted in distinctly traditional roles, and frequently had lower status than men. However, women were also portrayed more positively with regard to crime (only half as many female characters committed crimes) and they were far less likely to be villains.[35]

Gerbner and his associates identified another dimension of television that they called "cultivation analysis." They designed a multiple-choice questionnaire that included both correct statements about the actual demographic and social patterns in the United States and statements that corresponded to situations presented on television.[36] They then surveyed two samples, light viewers (persons who watched television less than two hours a day) and heavy viewers (persons who watched over fours hours per day). The authors found that heavy viewers tended to choose statements that reflected television's depiction of the world over statements that represented actual patterns found in the United States. The light viewers, on the other hand, chose answers that corresponded to actual conditions. For example, heavy viewers perceived senior citizens as making up a smaller proportion of the population than they did twenty years earlier. In fact, those over 65 years old are one of the two fastest-growing components of the American population.[37] In another example, the authors found that crime in prime time television occurred ten times more often than it does in reality. An average of five to six acts of overt physical violence occurred each televised hour and involved over half of all major characters.[38] Gerbner and his associates concluded that crime on prime time was at least ten times as rampant as in the real world.

Heavy viewers, regardless of socioeconomic class, overestimated the likelihood of being victims of crime. This caused Gerbner to warn of a "mean world syndrome," and speculate that this view of reality would result in support for simple, tough, hard-line solutions for crime. Gerbner's prediction was correct. Lawmakers *have* used the fear of crime to pass legislation that weakens individual protections. In 1996, when statistics showed an overall decrease in the crime rate, politicians continued to campaign on the issue.

The solutions proposed have been simplistic for the most part—the construction of more jails, three-strikes-and-you're-out rules, shortening of the appeals process, and increased use of the death penalty.

There are those who question the association between heavy viewing and judgments about the real world.[39] Some argue that while those who perceive a greater incidence of crime may modify their voting and other behavior, this link has not been established in the research.[40] Others argue that the cultivation effects tend to disappear when other standard variables of age, income, and education are controlled simultaneously.[41]

More recent studies by Robert Entman, Kathleen Hall Jamieson, and Jon Hurwitz and Mark Peffley have shown that network news portrayals of blacks do create a menacing impression. These researchers found that blacks are most often shown as criminals—in handcuffs, in mug shots, in physical custody, and often silent and unnamed. They are rarely shown in the news as lawful, contributing members of society.[42] This media image does not reflect the real world, but it causes many whites to have negative, stereotyped views of blacks. Dolf Zillmann has argued that there may be a reverse causality, that viewers who are by nature more fearful may seek out programs that reinforce their fears.[43]

As communication satellites and cable television gave viewers a greater programming selection, some believed this would decrease television's distorted picture of the world by increasing the diversity of programming. Robert Kubey and his colleagues addressed this question in their study of representation of gender, race, and age in network, cable, public broadcasting, and independent programming.[44] As Table 3.1 indicates, they found cable programming has slightly increased the underrepresentation of women in television programs. They also found that nonwhites and older people continue to be underrepresented as well.[45]

Three conclusions can be drawn concerning the media's impact on social development. First, the media present an unbalanced view of society, its problems, achievements, and composition. This widens social, economic, and political cleavages. Second, governing is made more difficult because what the citizen believes is real is frequently not. These misperceptions challenge the fabric of democracy, for the system presumes that citizens have sufficient and accurate information. Third, the media depict society in extremes—either a very negative side or a world most Americans can never hope to achieve. For these reasons, the way the media depict American society is one underlying reason politicians find it difficult to communicate accurately with those they represent.

psychological effects

The relationship between the mass media and politics has been a concern of rulers and social critics since the first medium, the printed word. In the

Table 3.1
Gender of Characters Across Channels

SOURCE	ALL OR MOSTLY MALE	MIXED	ALL OR MOSTLY FEMALE	TOTAL
Network				
N	128	40	54	222
Percent	57.7	18	24.3	30.7
Cable				
N	199	35	74	308
Percent	64.6	11.4	24	42.6
PBS				
N	44	12	12	68
Percent	64.7	17.6	17.6	9.4
Independent				
N	75	16	34	125
Percent	60	12.8	27.2	17.5
Total				
N	446	103	174	723
Percent	61.7	14.2	24.1	100

Source: Robert Kubey, Mark Shiffet, Niranjala Weerakkody, and Stephen Ukriley, "Demographic Diversity on Cable: Have the New Cable Channels Made a Difference in Representation of Gender, Race, and Age?" *Journal of Broadcast and Electronic Media*, 39(Fall 1995): 464.

United States throughout the 19th century there was growing anxiety about the power of the press to manipulate the public and perhaps undermine the democratic process. Those concerned viewed the rush by the press to sensationalize political issues as diverting the attention of the masses, arousing irrational passions, and lowering the level of political debate. Today these same criticisms are heard of the mass media.

Gordon Allport calls the concept of attitude "probably the most distinctive and indispensable concept in contemporary American social psychology, ... the keystone in the edifice of American social psychology."[46] Millions of dollars are currently spent each year on the media in an attempt to shape people's attitudes about political candidates, public policy, and consumer products. In most cases the objective of these campaigns is to influence people's behavior so they vote for a certain candidate, engage in a particular behavior, or purchase a specific product. The success of the media's campaign depends on whether the communications change the recipients' attitudes in the desired direction and then influence their behavior.

A recent example of this is the tobacco industry's attempts to change the public's attitudes toward the use of tobacco and related health problems. For many years the tobacco industry used the media to associate its product with desired social outcomes and there was little resistance to this approach. To persuade women to smoke, for instance, media campaigns suggested that women "Reach for a Lucky Instead of a Sweet" to play on women's concerns about weight. The campaign was very successful. (Later brand names incorporated this theme, as in the case of "Virginia Slims.") In the 1990s, however, the industry came under government scrutiny and large legal settlements were awarded to the states to reimburse them for tobacco-related medical care. At the same time the public's general attitude toward tobacco use became more negative as the public became more aware of the health problems associated with smoking and the financial consequences for taxpayers of those problems.

The early studies assumed the mass media produced a *direct* or *hypodermic effect* on receivers' attitudes and behavior. This was not a specifically articulated hypothesis, but an underlying assumption. Specifically, it assumed that everyone is exposed to mass media messages equally, everyone interprets them in the same general way, and so everyone is affected uniformly. Therefore, a cleverly designed message should produce a uniform response. This concept perceived audiences as captive, attentive, and gullible. Though this view may seem simplistic today, several factors supported it. These included propaganda campaigns in World War I, the behavior of the stock market of 1927, the mass hysteria following the radio broadcast of *War of the Worlds*, the rise to power of Adolf Hitler, and the popularity of radio personalities like the right-wing Catholic priest Father Coughlin and political figures like Huey Long. A pioneer in the study of mass media effects, Harold Lasswell, wrote in 1927 that "propaganda is one of the most powerful instrumentalities in the modern world."[47]

In 1935 Hadley Cantril and Gordon Allport wrote, "The radio is a recent innovation that has introduced profound alterations in the outlook and social behavior of men, thereby creating a significant social problem for psychologists. Radio, although a novel medium of communication, is preeminent as a means of social control and epochal in its influence upon the mental horizons of man."[48] In the 1930s the effect of the mass media (print and radio) was based on informal and anecdotal, rather than careful empirical, research.

During the 1930s and 1940s, the government and social scientists began to closely monitor the impact of the media, particularly the broadcast media. Harold Lasswell and his associates formed the Experimental Division of the Study of Wartime Communications, located in the Library of Congress, while Hans Spier was engaged in the study of "totalitarian communications" at the New School for Social Research. World War II intensified the study of the media's psychological effects, and a core group of scholars developed who were later to become leaders in the study of those effects.

The study of the mass media was not characterized by a single approach, but reflected the various disciplines of the researchers. Political scientists were concerned with how the mass media affected political behavior, psychologists studied how they affected individuals and small groups, and sociologists focused on the effects on organizations and society. This lack of a common focus has led some to describe the field of communications study as "one of the greatest crossroads where many pass but few tarry."[49]

The crossroads became more congested as new techniques in the study of media effects were introduced. In 1947 Herbert Hyman and Paul Sheatsley, using survey data from the National Opinion Research Center, concluded that simply increasing the flow of messages could not increase the effectiveness of mass communication campaigns. Rather, specific psychological barriers to effective information dissemination had to be considered and overcome.[50] This represented a sharp departure from the hypodermic effect theory. One assumption of this new *indirect* or *minimal effects* model was that people often distort incoming information to be consistent with prior attitudes. In addition, Hyman and Sheatsley argued that individuals have certain attitudes about politics and public issues that are not easily changed, and that the media's messages alone would not change them.

Similar conclusions were reached by Paul Lazarsfeld, Bernard Berelson, and Hazel Gaudet in their seminal work on the media's effect on the 1940 presidential election.[51] The mass media, according to the authors, tended to reinforce existing political views, rather than create new ones, due to what the authors called "selective exposure" and "selective attention." These existing views were found to be heavily determined by the community, family, and group affiliations. One of the most important findings was that respondents claimed that they discussed their political decisions more frequently than they were exposed to radio or print news. This led the authors to the concept of "opinion leaders" and a new hypothesis of a *two-step flow*. This hypothesis presumed that information flowed from the mass media to an opinion leader, who absorbed the information and then transmitted it to the final audience. This theory received support from sociologists during the 1950s and 1960s, while psychologists continued to investigate the media's effects on individuals.

This new view saw the media's threat to the democratic process as less than that posed by the view of a hypodermic effect. Individuals were not simply "injected" with messages and did not uniformly respond to those messages. The two-step flow model was generally accepted through the 1960s, and the "minimal effects" view of the mass media was predominant in the literature. Joseph Klapper refined the two-step flow model when he reviewed the communications literature[52] and concluded, "Persuasive mass communication functions far more frequently as an agent of reinforcement than as an agent of change. Within a given audience exposed to particular communication, reinforcement, or at least constancy of opinion, is typically found to be the most common, and conversion is typically found to be the most rare."[53] Klapper saw the potential effects of the mass media as limited by intervening forces. He suggested that people avoid media messages that conflict with their predispositions and focus on messages that reinforce their predispositions. According to this analysis, psychological mechanisms are the intervening variables between the mass media and audience response. Media messages have different effects, depending on receivers' personality traits. Thus, concern over the media's manipulation is lessened by two factors. Media messages are received indirectly through opinion leaders and group affiliations, and these psychological predispositions guide an individual's selection of compatible messages. Concern over the media's role in manipulating behavior is reduced under these circumstances because intervening variables (opinions of others, as well as one's own predisposition) filter the media's messages.

The rapid growth of television in the 1960s and 1970s increased the focus on this medium's effect on the population. Researchers began to question the underlying presumptions of earlier studies of media effects, arguing that they had too narrowly defined effects. These new researchers reasoned that to expect to find changes in attitudes, opinions, and voting behavior after single exposures to a message was unrealistic. Instead, they argued that attitudes, opinions, and behavior needed years of exposure. Maxwell McCombs and his colleagues argued that the minimal effects theory was valid only if one defined effects as changes in attitudes, opinions, or behavior. If effects were viewed as changes in attention, awareness, and information, then different results emerged, ones in which media effects were far from minimal. McCombs and Shaw reasoned that media affected "cognitions", or mental processes of knowing that include such elements as awareness, perception, reasoning, and judgment. In their work on agenda setting, they stated:

> People do learn from mass communication. Not only do they learn factual information about public affairs and what is happening in the world, they also learn how much importance to attach to an issue or topic from the emphasis placed on it by the mass media. Considerable evidence has accumulated that editors and broadcasters play an important part in shaping our social reality as they go about the day-to-day task of choosing and displaying news. . . .
>
> This impact of the mass media—the ability to effect cognitive change among individuals, to structure their thinking—has been labeled the *agenda-setting function of mass communication.* Here may lie the most important effect of mass communication, its ability to mentally order and organize our world for us. In short, the mass media may not be successful in telling us what to think but they are stunningly successful in telling us what to think about.[54]

Current research indicates that selective exposure and even selective attention occur far less than was earlier thought. Why the new skepticism? First, the nature of television and radio makes selective exposure and selective attention difficult. Many people "watch television" or "listen to the radio," rather than tuning in to specific programs. Second, research has found that exposure to information that is at odds with an individual's beliefs are not as troubling to the individual as once believed. Some people even seek out opposing views or see themselves as "open-minded".[55] There is evidence that the audiences of popular talk radio programs, for example, include many people who hold differing opinions from the program host and often disagree with the political messages.

physiological effects

The final type of mass media effects is physiological. The study of the media's effects on the human body is still in its infancy, yet there is at least anecdotal evidence that the media, particularly television, have such effects. While this study is concerned with the media and politics, should later findings indicate health problems are associated with extensive use of television or the Internet, those problems would become issues that would be dealt with in the political arena. Consider the case of tobacco. For years there was scant interest in the effects of tobacco use on human health. As studies found a link between tobacco consumption and lung cancer and other health problems, the subject became politicized. In the 1996 presidential campaign, Bob Dole's statement that nicotine was not habit forming and his financial support from tobacco companies became campaign issues. But it took years before tobacco consumption had this political impact. The same may be true with the physiological effects of television and the Internet.

As noted above, there is evidence that television viewing has physiological effects. The artificial light, its transmission of light and images, and the inactivity associated with television viewing have been linked to possible health problems, including hyperactivity, "television epilepsy," induction of a hypnotic state, eye damage, dangerous heart rate changes, and damage to the endocrine system. In 1997 a Japanese television network canceled the broadcast of a popular action-packed cartoon show that used brilliant flashing scenes when over 700 children were hospitalized with convulsions, spasms, and nausea.[56] In 1999 the American Academy of Pediatrics urged that children's television exposure be limited. The academy's recommendation was based on studies that found that children under the age of two years need close personal interaction for proper development of the brain, and that watching television did not provide this.[57]

early studies of the mass media

Among the first studies of the mass media by American social scientists were those that examined the media's effect on voting. The underlying assumption of these early voting studies was that votes change as a result of media coverage. In a study sponsored by Columbia University's Radio Research Department (which later became the Bureau of Applied and Social Research), Paul Lazarsfeld and colleagues applied their consumer marketing research skills to the study of the 1940 presidential election.[58] They interviewed 600 people in Erie County, Ohio, seven times before the election and once immediately after. The researchers believed that campaigns would reflect the marketplace and that successful candidates would be those who could best "sell" themselves. Instead they found that most voters had long-lasting loyalties, which limited the effectiveness of media campaigns. Among the strongest loyalties was that to a political party.

The study also isolated three major sociological factors in the voting process: class, religion, and place of residence. In addition, the researchers found that some voters were psychologically "cross-pressured." One factor might indicate they would vote Republican while another would predict a Democratic vote. For instance, an urban Protestant would be cross-pressured between Protestant Republicanism and Democratic urbanism. When cross-pressures occurred, voters either did not vote or sought additional information to make a decision. To the researchers' surprise, they did not seek information from the media, but from their friends, which caused the authors to conclude, "It is commonly assumed that individuals obtain their information directly from newspapers, radio, and other media. *Our findings, however, do not bear this out.*"[59] However, the researchers speculated that the media had an indirect effect through the two-step flow process. Information from the media first was received by an opinion leader and then transferred to the voter.

Since the 1960s the idea of "selling" a candidate, party, or issue has become a commonly accepted part of American politics, as witnessed by the increased number of media consultants and advisors, the growth in the Communications Office in the White House, and the sophisticated use of media appeals in modern politics. So while Lazarsfeld's study may have not uncovered the direct media connection the researchers were seeking, their notion that candidates can be marketed through the media has been accepted.

By today's standards this study, published as *The People's Choice*, is rather ordinary. It reflected only one Ohio county, so the authors could not draw sweeping conclusions. In addition, it lacked the sophistication of today's research in terms of both survey design and statistical methodology. Yet after nearly five decades, the findings have been replicated many times. Furthermore, the study ultimately gave rise to a wide range of other studies on the media's effects.[60]

When their initial findings failed to support a consumer model of voting behavior, the authors undertook a second project exploring the 1948 presidential election to determine if the findings could be extended beyond Erie County, Ohio. In this study, eventually published as *Voting*, the sample was expanded to 1,000 and the research was conducted in Elmira, New

York.[61] The authors again found that cross-pressure existed and that socioeconomic status was the best single predictor of how one would vote.

However, *Voting* made an important contribution to the study of the mass media—what the authors referred to as "selective perception."[62] They found that perceptual screening occurs when a voter has a distorted perception of a candidate's or party's position on some issue. This misperception is not intentional; instead, the voter subconsciously perceives agreement between his or her opinion and that of the candidate.

Another approach to the study of individual behavior was prompted by World War II. Administrators of the war bond program wanted to know why citizens bought and sold bonds. To assist in their research, the Department of Agriculture offered the services of its Division of Program Services. After the war, as government funding decreased, many people associated with this division left to establish the Survey Research Center at the University of Michigan. These included Rensis Likert, Angus Campbell, and Leslie Kish. Today the center is known as the Center for Political Studies and has become the preeminent electoral research organization in the world. The center has conducted national opinion surveys in conjunction with presidential elections since 1948, and has conducted national surveys of mid-term congressional elections since 1954.

While several books and numerous articles have been produced by the center, the seminal work is *The American Voter*, published in 1960.[63] *The American Voter* examined the 1952 and 1956 presidential elections, and remains the core of the "psychological" or "Michigan School" of electoral behavior research. The study approached the act of voting by examining the psychological orientations of voters. While it did not address the role of the media directly, it did find that people's perceptions of the political parties, candidates, and issues were the best measure of determining how they would ultimately vote. The psychological methods used in this study were later transferred to media studies. While these early psychological studies primarily focused on presidential elections, the findings have provided the foundation for an ongoing inquiry into the mass media and its effect in general and on democracy in particular.

The implications of the mass media for a democratic society are several. First, democracy needs informed, intelligent participants to survive, and the media are the channels of information. Second, the flow of information has increased and frequently does not reflect the realities of society. Third, the media are subject to manipulation and bias, often in very subtle ways. Finally, as we enter the 21st century, the mass media's role in sustaining democratic values and beliefs will be more important than at any other time in our history because of the weakening of political parties, local political organizations, and interpersonal communications. Once again, governing will be closely interwoven with the mass media. The media's role in the democratic process, coupled with the growth of the nation and the media, has resulted in a mediated democracy. The media are increasingly powerful as they provide the information necessary to a democratic system and are instrumental in acquiring democratic values.

summary

In this chapter we focused on the relationship between the media and democracy. First we examined fundamental principles of democracy—sovereignty, political equality, popular consultation (elections), and majority rule. The media's role in supporting and preserving these are one of their major contributions to society. The ideal of democracy was compared with the mediated world of modern politics, where the media's role has grown from that of a watchdog to an active participant in shaping government policies and practices.

How democratic norms are passed from one generation to the next was explored in terms of the media's role in political socialization and resocialization. Where until only a few years ago the family was viewed as the most important agent in these processes, now research indicates that the media are the primary agent of political socialization.

The media affect individuals' development in three areas: social, psychological, and physiological. All forms of the mass media have originated with upper-income groups and eventually become accessible to lower-income groups, and this pattern continues with the Internet. Concern about the psychological effects of broadcasting renewed the study of the mass media in a period when little was known about how individuals related to broadcast messages. Currently little is known about the physiological impact of the mass media, although there is evidence that watching certain types of programs may cause physical illness.

Finally, the chapter related studies of the 1940s to what has become today an important concern—the relationship between the mass media and the political process.

endnotes

[1]John Thompson, *The Media and Modernity: A Social Theory of the Media* (Stanford, Calif.: Stanford University Press, 1995).

[2]*Ibid.*, 3.

[3]Austin Ranney and Willmore Kendall, *Democracy and the American Party System* (New York: Harcourt, Brace & World, Inc., 1956), 6.

[4]It should be noted that a considerable part of the adult population of Athens was excluded from the class of "citizen," and therefore from any share in the city's decision-making powers. Neither women, slaves, nor resident foreigners were included.

[5]Benjamin I. Page, *Who Deliberates? Mass Media in Modern Democracy* (Chicago: University of Chicago Press, 1996), 4. Page's projections are based on a nation with 250,000 citizens.

[6]Dan Nimmo and James E. Combs, *Mediated Political Realities*, 2nd ed. (New York: Longman, 1990), xv.

[7]James Bryce, *Modern Democracies*, Vol. 1 (New York: The Macmillan Co., 1924), 20.

[8]Robert M. MacIver, *The Web of Government* (New York: The Macmillan Co., 1949), 9.

[9]Giovanni Sartori, *The Theory of Democracy Revised*, Vol. 1 (Chatham, N.J.: Chatham House, 1987), 86–87.

[10]Carl J. Friedrich, *Constitutional Government and Democracy*, 4th ed. (Waltham, Mass: Blaisdell, 1968), 502.

[11]Richard Dawson, Kenneth Prewitt, and Karen Dawson, *Political Socialization*, 2nd ed. (Boston: Little, Brown and Co., 1977).

[12]David O. Sears and Nicholas A. Valentino, "Politics Matters: Political Events as Catalysts for Preadult Socialization," *American Political Science Review*, 91(March 1977):59.

[13]*Ibid.*, 45.

[14]Richard M. Merelman, "Revitalizing Political Socialization," in Margaret Herman, ed., *Political Psychology* (San Francisco: Jossey-Bass, 1986), 279–319.

[15]Paul Allen Beck, "The Role of Agents in Political Socialization," in Stanley Allen Renshon, ed., *Handbook of Political Socialization: Theory and Research* (New York: Free Press, 1977), 115–141.

[16]*Ibid.*; Doris Graber, *Processing the News: How People Tame the Information Tide*, 2nd ed. (New York: Longman, 1988); Doris Graber, *Mass Media and American Politics*, 5th ed. (Washington, D.C.: Congressional Quarterly Press, 1997).

[17]Dawson *et al., op. cit.*

[18]Beck, *op cit.*; Dawson *et al., op. cit.*; Graber, *op. cit.*, 1997.

[19]Norris R. Johnson, "Television and Politicization: A Test of Competing Models," *Journalism Quarterly*, 50(Autumn 1973):474.

[20]Steven Chaffee, L. Scott Ward, and Leonard P. Tipton, "Mass Communications and Political Socialization," *Journalism Quarterly*, 47(Winter 1970):647–659.

[21]*Ibid.*, 658.

[22]Neil Hollander, "Adolescents and the War: The Sources of Socialization," *Journalism Quarterly*, 48(Autumn 1971):477. Emphasis added.

[23]Doris Graber, *Mass Media and American Politics*, 3rd ed. (Washington, D.C.: Congressional Quarterly Press, 1993), 11.

[24]George Gerbner, G. Gross, L. Morgan, and N. Signorielli, "Media and the Family: Images and Impact," paper presented at the Research Forum on Family Issues, National Advisory Committee of the White House Conference on Families, Washington, D.C., April 10–11, 1980 (ERIC Document Reproduction Services No. ED 198 919).

[25]Diana Owen, "Making Citizens in the Media Age: The Socializing Effects of Mass Communication," paper presented at the Annual Meeting of the Southern Political Science Association, Atlanta, Georgia, October 28–31, 1998. It should be noted that scholars from the communication discipline are more likely to push the position for the prominence of the mass media in the socialization process.

[26]Graber, *op. cit.*, 1997, 12.

[27]William G. Mayer, "The Polls: Trends in Media Usage" *Public Opinion Quarterly*, 57(Winter 1993):594.

[28]The Pew Research Center for the People and the Press, "One-in-Ten Voters Online for Campaign '96," *www.People-Press.org/tec96-1.htm*, December 16, 1996.

[29]*Ibid.*

[30]Bradley S. Greenberg and Brenda Dervin, "Mass Communications Among the Urban Poor," *Public Opinion Quarterly*, 34(1970):224–235.

[31]George Gerbner, Larry Gross, Michael Morgan, and Nancy Signorielli, "Living with Television: The Dynamics of the Cultivation Process," in Jennings Bryant and Dolf Zillmann, eds., *Perspectives of Media Effects* (Hillsdale, N.J.: Lawrence Erlbaum, 1986).

[32]George Gerbner, Larry Gross, Michael Morgan, and Nancy Signorielli, "The 'Mainstreaming' of American Violence," Profile No. 11, *Journal of Communications*, 30(1980):37–47.

[33]S. Robert Lichter, Linda S. Lichter, and Stanley Rothman, *Prime Time: How TV Portrays American Culture* (Washington, D.C.: Regnery, 1994).

[34]S. Robert Lichter, Linda S. Lichter, and Stanley Rothman, "From Lucy to Lacy: TV's Dream Girls," *Public Opinion*, 9(September/October 1986):16–19.

[35]*Ibid.*, 19.

[36]Gerbner *et al.*, "The 'Mainstreaming' of American Violence," *op. cit.*

[37]Senior citizens are the first- or second-fastest growing, depending on how Baby Boomers are measured. Senior citizens have become a highly organized and vocal group in American politics.

[38]Gerbner *et al.*, "The 'Mainstreaming' of American Violence," *op. cit.*

[39]See L.J. Shrum, "Assessing the Social Influence of Television: A Social Cognitions Perspective of Cultivation," *Communication Research*, 22(August 1995):402–429; P. Hirsh, "The Scary World of the Non-Viewer and Other Anomaliers: A Reappraisal of Gerbner et al.'s Findings on Cultivation Analysis," *Communication Research*, 7(1980):403–456; M. Hughes, "The Fruits of Cultivation Analysis: A Reexamination of Some Effects of Television Watching," *Public Opinion Quarterly*, 44(1980):287–302.

[40]L.J. Shrum, *op. cit.*

[41]R.P. Hawkins and S. Pingree, "Some Processes in the Cultivation Effect," *Communication Research*, 7(April 1980):193–226.

[42]Robert Entman, "Blacks in the News: Television, Modern Racism, and Cultural Change," *Journalism Quarterly*, 69(1992):341–361; Kathleen Hall Jamieson, *Dirty Politics: Deception, Distraction, and Democracy* (New York: Oxford University Press, 1992); Jon Hurtwitz and Mark Peffley, "Public Perceptions of Race and Crime: The Racial Stereotypes," *American Journal of Political Science*, 41(April 1997):375–401.

[43]Zillmann, *op. cit.*

[44]Robert Kubey, Mark Shiffet, Niranjala Weerakkody, and Stephen Ukrilley, "Demographic Diversity on Cable: Have the New Cable Channels Made a Difference in Representation of Gender, Race, and Age?" *Journal of Broadcast and Electronic Media*, 39(Fall 1995):459–471.

[45]*Ibid.*, 465–466.

[46]Gordon Allport, "The Historical Background of Social Psychology," in Gardner Lindzey and Elliot Aronson, eds., *Handbook of Social Psychology*, Vol. 1 (New York: Random House, 1985).

[47]Harold Lasswell, *Propaganda Techniques in the World War* (New York: Peter Smith, 1927), 220.

[48]Hadley Cantril and Gordon Allport, *The Psychology of Radio* (New York: Harper & Brothers Publishers, 1937), vii.

[49]Daniel Lerner and Lyle Nelson, eds., *Communication Research: A Half-Century Appraisal* (Honolulu: University of Honolulu Press, 1977), 31.

[50]Herbert Hyman and Paul Sheatsley, "Some Reasons Why Information Campaigns Fail," *Public Opinion Quarterly*, 11(1947):412–423.

[51]Paul Lazarsfeld, Bernard Berelson, and Hazel Gaudet, *The People's Choice*, 2nd ed. (New York: Columbia University Press, 1948).

[52]Joseph T. Klapper, *The Effects of Mass Communication* (New York: The Free Press, 1960).

[53]*Ibid.*, 15.

[54]Maxwell McCombs and Donald Shaw, *The Emergence of American Political Issues: The Agenda-Setting Functions of the Press* (St. Paul, Minn.: West Publishers, 1977), 5.

[55]See Lewis Donshew and Philip Palomgreen, "A Reappraisal of Dissonance and the Selective Exposure Hypothesis," *Journalism Quarterly*, 48(Autumn 1971):421–420; Michael Milburn, "A Longitudinal Test of the Selective Exposure Hypothesis," *Public Opinion Quarterly*, 43 (Winter 1979):507–517.

[56]Braven Smillie, "Japanese Cartoon Show Pulled After Hundreds of Kids Sickened," *Dallas Morning News*, December 18, 1997:23A.

[57]"Doctors Urge Limiting TV Time for Kids," *Dallas Morning News*, August 4, 1999:1.

[58]Lazarsfeld *et al., op. cit.*

[59]Paul Lazarsfeld, Bernard Berelson, and Hazel Gaudet, *The People's Choice*, 2nd ed. (New York: Columbia University Press, 1948), xxxv. Emphasis added.

[60]Joe McGinnis, *The Selling of the President* (New York: Pocket Books, 1974).

[61]Bernard Berelson, Paul Lazarsfeld, and William McPhee, *Voting* (Chicago: University of Chicago Press, 1954).

[62]*Ibid.*, Chapter 10.

[63]Campbell *et al., The American Voter.* Also see Angus Campbell and Robert Kahn, *The People Elect a President* (Ann Arbor, Mich.: Survey Research Center, Institute for Social Research, University of Michigan, 1952); Angus Campbell, Gerald Gurin, and Warren Miller, *The Voter Decides* (Evanston, Ill.: Row, Peterson & Co., 1954).

CHAPTER 4

understanding the changing media

One of the most complex tasks in studying the mass media involves determining their influence. As noted in the previous chapter, researchers have shifted from viewing the media as being all-intrusive to having only secondary effects. Meanwhile, the popular view is that the mass media exert immense political influence. For instance, in the 1996 and 1998 general elections, they were credited with making and selling candidates, manipulating issues, and contributing to the overall negative perception of the political process. But social science researchers have been unable to definitely attribute these effects to the media, perhaps because of problems inherent in measuring media effects, perhaps because of the complex ways individuals process media messages. This chapter focuses on seven approaches employed to study media effects and the problems associated with those approaches. These approaches include stimulus response, selective perception, uses and gratifications, schema, agenda setting, framing, and priming.[1]

The stimulus Response Approach

Studies of the media in the 1920s and 1930s were guided by the psychological concept of stimulus response. This approach to the media emphasized the media's ability to stimulate the audience into action in accordance with the media's message. It coincided with the formative years of radio and the interval between World Wars I and II, a period characterized by fear of the unknown and widespread use of propaganda. The stimulus response model assumes a passive audience that receives powerful media messages, which in turn produce a direct or "hypodermic" effect on that audience. These early studies were based not on scientific evidence, but on the "common wisdom" of the day. Journalist Walter Lippmann argued in 1922 that individuals exist in two distinct worlds, the *environment* (the world as it actually exists) and the *pseudo-environment* (individuals' private perceptions of the world). The latter world, Lippmann claimed, results from the media's depiction of the real world.[2] Lippmann's view was congruent with both the scholarly and popular assessments of the mass media of the period. Concern with the link between the pseudo-environment and the media led to attempts to discover how the media affected voters' attitudes.

The selective perception Approach

History has repeatedly shown that shifts in perspective alter outcomes. The change in perspective associated with the selective perception approach not only altered how the media were perceived, but replaced earlier assumptions about the media and how people received information. The most profound change was the media came to be seen as having an indirect effect caused by an active audience.

Stuart Rice wrote that behavior is a manifestation of political attitudes that "filter" objects in the individual's world.[3] Early studies of the media's effects on voters' behavior reflected this view. The authors of *Voting*, for example, found that Republican voters they surveyed who favored the Taft-Hartley Act were more likely to believe that Governor Dewey, the Republican presidential candidate in 1948, also supported the bill, when in fact he opposed it. They also found that less than half (40 percent) of Democrats who favored the legislation knew that President Truman had vetoed the bill in 1947 and campaigned against it during the 1948 presidential election. This type of perceptual screening occurred on other issues as well.[4] This approach to the study of media effects produced what is known as the "minimal effects" model, which held that important intervening variables change and filter media messages. In a recent study of the media's effects on people's understanding of economic conditions, H. Brandon Haller and Helmut Norpoth concluded that their findings "echo the minimal media effect conclusions of earlier studies" regarding the media's impact on citizens' understanding of economic conditions.[5]

Proponents of this theory believe people acquire bits of information that they perceive to be personally helpful and ignore others in their assessments of the political process, candidates, and issues. Various *cognitive balance theories* attempt to explain why people choose a particular item over another. Common to all is the concept that people avoid information that disturbs their peace of mind, offends their political or social taste, or conflicts with information, attitudes, and feelings already held. To avoid discomfort, people *select* information that is congruent with their existing beliefs. For example, two people reading the same article might have very different *cognitions*, or reactions. While one might find an essay by William F. Buckley or George Wills provocative and insightful, another might reject it because it conflicted with his or her views.

The selective attention approach to the media assumes an audience that actively seeks information that conforms to its perceptions and rejects information that does not. In addition, it holds that people filter information through a selection process that includes selective exposure, selective attention, and selective retention. As messages are received (in this case media messages), a variety of factors aid the individual in selecting some and disregarding others. These factors include political predisposition, issue orientation, socioeconomic status, ethnicity, and religion, to mention a few. The filtering process is important because it serves as a gatekeeper for accepted and rejected messages. There are many reasons a message may be rejected that have nothing to do with its content or structure. These include the person delivering the message and the medium.

The Filtering Process

Message ———⯈ Accept ———⯈ Action
⯇——— Reject

The uses and gratifications approach

The uses and gratifications approach also sees the audience as an active pursuer of media messages. During the 1960s and 1970s it was increasingly recognized that a more complex conceptualization of media usage was needed, one that explained how people interact with the media. Researchers began asking why people exposed themselves to particular media by investigating what uses they made of the media and what gratifications they received from their selection. Unlike previous approaches, this approach stressed the individual's uses of the media.

Paul Lazarsfeld, Robert Merton, and Harold Lasswell were among the first to employ this approach. Lazarsfeld and Merton proposed that status conferral (the status one places on oneself or others) and ethnicity helped explain why people chose certain radio programs.[6] Harold Lasswell suggested that by performing certain activities, such as surveillance (also known as the watchdog function), media content produced common effects on people. [7] Later researchers found that television provided viewers with a sense of parasocial interaction with media personalities.[8] That is, viewers tend to regard those personalities as part of their daily social structure. L.L. Pearlin, for instance, found that viewing television allowed people to escape from unpleasant life experiences,[9] while Harold Mendelson demonstrated that media entertainment reduced anxiety created by the media news.[10] Through the years, researchers have found that the media have a variety of uses and provide a variety of gratifications for their audiences, and some are related to politics.

Elihu Katz, Jay Blumler, and Michael Gurevitch have outlined three objectives of this approach: to explain how people use the media to gratify their needs, to understand the motives for their media behavior, and to identify the consequences that follow from the needs, motives, and behavior.[11] The authors have focused on the social and psychological origins of needs, arguing that needs generate expectations of the mass media. These expectations result in different patterns of media exposure (or engagement in other activities), which lead to various consequences, including unintended ones.[12] This approach to the media is based on six assumptions: (1) Audiences are variable. (2) Communication behavior is goal oriented, purposive, and motivated, so people are active participants in the process of selecting and interpreting the media. (3) People take the initiative in selecting and using the media to satisfy their felt needs or desires. (4) A host of social and psychological factors mediate individuals' media behavior and expectations, including predispositions, interactions, and environment. (5) The media compete with other forms of communications for selection, attention, and use. (6) People are typically more influential than the media in the relationship.[13] A citizen who knows a candidate personally or is highly involved with an issue may depend less on the media than others. The principle elements in this approach are the individual's communication *needs* and *motives*.

Table 4.1 shows typologies developed by Ehilu Katz and colleagues and by Denis McQuail and associates. The typologies represent the two essential components of the uses and gratifications approach to the study of the mass media. This approach incorporates many concepts of earlier approaches, but it is more complex and shifts the focus from the media themselves to how and why they are used.

Uses and gratifications has been primarily utilized by those in the field of communications studies, but numerous studies have applied it to the study of the media's role in the political process, attempting to explain the media's uses and effects. Jay Blumler identified the three primary uses of the media as cognition, diversion, and personal inquiry.[14] There are some empirical data to support this. For instance, at a minimum, cognitive motivations appear to lead to news and information program viewing.[15] Other studies have found links between the surveillance or information-seeking motive and information gained during political campaigns.[16] In their research on the uses and effects on political advertising, Charles Atkins and colleagues found individuals viewed political ads for information, rather than being captive audiences of the ads.[17] In addition, they found a strong correlation between exposure and personal affect for candidates. More important, the authors discovered that whether or not one was in the "information-seeking mode" was the strongest predictor of attention to political ads.[18]

Gina Garramone, in a study assessing the influence of audience motivation in the 1982 Michigan gubernatorial race, found support for "the assertion that audience motivation for attending to political advertising influences the processing and effects of the advertising."[19] This approach to the study of the media has been particularly helpful in determining why people use campaign messages presented in the media.

Table 4.1
Typology of Needs and Motives

NEEDS	MOTIVES
Strengthen understanding of self, friends, others or society	Diversion (escape, emotional release)
Strengthen states of self or society	Personal relationships (companionship, social utility)
Strengthen contacts with family, friends, society, and culture	Personal identity (personal reference, reality exploration, value reinforcement)
	Surveillance (acquisition of news and information)

Source: Ehilu Katz, Michael Gurevitch, and H. Hass, "On the Use of the Mass Media for Important Things," *American Sociological Review,* 38(1973):164–181; and Denis McQuail, Jay Blumler, and J. Brown, "The Television Audience: A Revised Perspective," in Denis McQuail, ed.), *Sociology of Mass Communications* (Middlesex, England: Penguin, 1972), 135–165.

The schema Approach

Since the 1980s mainstream social psychology has moved from cognitive consistency theories[20] to schema theory, which contends that the way people with limited time, inclination, and capacity operate in the face of a flood of information and impressions is by developing structures of understanding. These structures, called *schema* (or *schemata*), are formed through the accumulation of learning and life experiences. Schema are more or less organized general conceptions that tie clusters of bits of knowledge and information together.

Suppose, for example, a hypothetical voter formed a schema of Governor George Bush during the 2000 presidential campaign. Positive bits of information included the governor's ability to lead a large state, his youth, his family, the campaign techniques he employed, and his positions on issues important to the voter. However, the schema also included areas of concern, such as the governor's unwillingness to discuss his past, lack of foreign policy experience, and use of his family connections to avoid combat during the Vietnam War. Both positive and negative information would go into the voter's schema regarding Governor Bush.

Vincent Price explains, "Researchers have hypothesized a variety of structural forms of schema. Some propose hierarchical systems of interconnected propositions . . . whereas others propose simpler, associative structures like event sequences or scripts."[21] Regardless of the level of conceptualization— hierarchical or simplistic—all schema help people receive messages and sort information into manageable categories. Individuals usually resist basic disconfirmation of their schema by making minor modifications or creating new categories to handle the disconfirming information.[22] The schema concept has been particularly useful in explaining how people use their knowledge, as well as the structure of their thought processes.

In a landmark study, Doris Graber used the schema concept to help explain "how people tame the information tide" in processing political matters.[23] The central questions explored in her study were how people select and process information for incorporation into their thinking and what patterns they impose on the information. Graber repeatedly interviewed a panel of twenty-one registered voters in Evanston, Illinois, from January 1976 through January 1977. She divided the sample into groups, based on their use of the media (high or low) and the availability of media (easy or difficult). She found the surveyed voters excluded two out of three newspaper stories and read in full only 18 percent. Nearly half of the newspaper stories panel members noticed were only partially read. The pattern held for television and radio as well. Of fifteen to eighteen stories in a television newscast, only one was retained sufficiently to be recalled. Many television stories were lost because panel members recognized them as repeated information. From these data, Graber drew some conclusions about what people tend to grasp from the media:

> They scan the information haphazardly to extract portions that are useful to them either to flesh out existing perceptions, or amend them, or confirm and, occasionally, disconfirm them. The failure to retain a wealth of details, or to always mirror the media stimulus faithfully, springs from media consumers' practices of limiting processing to information suitable for incorporation into their schemata. Questions [asked of people] about the media content thus tend to tap what remains of the original stimulus after processing, as well as what has been recalled from previously stored information as a consequence of the media stimulus.[24]

The schema concept helps explain how people with low levels of information can participate in the democratic process and cast votes in a manner similar to those with high levels. Samuel Popkin, in his analysis of elections, concludes that people use "low information" or "gut rationality" in selecting candidates. In doing so, they employ decision-making shortcuts, such as evaluating the candidate's personality, character, and campaign skills to draw conclusions about the candidate's likely performance in office.[25] The 1992 and 1996 presidential elections found Bill Clinton battling the "character" issue while his personality and campaign style appealed to most voters. Schema are tapped when less-informed individuals are moved in a given direction through the use of symbols in the mass media. The schema approach helps explain how a democratic system can operate effectively when some citizens have low levels of information.

The Agenda-setting Approach

The agenda-setting approach also helped explain the media's impact on attitudes and what people learn from the media. Bernard Cohen introduced the concept of agenda setting as he attempted to find connections between public opinion and American foreign policy.[26] Cohen set forth the agenda-setting hypothesis:

> The press is significantly more than a purveyor of information and opinion. It may not be successful in telling its readers what to think, but it is stunningly successful in telling its readers what to think about.[27]

Maxwell E. McCombs and Donald L. Shaw studied the media's capacity to set the topical agenda during the 1968 presidential campaign. They asked survey respondents to name the "main things . . . government should concentrate on doing something about."[28] The issues mentioned were the same as those stressed in newspaper and television coverage of the campaign. McCombs and Shaw argued that this relationship was more than a sharing of concern by the public and the decision-makers, since the public obtains its information from the media. This study shifted attention from the attitudinal effects of the mass media to an examination of what people actually learn from the media.

The effects of the media on agenda setting have been studied systematically in a series of experimental and quasi-experimental studies conducted by an interdisciplinary research team at the Center for Urban Affairs and Policy Research at Northwestern University. One of the first of these studies used an experimental design to test the effect of a televised investigative report on home health care.[29] Among the general public, there was a clear agenda-setting effect: Those who viewed the program became more interested in home health care and more likely to see the need for governmental assistance. Government policymakers who viewed or heard about the program were significantly more likely to become more concerned about fraud and abuse in home health care. Interest group leaders were also significantly more interested in the problem after viewing or reviewing the media report. The result was an elevation of the issue of home health care on the public's agenda.

A second study in this series used a quasi-experimental design to examine the agenda-setting effects of a *Chicago Sun-Times* investigative report on government improprieties in the reporting and handling of rape cases in the Chicago area.[30] The agenda-setting effects of the newspaper series were more limited than those for the televised report on home health care, in part, perhaps, because of the already high level of concern about the crime among all groups.

The third study used a pre-test, post-test experimental design to study the effects of a five-part televised investigative series on police brutality in Chicago.[31] This study found that exposure to this series increased awareness of police brutality among the general public. In elite groups, however, no significant change was demonstrated.

Shanto Iyengar and Donald Kinder found evidence for agenda setting by television news in carefully designed experiments that manipulated the levels of news according to issues.[32] They inserted a modest degree of news coverage about particular issues into prerecorded network newscasts, which then produced significant shifts in viewers' beliefs about the issues. In one experiment, viewers were shown a series of telecasts containing three, six, or no stories about America's dependence on foreign energy sources. Among those in the group who were exposed to no news coverage on the issue, 24 percent cited energy as among the three most important problems facing the nation. Among those who viewed newscasts with three stories on the United States' dependency on foreign energy sources, 50 percent believed energy to be one of the most important problems. Among those whose newscasts contained six stories, 65 percent believed energy was one of the most important problems.[33] Thus, the more frequently the news draws attention to a problem (sets the agenda), the more the audience will be aware of it and consider it important.

Using data collected from identically worded questions on public policy between 1968 and 1983, Benjamin Page and Robert Shapiro showed that television has a direct impact on public opinion.[34] They found that for nearly half of the policy issues, opinion changed significantly from the period of the initial question to when it was next asked, and concluded that "what appears on TV news accounts in large part for the relatively short-term . . . changes public opinion."[35] Further investigation indicated that news commentators (news anchors, reporters in the field, or special commentators) had the most dramatic positive impact. Each commentary was associated with a change in opinion of more than 4 percentage points.[36] This is not a particularly compelling amount of change, but it suggests a need for future studies.

Donald Jordon addressed the question of a newspaper's influence on public policy by examining the *New York Times*. He found that, like television, the newspaper's greatest impact came from commentators and experts, and, as with television, presidents and members of their administrations had little impact.[37] Jordon concluded that "different actors or news sources do indeed have different impacts on public opinion and that in both newspaper items and television broadcasts experts and commentators wield heavy influence."[38] He further found both the president and members of his administration and other partisan supporters had relatively little effect on public opinion.[39]

John Zaller's study of *Newsweek's* coverage of 1980 defense spending provides another example of this medium's agenda-setting function. In the twenty-four-month period prior to the 1980 presidential election, the magazine carried fifty-seven stories on the issue of defense spending, forty-six of which (80 percent) wholly or predominantly favored more defense spending. In the twenty-four-month period following the election of Ronald Reagan, the magazine carried six stories on defense spending, with four (66 percent) opposing any increase in defense spending. Zaller concluded that public opinion moved in tandem with these shifts in the media.[40] As the magazine's emphasis on defense spending dwindled, so did the public's support for increased spending in this area. In this instance the public's position reflected *Newsweek's* agenda.

These studies on the agenda-setting function of the media support the common impression that the media possess significant power in political affairs. The agenda-setting approach to the media is generally accepted by scholars. Two narrower interpretations of the media's impact have been developed from the agenda-setting approach, framing and priming.

The framing Approach

Building on the agenda-setting principle, scholars are currently refining their examinations of the effect of the mass media on the public. Shanto Iyengar, for instance, argues that people's attitudes toward social problems depend on whom they see as responsible for the problems.[41] For example, some contend that the poor are responsible for their poverty, that they prefer welfare to work. Others argue that social forces and institutions perpetuate poverty. Iyengar contends the way the media present the poverty issue determines the public's attitudes. Studies in psychology indicate that attributing responsibility, either positive or negative, is a way of simplifying and understanding complex issues. The political world is not exempt from this rule. When issues become part of the public agenda, citizens instinctively assign responsibility in the form of blame or praise.

Television is one of several sources that influence attribution of responsibility for political issues. Nightly newscasts not only set the agenda on an issue, but also determine how the issue is "framed." According to Iyengar, framing refers to "the effects of presentation on judgment and choice." Ansolabehere and colleagues have noted that news is framed in two ways.[42] With *episodic* framing, concrete examples of the issue are presented in the story without in-depth coverage of the issue or its cause. With *thematic* framing, depth is provided but the topic is usually less appealing to the public. How issues are presented or framed affects whom the public perceives as responsible. Iyengar found that 89 percent of network news reports on crime between 1981 and 1987 focused on a specific perpetrator, victim, or criminal act.[43] During the same period, nearly 2,000 stories on terrorism were reported, of which 74 percent were live reports of some specific terrorist act, victim, or group and 26 percent covered terrorism as a general problem.[44] Such coverage presents individual acts of terrorism without explaining the motivations that led to them. Iyengar also found that news reports involving the economy conveyed information about the latest economic indicators, as well as interviews with economists, businesspeople, and public officials.

The author found that how issues were framed, with concrete examples (episodic) or more in-depth treatment (thematic), affected attributions of responsibility. Viewers who were exposed to news coverage that is framed in a thematic manner tended to assign responsibility for national issues to social factors—cultural values, economic circumstances, or motives and actions of governmental figures. When issues were covered in an episodic manner, responsibility was assigned not to social factors, but to private individuals.[45] In the case of crime, viewers assigned responsibility to those committing the offense, not to politicians or society. Thus, the manner in which media (television in the cases above) frame national problems has the effect of either shielding politicians or exposing them to public blame (or praise). Conversely, when issues are framed in episodic terms, the public is less likely to hold government, society, or politicians responsible.

W. Russell Neuman and colleagues contend that the media and public use five types of frames: economic, conflict, powerlessness, human impact, and morality.[46] Economic presentations focus on the "bottom line," profits and losses, or the value of capitalism. Conflict presentations include "race-horse" accounts of campaigns and stories that polarize the audience by focusing on the criminal versus the victim or one region against another. In the powerless frame, the government is depicted as unable to help in the face of a major event, such as stock market problems, epidemics such as AIDS, and drug addiction. The human impact frame, which involves reporters placing a "human" face on a story in an attempt to personalize it, is increasingly used. The final frame is that of morality. While reporters might not themselves assign a moral to a disease like AIDS, they can inject a moral element in their selection of those they interview. For example, if Jerry Falwell were interviewed, he would raise moral questions.

Matthew Kerbel and Marc Ross, in a study of the framing effects of network television during the presidential elections of 1984–1996, found framing was predominantly negative and impugned the motives of those seeking office.[47] They argued that such framing helps perpetuate cynicism about politics and makes informed political choice increasingly difficult. The authors found the most prevalent frame during the primaries was conflict, with "horse-race" stories accounting for 48.8 percent of presidential campaign stories. Next most common were personal attributes at 27.7 percent and issues at 20.6 percent.[48]

During the 2000 presidential election, members of Governor Bush's campaign staff expressed concern over the number and content of nightly jokes by Jay Leno and David Letterman. They were concerned that such remarks were creating an image of their candidate as an ex-fraternity boy, an anti-intellectual, a former drunk, and a cocaine user. It appears likely that the line between entertainment and hard news will become increasingly blurred in the future.

The priming Approach

The priming or cognitive-neo-association approach posits a more direct link between the mass media and their effects on their audience. According to Iyengar and Kinder, priming refers to "changes in the standards that people use to make political evaluations."[49] Eunkyunk Jo and Leonard Berkowitz explain that "when people witness, read, or hear of an event through the mass media, ideas having similar meaning are activated in them for a short time afterwards, and that these thoughts in turn can activate other semantically related ideas and action tendencies."[50] Gathering information requires time and effort, so citizens tend to use and to be influenced by readily available information. Television is particularly important in this model, since it is the most accessible source of information. Scholars argue that the media call attention to some matters while ignoring others (agenda setting), and priming occurs in the process.

An example of priming emerged during the last years of the Bush administration. The administration was engaged in building an international coalition to drive Saddam Hussein's forces from Kuwait. As the media focused on President Bush's handling of the situation, the president's job approval ratings reached record highs in the Gallup polls. A few months later the media began questioning Bush's economic leadership at home, and the president's approval ratings soon fell to the lowest of his administration. According to the priming principle, the shift in the media's attention from foreign success to domestic failure changed the standards by which President Bush was judged. By focusing on particular issues, events, or themes, the media set the criteria by which politicians, and particularly presidents, are evaluated.

The change in President Bush's standing occurred over months, but priming can work more rapidly. The disclosure in 1986 that funds were being secretly channeled to the Nicaraguan contras from money obtained from covert arms sales to Iran had an immediate priming effect. The Iran-contra affair dominated the media and changed the standard of evaluation for President Reagan.[51] Since most Americans opposed such aid, the story quickly led to President Reagan's decline in approval ratings. Priming is particularly strong when news stories explicitly suggest that incumbent politicians are directly responsible for a state of affairs, as in the House of Representatives' check-bouncing scandal or the Whitewater investigation. However, priming also occurs when politicians have been successful, as with

President Bush's popularity during the Gulf War and President Clinton's popularity during the budget fight with congressional Republicans during his first term.

There has been a continual evolution in the methods researchers have used to examine the media. While there is no agreement concerning the best approach, it is clear that the relationship between the media and political institutions is far more complex than was once thought. It is also clear that the mass media do more than entertain their audiences or transmit news. They can also influence the thoughts and behaviors of their audiences. There is widespread agreement that the media set the political agenda. The concern today is that the media are going beyond telling us "what we need to know" to telling us "how we should react."

measuring the media

While the approaches to the study of the mass media have continued to evolve through the years, the problems associated with measuring the impact of the media continue to represent the most serious obstacle to those attempting to address the relationship between the media and the political process. As the media's role in the process has expanded, so too has interest in the problems of measurement. There are four prominent methods used in attempts to measure the media's impact: surveys, experimental designs, content analysis, and in-depth interviews. None can prove a causal relationship between the media and politics, nor are they mutually exclusive—many studies incorporate multiple methods. Their use can suggest certain relationships and improve our understanding.

Surveys

The most common method of ascertaining the mass media's impact has been "self-reporting" by respondents in surveys. However, this method has its own problems. First, self-reporting is not as reliable as one would like, for respondents commonly overreport. For example, the 1989 National Elections Studies pilot study found that 35 percent of respondents claimed to have listened to National Public Radio (NPR) once a week, but Arbitron diary reports indicated that only 6 percent listened to NRP, thus producing a possible overreporting of 29 percent.[52] Second, self-reporting cannot determine if the media actually provided new information if the person did use the media. Since researchers rarely know all the information a person has before he or she has contact with the media, it is impossible to pinpoint the exact influence of the media on the individual. Third, since the impact of the media varies with the subject matter and the way individuals process material, it is difficult to accurately assess the media's impact. For instance, research indicates that new stories have a greater impact than old stories, yet there is no assurance that an "old" story is in fact old to the person receiving it. In addition, people differ in the amount of information they absorb from the same media. The underlying problem is that we cannot directly link media to individual behavior.

Attempts to measure the media's impact have found that the media can produce unanticipated effects. A study by William C. Adams and colleagues of ABC's 1984 broadcast of the highly publicized drama *The Day After*, concerning the horrors of nuclear war, found such unanticipated effects.[53] It was anticipated that many of the 80 million viewers would become more concerned about nuclear war, but that reaction did not occur, leading some observers to proclaim it had no effect. However, most observers failed to notice several unanticipated effects of the broadcast. The percentage of people who had previously criticized President Reagan for pursuing policies likely to lead to war dropped sharply, from 57 percent to 43 percent, after the program aired. In political terms, this translated into a decrease in the number of people who opposed the Reagan administration's military policies. At the same time, viewers became more conciliatory toward the Soviet Union and more supportive of general arms limitation agreements between the two superpowers.

Many measurement challenges are inherent in the social sciences, such as determining what individuals are thinking when they receive information or what factors they include in the processing process. Others, like unexpected consequences, call for larger and more comprehensive approaches to the study of the media. It is important to be aware of the limitations measurement challenges impose on our understanding of the relationship between the media and the political process.

Experimental Designs

The use of experimental designs is one of the oldest techniques in the social sciences, and in many ways closest to the "pure" sciences. While there are many variations, a common factor is the researcher's effort to examine before and after effects. In the case of the media, these would be the media's reporting and the public's reaction. Experimental designs have been used extensively to determine the impact of television on viewers' preferences. For instance, this method is frequently used to ascertain if more exposure heightens a viewer's awareness of issues. In the case of television, after completing a questionnaire, participants might view a newscast the content of which researchers have altered. This method gives the researchers control of the viewing environment as well as the content. A typical design would include groups of individuals separated by some criteria that are important to the investigation. A study to measure the media's effect on support for the United States military intervention in Kosovo might have three groups view different news accounts of Kosovo. One group could receive the actual news telecasts for a given period, the next an altered version with more or less Kosovo coverage, and the final group no news on Kosovo. The groups could then be compared to ascertain their views on the Kosovo situation and thereby inferring the media's impact on those views.

There are serious problems with experimental designs. First, they typically provide no useful descriptive data. If, for example, an experiment indicated that 30 percent of each group opposed federal gun control, it would not tell much about the 70 percent who favored gun control. Second, control groups represent an artificial test of a hypothesis. The relevance of the experiment to the real world is always subject to question, for the subjects are not in their normal environments when tested, which raises questions about the effect of the testing environment on the outcomes. Finally, the findings in an experimental design may not be generalizable to other segments of the population.[54] Frequently experimental studies do not select their subjects randomly, so the findings cannot be viewed as representative of the general population. Many experimental studies use college students or some other specialized subgroups, thereby reducing the significance of the findings.

Despite these limitations, experimental designs, like surveys, have aided those interested in the impact of the media on citizens. Experimental designs have provided a greater understanding of how citizens engage the media.

Content Analysis

While content analysis is used in many disciplines, ranging from English to religion, it is particularly well suited to the study of the media. This type of measurement attempts to clarify assumptions about how the media represents items. Often it is said that a newspaper, magazine, or television program favors one side of an issue or one political party more than the other. Content analysis is a method of measuring the accuracy of such assertions. It provides a systematic way of examining materials that are typically evaluated on an impressionistic basis. Suppose one believed that a television news program favored Republican candidates over Democrats. One way to determine the validity of this assertion would be to count the number of stories aired on each party over a period of time. This could be extended by analyzing the placement and time given to each.

Content analysis is a widely used technique in media studies and aids attempts to move from impression to fact. There are disadvantages to this approach, as well. First, the type of documents examined might not be the most appropriate. In television, examining those who make reference to the issue being measured might be more important than measuring the number of stories or the time allotted. Also, there is evidence that commentators and anchors have a greater impact on the public than outside experts. Assigning scores to comments can be difficult. In the partisanship example above, a determination must be made on what is "pro" Republican or Democrat. This can be difficult, for most statements are not clearly slanted toward either party. In addition, there must be solid rules for the coding process, with multiple coders to prevent bias on the part of the investigator.

In-depth Interviews

The final method of measuring the media's effect is to conduct intensive interviews of individuals over a period of time. While political scientists have not used this technique as frequently as other social scientists, several important works have employed it. This method allows the interviewer to use probing and follow-up questions. Doris Graber, who used this method in her book *Processing the News*,[55] cites four additional advantages. One, the method allows those interviewed to pursue their own trains of thought. Two, these intense interviews are dialectical; they permit give and take, which gives the interviewer a better understanding of how and why those interviewed arrived at their decisions. Three, they provide an accurate textual account of everything said. Finally, they provide a biographical referent, as they allow one's life experiences to be related to information-processing and reasoning patterns.

Like the other methods, this one also has disadvantages. The group is necessarily small, which makes it difficult to generalize from the findings to a larger population. Some researchers doubt whether those interviewed fully and accurately report their thoughts. Both problems can alter findings, but with a small group the margin of error is magnified many times more than in a traditional random sample.

summary

This chapter has addressed approaches scholars have used to studying the media's impact and to measuring that impact. The growth of media research coincided with the development of radio broadcasting in the 1920s and 1930s, and it increased with World War II. Some of the initial research focused on determining what direct effects radio was having on the public. The first approach used, stimulus response, grew out of the fear that radio broadcasts could be used to spread propaganda. The next approach, selective perception, argued that people selectively perceive information based on party affiliation, socioeconomic background, and other factors.

By the 1960s and 1970s the uses and gratifications approach had become a dominant means of explaining the media's impact. These researchers argued that people used the media to achieve gratification, primarily in the form of entertainment, rather than political information.

The schema approach followed. It held that people form mental pictures (schema) about a wide variety of the things, including the political world. The media help reinforce or undermine these schema.

The preceding approaches were based on what psychologists call the cognitive world, or one's mental pictures of the world. Since the late 1960s a great deal of attention has been paid to the media's role in agenda setting. The idea is rather straightforward—the media may not tell us what to think, but they tell us what to think about. Unlike earlier approaches, this one can be tested. Through the use of experiential designs, researchers can see the impact of the media's coverage, or lack of coverage, of a story.

In a related approach, framing, scholars argue that how a story is framed affects how it is received. For example, when a story involving AIDS focuses on those afflicted, the public is more likely to perceive the individuals as responsible for their condition. If the story examines the social and economic costs of the disease, the public is more likely to view society as responsible. Finally, the issue of priming is currently under investigation, which is particularly important for politics. It is argued that how a story is presented "primes" the audience and prepares them for an interpretation that is formed by the media.

The issue at the heart of all media research is how the media's impact can be measured. Researchers have relied on four methods: surveys, experimental designs, content analysis, and in-depth interviews. Currently the most widely used are surveys, followed by experimental designs and content analysis.

Endnotes

[1]See Dan Nimmo and Keith Sanders, eds., *Handbook of Political Communications* (Thousand Oaks, Calif.: Sage Publications, 1981; Melvin L. Defleur and Sandra Ball-Rokeach, *Theories of Mass Communication* (New York: Longman, 1989); Denis McQuail, *Mass Communication Theory: An Introduction*, 3rd ed. (Thousand Oaks, Calif.: Sage Publications, 1994); and Jennings Bryant and Dolf Zillmann, eds., *Media Effects: Advances in Theory and Research* (Mahwah, N.J: Lawrence Erlbaum Associates, 1994).

[2]Walter Lippmann, *Public Opinion* (New York: Macmillan Co., 1949).

[3]Stuart Rice, *Quantitative Methods in Politics* (New York: Alfred A. Knopf, 1928).

[4]Bernard Berelson, Paul Lazarsfeld, and William McKee, *Voting* (Chicago: University of Chicago Press, 1954), 221.

[5]H. Brandon Haller and Helmut Norpoth, "Reality Bites: News Exposure and Economic Opinion," *Public Opinion Quarterly*, 61(Winter 1997):572–573.

[6]Paul Lazarsfeld and Robert Merton, "Mass Communications, Popular Taste and Organized Social Action," in Lyman Bryson, ed., *The Communication of Ideas* (New York: Harper, 1948), 95–115.

[7]Harold Lasswell, "The Structure and Function of Communication in Society," in Bryson, *op. cit.*, 37–52.

[8]D. Horton and R. Wohl, "Mass Communications and Para-Social Interaction," *Psychiatry*, 19(1959):215–229.

[9]L.L. Pearlin, "Social and Personal Stress and Escape Television Viewing," *Public Opinion Quarterly*, 23(1959):255–259.

[10]Harold Mendelson. "Socio-Psychological Perspective on the Mass Media and Public Anxiety," *Journalism Quarterly*, 40(1963):511–516.

[11]Elihu Katz, Jay Blumler, and Michael Gurevitch, "Utilization of Mass Communications by the Individual," in Jay Blumler and Elihu Katz, eds., *The Uses of Mass Communications: Current Perspectives on Uses and Gratifications Research* (Thousand Oaks, Calif.: Sage Publications, 1994), 19–32.

[12]*Ibid.*, 20.

[13]Alan M. Rubin, "Media Uses and Effects: A Uses-and-Gratifications Perspective," in Jennings Bryant and Dolf Zillmann, eds., *Media Effects: Advances in Theory and Research* (Mahwah, N.J.: Lawrence Erlbaum Associates, 1994), 286.

[14]Jay Blumler, "The Role of Theory in Uses and Gratifications Studies," *Communication Research*, 6(1979):9–36.

[15]Alan Rubin, "A Multivariate Analysis of 60 Minutes Viewing Motivations," *Journalism Quarterly*, 58(1981):529–534.

[16]J. McLeod and L. Becker, "Testing the Validity of Gratification Measures Through Political Effects Analysis," in Jay Blumler and E. Katz, eds., *The Uses of Mass Communications: Current Perspectives on Gratifications Research* (Thousand Oaks, Calif.: Sage Publications, 1974), 137–164.

[17]Charles Atkins, Lawrence Bowen, Oguz Nayman, and Kenneth Sheinkopf, "Quality Versus Quality in Televised Political Ads," *Public Opinion Quarterly*, 37(1973):209–224.

[18]*Ibid.*

[19]Gina M. Garramone, "Audience Motivation Effects: More Evidence," *Communication Research*, 11(January 1984):93.

[20]Shelley E. Taylor, "The Interface of Cognitive and Social Psychology," in John Harvey, ed., *Cognition, Social Behavior and the Environment* (Mahwah, N.J.: Lawrence Erlbaum Associates, 1981), 189–211.

[21]Vincent Price, *Public Opinion* (Thousand Oaks, Calif.: Sage Publications, 1992), 52.

[22]Doris Graber, *Processing the News*, 2nd ed. (New York: Longman, 1978), 184–186.

[23]*Ibid.*

[24]Doris Graber, "Information Processing and the Media," in Stanley Feldman et al., "Political Applications of Information Processing Theory," paper prepared for presentation at the Annual Meeting of the Midwest Political Science Association, Chicago, April 1985:2.

[25]Samuel Popkin, *The Reasoning Voter* (Chicago: University of Chicago Press, 1991).

[26]Bernard Cohen, *The Press and Foreign Policy* (Princeton, N.J.: Princeton University Press, 1963).

[27]*Ibid.*, 15.

[28]Maxwell McCombs and Donald L. Shaw, "The Agenda-Setting Function of the Mass Media," *Public Opinion Quarterly*, 36(Summer 1972):176–87.

[29]Fay Lomax Cook *et al.*, "Media and Agenda Setting: Effects on the Public Interest Group Leaders, Policy Makers, and Policy," *Public Opinion Quarterly*, 47(Summer 1983):16–35.

[30]David L. Protess, Donna Leff, Stephen Brooks, and Margaret Gordon, "Uncovering Rape: The Watchdog Press and the Limits of Agenda-Setting," *Public Opinion Quarterly*, 49(Spring 1985):19–38.

[31]Donna Leff, David Protess, and Stephen Brooks, "Crusading Journalism: Changing Public Attitudes and Policy-Making Agendas," *Public Opinion Quarterly*, 50(Fall 1950):300–315.

[32]Shanto Iyengar and Donald Kinder, *News That Matters: Television and American Opinion* (Chicago: University of Chicago Press, 1987).

[33]*Ibid.*, 24.

[34]Benjamin Page and Robert Y. Shapiro, *The Rational Public: Fifty Years of Trends in America's Policy Preferences* (Chicago: University of Chicago Press, 1982).

[35]*Ibid.*, 344.

[36]*Ibid.*

[37]Donald Jordon, "Newspaper Effects on Policy Preferences," *Public Opinion Quarterly*, 57(Summer 1993):191.

[38]*Ibid.*, 197.

[39]*Ibid.*

[40]John Zaller, *The Nature and Origins of Mass Opinions* (New York: Cambridge University Press, 1992), 15.

[41]Shanto Iyengar, "Framing Responsibility for Political Issues," *The Annals*, 546(July 1996):61.

[42]Stephen Ansolabehere, Roy Behr, and Shanto Iyengar, *The Media Game: American Politics in the Television Age* (New York: Macmillan Co., 1993),143.

[43]Shanto Iyengar, *Is Anyone Responsible? How Television Frames Political Issues* (Chicago: University of Chicago Press, 1991).

[44]*Ibid.*

[45]*Ibid.*

[46]W. Russell Neuman, Marion R. Just, and Ann N. Crigler, *Common Knowledge* (Chicago: University of Chicago Press, 1992), Chapter 4.

[47]Matthew R. Kerbel and Marc Ross, "Television News Frames and Informed Political Choice: A Longitudinal Analysis of U.S. Presidential Elections," paper presented at the Annual American Political Science Association Meeting, Boston, Mass., September 3–6, 1998.

[48]*Ibid.*

[49]Shanto Iyengar and Donald Kinder, *News That Matters: Television and American Public Opinion* (Chicago: University of Chicago Press, 1987), 63.

[50]Eunkyunk Jo and Leonard Berkowitz, "A Priming Effect Analysis of Media Influence: An Update," in Jennings Bryant and Dolf Zillmann, *Media Effects: Advances in Theory and Research* (Mahwah, N.J.: Lawrence Erlbaum Associates, 1994), 45.

[51]Jon Kronsnick and Donald Kinder, "Alternating the Foundations of Political Support for the President Through Priming: Reagan and the Iran-Contra Affair," *American Political Science Review*, 86(1980):497–512.

[52]Vincent Price and John Zaller, "Who Gets the News? Alternative Measures of News Reception and Their Impacts for Research," *Public Opionion Quarterly*, 57(Summer 1993):136.

[53]William Adams, Dennis Smith, Allison Salzman, Ralph Crossen, Scott Hieber, Tom Naccarato, William Vantine, and Nine Weisbroth, "Before and After the Day After: The Unexpected Results of a Television Drama," *Political Communications and Persuasion*, 3(1986):191–213. Also see Stanley Feldman and Lee Sigelman, "The Political Impact of Prime-Time Television: The Day After," *Journal of Politics*, 47(May 1985):556–578.

[54]See Earl R. Babbie, *Survey Research Methods* (Belmont, Calif.: Wadsworth Publishing, 1973).

[55]Doris Graber, *Processing the News: How People Tame the Information Tide* (New York: Longman,1984).

CHAPTER 5

freedom and Regulation

One of the most dramatic and lasting transitions in mass media history occurred in the 1920s, with the development of the broadcast media. This signaled the end of the print monopoly and the beginning of decades of renewed conflict over the proper role of the mass media in American politics. In this chapter we explore two conflicting concepts vital to the mass media and the political process—freedom and regulation. The continuing challenge democracies face is to ensure freedom for individuals and the media while also ensuring protection for each. A long history of legislative and judicial actions illustrates the challenge and different attempts to deal with it.

Freedom of the press has always been perceived as a cornerstone of the American political system. The framers of the Constitution viewed a free press as fundamental to an informed citizenry, as well as critical to proper monitoring of the government's actions. The media provide the vital linkage between citizens and their government, as well as an institution that helps keep the government accountable. The First Amendment, which also establishes the right of free speech, is the constitutional basis for press freedom in America. It makes the press the only private enterprise in America that is granted a privileged status by the Constitution.

Three episodes in the nation's early history demonstrate significance of a free press to the new nation. The first was the trial of New York printer John Zenger in 1734–1735. In England at the time, a verbal attack on a public official, whether true or false, was considered libelous. The jury at Zenger's trial in Philadelphia concluded that criticisms of the government were not libelous if factually true. The second was the passage of the First Amendment to the Constitution in 1791, which declared, "Congress shall make no law respecting an establishment of religion, or prohibiting the free exercise thereof; or abridging the freedom of speech or of the press; or the right of the people to peaceably assemble and to petition the Government for a redress of grievances."

The third event, in 1798, was the passage by the Federalist-controlled Congress of the repressive Alien and Sedition Acts. The Alien Act authorized the president to order the deportation of any foreigner he considered dangerous. The Sedition Act applied to native Americans as well as foreign born, and provided for punishment by fines of up to $2,000 and imprisonment for up to two years for anyone who wrote, uttered, or published any words disrespectful of Congress or the president, or any words calculated to stir up sedition (resistance to the government). While President Adams never invoked the Alien Act, his administration did enforce the Sedition Act, arresting about two dozen men and convicting ten. Most were Republican newspaper editors whose writings, while tending to bring the Federalists into disrepute, were not seditious. Critics pointed out that these acts were in conflict with the First Amendment, and the resulting confrontations helped mold the public's understanding of the need for a strong and free press. While interpretations of freedom of the press have varied over the years, the concept has generally been broadly construed. Similar clauses in state constitutions have often been construed in ways that differ from the United States Constitution.[1]

The founding fathers granted special status to the press because they considered the right to express opinions and to collect and disseminate information free from government controls essential for a free society. If restraints were needed to protect society from harmful publicity, the founders felt they must come from the deterrent effects of fear of punishment after publication, not from "prior restraint." Publication could be prevented only if it "will surely result in direct, immediate, and irreparable damage to our nation or its people."[2] The belief in the importance of a free press has withstood the test of time, and any interpretation that alters its meaning is therefore politically significant. But two centuries after the constitutional guarantee, the means of communication are vastly different and have transformed the relationship between the government and the media. How have these changes affected the concept of a free press? Some, such as Carl Friedrich, have argued that "the possibilities of broadcasting the spoken word and projecting visual materials to the Four Corners of the globe have profoundly altered the realities of modern politics. . . . Inevitably, therefore, the issue of who shall control this channel of communications presents problems of decisive importance, at least in a constitutional democracy."[3] An examination of the freedom and regulation of the media can help us understand the importance of not only the changing media, but also the standards by which they are held accountable.

Regulation of the Media

While the printed word has special protection under the Constitution, this protection is not absolute. There are limits on the constitutional guarantees, including laws governing libel, copyright, and the right of privacy, prior restraint, and shielding of journalists. These regulations are not exclusive to print, but their origins can be traced to that medium.

Libel

Libel, or written defamation of character, is not a protected right under the First Amendment. Statements that expose individuals to hatred, contempt, or ridicule, that injure their reputations by imputing to them a criminal act, or that harm them in their trade or profession fall into this category. Libel usually involves civil damages, but it may also be punished under criminal laws. It is viewed as more serious than *slander*, which involves the spoken word (although there are laws against slander as well), because libel is seen as more durable than a passing remark. Laws against libel and slander are limitations on freedom of speech and the press, and many state constitutions recognize the distinction between protected and unprotected speech.

There are restrictions on libel. For instance, libel is very difficult to prove when the person is a celebrity, public official, or "newsworthy" in some other way unless malicious intent is proven. The courts have held that since these individuals use the media to their advantage, they have a special interest in the media and the legal standard is therefore higher in such cases. The proof of malice is subject to special judicial scrutiny. The courts have struggled over the decades to come to a proper proof of malice. They have narrowed the definition of a public figure through the years, but have maintained that elected officials and entertainers must meet a higher burden of proof than others.

A landmark case in libel was the *New York Times* v. *Sullivan* in 1964. The *New York Times* ran an advertisement that claimed the chief of police in Montgomery, Alabama had mishandled civil rights demonstrations, and the chief brought suit against the newspaper. The United States Supreme Court absolved the newspaper from libel, stating in its ruling that a public official who claims libel must be able to show that libelous information was published "with knowledge that it was false or with reckless disregard of whether it was false or not."[4] This decision established a new and more restrictive standard for public officials in their pursuit of libel claims because it made it difficult for them to prove libel, malicious intent, or extraordinary carelessness. The court's ruling thus gave the media wider latitude. The court argued that the limitation on libel suits was necessary to ensure free discussion of public affairs, a major purpose of the First Amendment guarantees. Later decisions extended the ruling to "newsworthy" people engaged in public controversies.[5]

By the 1970s the courts had begun to place limitations on ordinary citizens involved in events of general interest. In one of these cases, *Gertz* v. *Robert Welch, Inc.*, the Supreme Court restricted its definition of "public figure."[6] Gertz was a lawyer retained by relatives of a man who had been charged with killing a Chicago police officer. Robert Welch, in his monthly John Birch Society publication, *The American Opinion*, described Gertz as a "Marxist" and a "Communist fronter," as well as a member of several left-wing groups. In the ruling, the court stated that "these statements contained serious inaccuracies" and that Welch had made "no effort to substantiate these charges."[7] The court ruled that the fact that Gertz's name had been widely reported in the media did not make him a public figure, and therefore he could sue for libel.

The courts have left unclear under what circumstances a person who does not seek publicity could be considered a public figure, but have generally construed "public figure" more narrowly in recent years. As a result, private individuals have substantial rights to bar the media from publishing politically libelous or embarrassing facts that are not a matter of public record. As we will see, these restrictions are intertwined with the issue of privacy. Several states have passed statutes aimed specifically at restricting the "disparagement" of food products. The statutes generally authorize food producers to sue anyone who disparages a food product with information unsupported by reliable scientific data.[8] In January 1998 the first court test of the disparaging food laws, known as "veggie libel," occurred in Amarillo, Texas. Texas cattlemen sued television talk show host Oprah Winfrey, alleging that her televised comments about "mad cow" disease had caused the beef market to plummet, costing them millions of dollars. They sought an $11 million judgment in the case. After five weeks of testimony the jury found Winfrey not guilty. As one juror explained, "We felt that a lot of rights have eroded in this country. Our freedom of speech may be the only one we have left to regain what we've lost."[9]

Beyond Libel

In 1997 a new legal strategy was initiated by Food Lion, Inc., in response to a segment of the ABC program *Prime Time Live*. The program had reported that Food Lion stores sold spoiled meat.[10] Rather than contesting the program's content, Food Lion accused Capitol Cities/ABC of engaging in fraud and trespassing because undercover reporters lied about their work histories to secure employment by Food Lion and used hidden cameras and microphones to collect evidence for their story. A federal jury in 1996 found Capitol Cities/ABC guilty of fraud and awarded damages to Food Lion, Inc. In 1999 the 4th U.S. Circuit Court of Appeals threw out the jury's verdict and the $315,000 judgment against ABC. The court ruled 2–1 that Food Lion was not damaged by the reporters' deception, but it upheld a dollar in damages against each reporter for trespassing and breaching their duty to be loyal to Food Lion. This case gave those fighting perceived media transgressions new legal alternatives to libel that are easier to prove in court.

Copyright

Creative products by writers, composers, dramatists, photographers, and others are protected by copyright. A notice of copyright registration is issued to the creator or his or her representative following submission to the Copyright Office. (While works need not be registered to be copyrighted, registration makes enforcement easier.) A copyright confers an exclusive privilege for the life of the creator plus fifty years. This power is based on the constitutional grant to Congress to promote science and the arts by granting authors "the exclusive right to their respective writings. . . ." The significance of copyright is that it fosters creative efforts and rewards talent. The Copyright Office makes no effort to enforce the grant, but individual grantees may file civil suit or take injunctive action through the federal courts when they believe their copyright has been infringed. While infringement of copyright is not nearly as significant politically as libel, the concept of copyright does extend protections for written and recorded works.

Privacy

The concept of a legal right to privacy first appeared in an 1890 article in the *Harvard Law Review* by Louis Brandeis and Samuel Warren.[11] The authors wrote:

> In general, then, the matters of which the publication should be repressed may be described as those which concern the private life, habits, acts, and relations of an individual, and have no legitimate connection with his fitness for a public office which he seeks or for which he is suggested, or for any public or quasi public capacity.[12]

A decade and half later a Georgia Supreme Court found that an individual's privacy had been violated when his photograph was used without permission in a newspaper advertisement.[13] Today nearly every state recognizes some right of privacy either in their statutes or by common law. States attempt to strike a balance between the individual's right to privacy and the media's legitimate pursuit of the public interest under the freedom of the press. The media have frequently violated privacy in their pursuit of stories. These violations have generally taken four forms: intrusion, publication of private facts, false light, and misappropriation.

Intrusion occurs when the media intentionally intrude, physically or otherwise, on a person's solitude or into his or her private affairs. Intrusion by the media most often occurs during the news-gathering phase. Trespassing and the wrongful use of tape recorders and cameras are common means of media intrusion.

The publication of truthful information about the private life of a person that would be both highly offensive to a reasonable person and not of legitimate public concern is referred to as *publication of private facts*. Publication of information about a person's sexual behavior, health, or economic status could be considered an intrusion into a private life and therefore a publication of private facts. However, reporting events that take place in public is not generally considered an invasion of privacy, for the courts have held that individuals have no "reasonable expectation of privacy" when they are in public. Therefore, publishing information obtained from public records, such as birth certificates, police reports, or transcripts of judicial hearings, is not generally considered a publication of private facts. The media can, for instance, print the names of persons who have received a divorce.[14] However, in one case a report of a woman's involvement in an auto accident revealed that she was living with a man who was not her husband. The court ruled that this fact was not pertinent to the story of the accident, which otherwise was newsworthy, and the reporter was held liable for intrusion and publication of private facts.[15]

The violation of *false light* occurs when information about a person is published that is false or places the individual in a "false light" by portraying him or her in a false and highly offensive manner. False light cases most commonly arise when the media attempt to condense or fictionalize a story.

The final violation of privacy, *misappropriation*, occurs when a person's name or likeness is used for commercial purposes without the individual's consent. The courts have generally held that use of a photo to illustrate a newsworthy story, even if the photo also promotes the sale of a magazine on a newsstand, is not misappropriation.

privileged communication

One of the most important issues for the media is that of privileged communication. The courts have long held that discussions between specified individuals constitute "privileged" speech, and their contents cannot be legally compelled. This privilege extends to husband and wife, attorney and client, priest and penitent, and physician and patient. The concept of privileged communication is significant to the media for they frequently can obtain information only through the use of confidential informants, to whom they promise that they will not disclose the source of their information. During the Whitewater investigation, federal prosecutor Kenneth Starr's office quietly, and without much comment from the media, subpoenaed audiotapes, videotapes, and notes from CBS News, ABC News, the *Wall Street Journal*, the *New Yorker*, and local television stations in Pennsylvania and Florida. Twenty years earlier these actions would have brought outcries of abridgement of First Amendment rights, but the Whitewater investigation did not receive the same media attention that Watergate did. Many journalists believe that it is essential to fight such efforts in order to protect the public's right to know. If the media's rights are compromised, the public's access to information is reduced.[16]

Journalists' efforts to protect their sources have sometimes become the focus of judicial action. The United States Supreme Court ruled in a 1972 trilogy of cases, known as *Branzburg* v. *Hayes*, that the press had no special right to withhold evidence received in the course of gathering the news. After Paul Branzburg, a reporter for the *Louisville Courier-Journal*, observed two persons synthesizing hashish from marijuana, a violation of local law, he incorporated this information in an article and was called before the grand jury. He refused to identify the persons involved, claiming protection under the First Amendment of the Constitution. Branzburg was joined in his petition to the U.S. Supreme Court by two other reporters who had refused to reveal the sources of information they had obtained while investigating the Black Panthers. The three cases were joined because they raised the issue of whether requiring reporters to testify before state and federal grand juries abridged the freedom of speech and press guaranteed by the First Amendment. The court ruled that the reporters did not have a privileged communication status. In its decision, it recognized the importance of some protection for the media in their news-gathering efforts: "[W]ithout some protection for seeking out the news, freedom of the press could be eviscerated. But this case involves no intrusions upon speech or assembly, no prior restraint or restriction on what the press may publish, and no express or implied command that the press publish what it prefers."[17] The issue before the court was whether reporters were subject to the same obligation to respond to grand jury subpoenas and to answer questions relevant to the investigation. The decision in the *Branzburg* v. *Hayes* case was viewed by most of those in the media as a limitation of their First Amendment rights.

shield laws

Following the Branzburg decision, a number of bills were introduced in Congress in an effort to pass a federal law that would shield the press. There were many reasons why these efforts failed, but two major problems surfaced that Congress could not resolve. The first concerned the definition of a journalist. While prominent journalists and their publications were easily identified, attempts to limit the law to these journalists raised new First Amendment issues. The second problem involved the issue of "prescient witnesses," those who actually witness a crime, as did Branzburg. There was wide disagreement on the scope of the proposed bills regarding persons who had firsthand knowledge of a crime. These and other problems contributed to Congress's failure to pass a shield law. The courts, however, do recognize journalists' needs to protect their sources. In *Riley* v. *City of Chester*, a federal court stated, "The relationship between newsgathering, news dissemination, and the need for a journalist to protect his or her source is too apparent to require belaboring."[18]

While there is no federal statute protecting journalists, twenty-nine states plus the District of Columbia have enacted shield laws. In several states without shield laws, the courts have recognized some form of qualified privilege. Some states have added "free press" provisions to their constitutions to protect qualified news gathering by the media. However, in other states, most notably Hawaii and Wyoming, the courts and legislatures have ruled that there is no privilege for unpublished sources of information.

The idea of shield laws is not new. The first shield law, enacted by the state of Maryland in 1896, read:

> [N]o person engaged in, connected with or employed on a newspaper or journal shall be compelled to disclose in any legal proceeding or trial before a committee of the legislature or elsewhere the source of any news or information procured or obtained by him for and published in the newspaper on and in which he is engaged, connected with or employed.[19]

State shield laws vary in their scope, but commonly address two areas: the reporter's source of information and the information itself. The protection states extend ranges from "absolute" to "qualified." An example of a qualified protection would be not protecting a source if the article was written in "bad faith, with malice, and not in the interest of the public welfare" or if failure to disclose would cause a "miscarriage of justice." Table 5.1 lists the states that have enacted shield laws. In the fourteen states that grant absolute privilege, as well as the District of Columbia, reporters can under no circumstance be forced to reveal their sources. The remaining states grant qualified privileges, which require reporters to divulge confidential sources under certain limited conditions. The information gathered by reporters is given absolute protection in only five states, while an additional nineteen and the District give qualified protection to information. In seven states the shield laws do not specify this area of protection.

Even absolute protection is not really absolute, for when the right of a reporter to withhold names of his or her sources clashes with the right of an individual to obtain a fair trial or in the case of serious crimes, state shield law protections do not hold. One of the most notable examples involved CBS News. When a CBS documentary on the Vietnam War alleged that General Westmoreland had falsified enemy troop figures, the general sued the network for libel. During the course of the trial, General Westmoreland sought all material used in preparing the story. The network contended this material was protected under the First Amendment guarantee, but the court rejected CBS's contention.[20]

prior restraint

Can a government or other party stop the dissemination of a story it does not like? Intervention in the media's ability to express opinion *prior* to release

Table 5.1
Shield Laws States and the Scope of the Laws

STATE	SOURCE'S PRIVILEGE	INFORMATION'S PRIVILEGE
Alabama	Qualified	Not specified
Alaska	Qualified	Qualified
Arizona	Absolute	Not specified
Arkansas	Qualified	Qualified
California	Absolute	Not specified
Colorado	Qualified	Qualified
Delaware	Absolute	Qualified
D.C.	Absolute	Qualified
Florida	Qualified	Qualified
Georgia	Qualified	Qualified
Illinois	Qualified	Qualified
Indiana	Absolute	Not specified
Kentucky	Absolute	Not specified
Louisiana	Qualified	Not specified
Maryland	Absolute	Qualified
Michigan	Qualified	Qualified
Minnesota	Qualified	Qualified
Montana	Absolute	Absolute
Nebraska	Absolute	Absolute
Nevada	Absolute	Absolute
New Jersey	Absolute	Absolute
New Mexico	Qualified	Qualified
New York	Absolute	Qualified
North Carolina	Qualified	Qualified
North Dakota	Qualified	Qualified
Ohio	Absolute	Not specified

Table 5.1 (continued)
Shield Laws States and the Scope of the Laws

STATE	SOURCE'S PRIVILEGE	INFORMATION'S PRIVILEGE
Oklahoma	Qualified	Qualified
Oregon	Absolute	Absolute
Pennsylvania	Absolute	Qualified
Rhode Island	Qualified	Qualified
South Carolina	Qualified	Qualified
Tennessee	Qualified	Qualified

Source: The Reporters' Committee for Freedom of the Press, "Confidential Sources & Information," Summer 1998, at *www.rcfp.org*.

of the information for mass consumption is referred to as "prior restraint." The concept of prior restraint originated in the privacy article by Louis Brandeis and Samuel Warren cited above.[21] Since 1931 the courts have consistently held that government cannot stop the dissemination of material that it views as scurrilous or negative.[22]

This position was first expressed in a case that involved the editor of a newspaper, the *Saturday Press*, that indulged in anti-Semitic, anti-black, anti-Catholic, and anti-labor union comments. In 1927 the state of Minnesota passed a public nuisance law that had the effect of forbidding Jay Near from publishing the paper. The law, which became commonly known as the "gag law,"[23] allowed a single judge to bar publication of any newspaper that printed "malicious, scandalous or defamatory" material. In overruling the Minnesota statute, the Supreme Court found that the law was "an infringement of the liberty of the press guaranteed by the 14th Amendment."[24]

In 1971 the Supreme Court ruled that any prior restraint of freedom of expression by the government carried a heavy presumption of unconstitutionality. The case that produced this ruling, also known as the "Pentagon Papers" case, involved the publication of secret documents on American policy in Vietnam that had been leaked to the press by Daniel Ellsberg. This was the first case in which the federal government attempted to restrain a newspaper's publication of material in its possession. While holding that the Nixon administration could not forbid publication, since the government had failed to prove justification of censorship, the ruling left unclear whether the government could enjoin publication of information that presented a serious threat to national security.[25]

In 1993 Federal Beef, a meatpacker, attempted to enjoin CBS from airing a videotape recording of its processing operations. A Federal Beef employee had recorded the operations on his shift with a hidden camera and gave the tape free of charge to a reporter for CBS's program *48 Hours*, which was preparing an investigative report on contaminated food. A circuit court granted Federal Beef a temporary restraining order and later a preliminary injunction against CBS. The network then filed a motion for an emergency stay with the U.S. Supreme Court and the injunction was lifted the next day. In its decision, the Court stated that gags on the media are permitted only in exceptional cases and that Federal Beef had as its remedy civil or criminal damages, but not prior restraint.[26]

There have been numerous cases involving citizens' attempts to stop publication of materials. In December 1994 Paula Jones, who had accused President Clinton of sexual harassment, sought and received a preliminary injunction against *Penthouse* magazine, which had printed nude photos of her in its January 1995 issue. *Penthouse* sought to have the injunction lifted and appealed to a district court in New York. The court lifted the injunction two days later, stating that the photographs had a relationship to an editorial questioning Jones' credibility and that the matter was a public issue.

The courts have ruled on prior restraint in a wide range of areas, including corporate information, individuals' information, obscenity, commercial speech, and restrictions on compensation. They have generally upheld the original decision, expressed in *Near* v. *Minnesota*, that media have a right of free expression and that if these expressions are offensive, the remedy occurs *after* their release, not before.

Broadcast Media

Some regulation of the media has been a common method of government control, and has been used since the invention of the printing press. No country allows complete freedom of the press. The question then becomes how, and under what circumstances, should the government be involved in regulating the media? The delicate balance between regulation and media freedom has undergone considerable modification through the years. The concept of freedom of the press was not firmly grounded in American culture in the early years of the nation, as was demonstrated by the enactment of the Alien and Sedition Acts of 1798. However, while the press was granted a special status in the Constitution and gained greater independence through the years, the situation has not been the same for the broadcast media. Since their inception, the broadcast media have been more closely regulated than the print media. The newer media of networked computers and the Internet appear to enjoy a status closer to print than broadcasting, although their rights are only beginning to be tested in the courts.[27] The differences in standards stem in great measure from the issue of ownership.

Print ownership is easily distinguished—the person who owns the paper is accountable for its content. However, with broadcasting the issue of ownership is more complex, for it raises the issue of who owns the airwaves. A second reason for more broadcasting regulation is practical: regulation is needed to ensure the clear transmission of signals.

The regulation of radio broadcasting began with the Wireless Ship Act of 1910, which forbade any steamer carrying fifty or more persons to leave an American port unless equipped with efficient apparatus for radio communication in the charge of a skilled operator. The enforcement of the legislation was entrusted to the secretary of commerce and labor. In 1912 the United States ratified the first international radio treaty, which resulted in Congress enacting the Radio Act of 1912. This act forbade the operation of radio apparatus without a license from the secretary of commerce and labor. In addition, it allocated certain frequencies for the use of the government, and imposed restrictions on the character of sound waves and transmission of distress signals.

The rapid growth of the radio in the early 1920s led to inaudible transmissions, as stations commonly used the same frequencies to send their messages. Radio station owners soon requested congressional regulation of the air waves, and Congress complied by passing the Radio Act of 1927. The act established the Federal Radio Commission (FRC) to regulate radio. However, the legislation reflected the *laizze faire* capitalism of that era, and the FRC was perceived to be more a servant of the industry than a regulator. The regulation that did occur focused on technical aspects of the new medium, not content. Herbert Hoover, the secretary of commerce and labor, viewed the broadcast media as publicly owned utilities that should be subject to greater government scrutiny than print. This view did not long prevail, and even Hoover soon modified it. However, it is noteworthy that early perceptions of radio were different from those of print, and this helps explain differences in the treatment of the two media through the years. Complaints about the FRC and the desire to combine radio, telephone, and telegraph under one piece of legislation led to the passage of the Federal Radio Act of 1934, which established the Federal Communications Commission (FCC).

The Federal Communications Commission

The Federal Communications Commission consists of five commissioners appointed by the president and confirmed by the Senate for five-year terms except when filling unexpired terms. The president designates one of the commissioners to serve as chairperson. Only three commissioners may be members of the same political party. None can have a financial interest in a Commission-related business. The FCC's initial charge was to regulate the broadcast media in "the public interest, convenience, or necessity." The commission has operated through the years on the basis of this vague language. It has been the FCC's responsibility to establish the rules and guidelines for implementing the policies that regulate broadcasting. Congress has given the FCC a great deal of discretion.

Few cases challenged the commission's power to regulate in the years immediately following its creation. The first major challenge occurred in *National Broadcasting Company* v. *United States*, in 1943. In 1941 the commission examined business practices and ownership patterns of radio networks and concluded that the major networks (NBC and CBS) exerted too much influence over broadcasting by controlling local station programming. To rectify this, the commission issued the chain broadcast regulations, which defined the permissible relationship between networks and their affiliates.[28] NBC challenged the commission's authority to adopt regulations controlling licensee behavior not related to technical or engineering matters. Its challenge was based on three contentions. First, Congress had not authorized the FCC's adoption of such regulations. Second, if Congress had authorized their adoption, then the congressional statute itself was unconstitutional because the term "public interest" was too vague. Finally, the regulations violated NBC's First Amendment rights. The court upheld the statute, and in its decision it explained why broadcasting is different from other forms of communication:

> We come, finally, to an appeal to the First Amendment. The Regulations, even if valid in all other respects, must fall because they abridge, say the appellants, their rights of free speech. If that be so, it would follow that every person whose application for a license to operate a station is denied by the Commission is thereby denied his constitutional right of freedom of speech. Freedom of utterance is abridged to many who wish to use the limited facilities of radio. Unlike other modes of expression, radio inherently is not available to all. That is its unique characteristic, and that is why, unlike other modes of expression, it is subject to governmental regulation. Because it cannot be used by all, some who wish to use it must be denied.[29]

Licensing

The primary mechanism established by the FCC for implementing federal policy regarding broadcasting has been the commission's authority to grant licenses. Through the years, the FCC has established a number of rules that it applies to new applicants and those seeking renewal. Two assumptions underlay the licensing function. The first was the need to regulate radio frequencies, since channel scarcity was initially an important consideration for the new commission. The second principle was the assumption that the public interest needed to be protected. Licenses were granted for three years, after which stations could seek renewal. If a station did not perform in the public interest, the owner could theoretically lose its license. All new channel assignments were made on the *promise* of good performance as spelled out in the application submitted to the FCC.

In fact, however, the FCC has never refused to renew a station's broadcast license when another organization has challenged the existing license holder by asserting that it would serve the public interest better. Such "comparative challenges" are usually based on the contention that the current license holder has failed to perform in the public interest. In 1982 the United States Court of Appeals (D.C. Circuit) noted that fact in a decision involving a television station:

> Finally...we are still troubled by the fact that the record remains that an incumbent television licensee has never been denied renewal in a comparative challenge. American television viewers will be reassured, although a trifle baffled, to learn that even the worst television stations—those which are, presumably, the ones picked out as vulnerable to a challenge—are so good that they never need replacing. We suspect that somewhere, sometime, somehow, some television licensee should fail in a comparative renewal challenge, but the FCC has never discovered such a licensee yet.[30]

The case established two important findings. The first was that Congress was within its authority to establish the FCC and its regulatory functions. The second was that radio broadcasting did not have the same First Amendment protections as other modes of expression. In the rare instances in which stations have lost their licenses, those decisions have been based on other grounds, such as deceit in the financial operations of the station or in the license application.

Licensing Criteria

From its inception, the FCC has been left to its own judgment of what criteria should be used in making the critical license and renewal decisions. Dean Alger, drawing from a 1965 "Policy Statement" and other statements of particular case decisions, isolated five major criteria used by the FCC: (1) *diversity of control* of the mass media, which originally focused on preventing a concentration of media ownership, (2) *full-time participation* in the operation of the station, which pertains to the owner's connection to the station's daily operations, (3) the actual performance of program *service* as proposed in previous applications, (4) the pattern of actual performance, or *past record*, which applies to the renewal of licenses, and (5) the *character* of the owner, which focuses on the owner's truthfulness to the commission about the other criteria.[31]

These criteria have been reinforced and expanded over the years. For instance, in the 1970s the FCC, in an effort to encourage attention to programming in public affairs, established a formula for programming, ruling that 5 percent of total programming had to be devoted to local affairs, 5 percent to news and local public affairs, and 10 percent to nonentertainment programs. To assist it in monitoring stations' performances, the FCC required radio and television stations to maintain detailed logs of their programs' content.[32] These logs were then used to document the amount of time the stations spent on news, public affairs, and so forth.

Licensing Reality

In theory, the FCC is to apply the same criteria to the granting of new and the renewal of old licenses. In reality, however, the dominant orientation of the FCC has been the *expectation* that these criteria will be or are met, since new stations have no previous record and renewals are rarely denied. Therefore, unless there has been blatantly abnormal behavior on the part of the licensed station, renewal is automatic. One FCC commissioner, commenting on the decision process stated, "To the perceptive observer . . . [it is] apparent by now that there is less to such [removal] 'contests' than meets the eye, that in fact it is not a real contest between two applicants but a pretend game played between the commission and the public. The outcome of the game is predetermined."[33]

The FCC and Media Access

In addition to licensing, three other areas have been important to the FCC's ensuring that broadcasters meet their responsibilities to the public interest. When an outside agency becomes involved in determining the media's responsibility, the issue usually becomes hotly contested, and the issue of access is no exception. The underlying questions here are who has the right to assess the mass media's messages and under what conditions. The FCC has dealt with these questions over the years by the establishment of three provisions to the Federal Communications Act of 1934. Through the years the act has been amended by many administrations.

The Equal Time Provision

The equal time provision applies only to candidates seeking federal office, for the FCC has no specific rules for state and local races. It was enacted into law as Section 315 of the Federal Communications Act of 1934, and states that each station must have a policy on selling or donating political advertising time to candidates for public office. That "policy must provide equal opportunity for all certified [legally qualified] candidates to purchase time at least equal to the time purchased by any one candidate"[34] for a given office. This requirement does not apply to bona fide news events, like nightly news programs or public affairs interviews of candidates on such programs as *Larry King Live*, *Meet the Press*, and *Nightline*.

This provision has been applied in varying ways. For the first televised presidential debates, in 1960, Congress circumvented the provision by enacting legislation that set it aside for the period of the debates. In 1976 and 1980 the FCC ruled that events arranged by some private organizations, in this instance the League of Women Voters, were news events and therefore not in violation of the equal time provision. In 1983 the FCC began allowing news organizations to arrange debates, again circumventing the provision. In the 1996 presidential campaign H. Ross Perot, the United We Stand candidate for president, was denied a place in the presidential debates even though he had qualified for federal matching funds. The Presidential Debates Commission ruled that Perot was not a serious candidate, based on his low standing in the public opinion polls.

The Fairness Doctrine

When radio was introduced, it was believed, because of the pervasiveness, reach, and impact of this new medium, that individuals must be ensured fair treatment of issues. The doctrine arose from a case in the 1940s in which an owner of three radio stations ordered his news staff to "slant, distort, and falsify" news against politicians he disliked, such as President Roosevelt. Among other things, he ordered stories about the president to be reported with those about "communists" and criminals so they might seem related. When the issue of fairness was raised by listeners and members of the press, the owner replied, "This is my station and I'll do what I want with it."[35] The FCC responded to such behavior in 1949 by issuing a report directing license holders to "operate in the public interest." The report required that stations devote a reasonable amount of time to the coverage of controversial issues of public importance, and do so fairly by affording a reasonable opportunity for contrasting viewpoints to be voiced.[36] Though the years, a number of court cases have challenged the fairness doctrine, and in 1987 the Reagan administration abolished it. However, the principle remains an issue of considerable debate with partisan overtones.

The Right of Rebuttal and Personal Attack Rule

The third provision was based on the responsibilities of broadcasters and the issue of access that is part of the fairness doctrine: the right to rebut personal attacks. While the fairness doctrine was abandoned by the Reagan administration in 1987, the portion pertaining to the responsibilities of broadcasters remains. This provision produced the first case heard by the Supreme Court regarding access to the broadcast media: *The Red Lion Broadcasting Co.* v. *FCC* (1968). The Reverend Billy James Hargis, an extremely conservative "radio minister" and host of the "Christian Crusade," aired by WGCB and other stations, aired an attack on the book *Goldwater:*

Extremist to the Right and its author, Fred J. Cook. Reverend Hargis believed that the book was instrumental in Goldwater's failed presidential bid and spent two minutes attacking it and its author. Cook, with assistance from the Democratic Party, wrote over 200 stations that carried the Hargis attack requesting free time to respond. WGCB was one of several stations that were willing to provide Cook reply time if he paid for it. Cook sought the aid of the FCC, which eleven months later supported him. The commission's ruling was then appealed to the United States Supreme Court, which ruled in support of the FCC.[37] In its ruling the court noted: "There is no question here of the Commission's refusal to permit the broadcaster to carry a particular program or to publish [his or her] own views. . . .Such questions would raise more serious First Amendment issues. But we do hold that Congress and the Commission do not violate the First Amendment when they require a radio or television station to give reply time to answer personal attacks and political editorials."[38] The court did not say how soon the rebuttal should be aired and how much time should be devoted to it, leaving a great deal of discretion to the broadcaster.

Do these provisions apply to all forms of media? In 1974 the Supreme Court answered this question when it issued an opinion that provided the print press wide discretion.[39] At issue was the constitutionality of a Florida law that gave a right to immediate reply to candidates for public office who had been personally attacked by newspapers. The law provided for a matching format and placement in the newspaper for a candidate who had been attacked. The case involved Patrick Tornillo, Jr., a former leader of the Dade County Teachers Union, who was running for the Florida State Legislature. Just before the primary, the *Miami Herald* published two editorials objecting to Mr. Tornillo's election because he had led teachers in a strike. Tornillo demanded that the paper print his replies to the editorials, but the paper refused. After his primary defeat, Mr. Tornillo sued the *Miami Herald.* In 1974 the case reached the United States Supreme Court, which ruled unanimously that newspapers could refuse to print anything they liked. The court held that no one, even candidates whose reputation had been damaged, had the right to space in a newspaper. This decision reaffirmed a long tradition of newspaper independence, a position not shared by the broadcast media.

Why did the court rule in favor of the press over Tornillo's claim for access? Scholars have put forth five possible reasons. First, the court may have regarded the print media as having a longer-lasting effect. Second, the court may have considered newspaper readers more sophisticated and intelligent in forming opinions than the broadcast audience. Third, the court may have distinguished between the two media because it saw a scarcity of frequencies in broadcast that is not present in print. Fourth, the court may have felt government licensing of stations imposes public service requirements on broadcasters. Fifth, the court may have ignored references to the Red Lion decision in the Tornillo case because it was uncomfortable with its earlier ruling.[40]

The FCC in the Era of Deregulation

Since its inception in 1934, the FCC has had as its stated purpose protection of the public interest in the use of the airwaves. In the 1980s two major factors significantly altered the way the public interest was perceived. The first involved the technical character of broadcasting. From the enactment of the Radio Act of 1927 through the establishment of the FCC, the major focus of attention was on regulation of the airwaves. To safeguard the public interest, the FCC established frequencies, licensed radio and television stations, and acted as an arbitrator in disputes involving stations and the public interest. The agency ensured the clarity of broadcast and programming through its licensing process. By the 1980s advances such as satellite network transmission for both radio and television, cable transmission for television, and low-power stations had relieved the early scarcity of broadcast frequencies, and the resulting vast number of radio and television stations provided the public with diverse programming and relieved fears about a monopoly of ideas.

The technical advances reinforced the argument for more limited governmental regulation of business. By the time Ronald Reagan was elected a majority of FCC members were arguing that the government should allow market forces to dominate the broadcast industry. They also felt the broadcasting media should be accorded the same rights under the First Amendment as the print media. These members were among the proponents of a political philosophy that viewed federal agencies as obstacles to progress, a philosophy that had a popular spokesperson in Ronald Reagan. Thus, the Reagan years saw a pronounced shift toward deregulation in the FCC. The commission itself was reduced from seven to five members, and the length of licenses was extended from three to five years. The requirement that radio and television stations maintain daily logs of their programming was abolished, as was the fairness doctrine. News organizations were allowed to stage presidential debates. Finally, the rules limiting ownership of multiple stations were relaxed. Together, these changes amounted to the most significant revolution in media regulation since the establishment of the FCC.

Rules regarding ownership best illustrate the new era of deregulation. Until 1984 companies were limited to owning seven AM radio stations, seven FM radio stations, and seven television stations. In 1984 the numbers were increased to twelve of each, and in 1992 they were expanded to eighteen. Companies were allowed up to six additional radio stations if women or ethnic minorities had controlling interest. Concerns over concentrated ownership of the media were noted by the Supreme Court in its decision in *Miami Herald Publishing Co. v. Tornillo*:

> The elimination of competing newspapers in most of our large cities, and the concentration of control of media that results from the only newspaper's being owned by the same interests which own a television station and a radio station,

are important components of this trend toward concentration of control of outlets to inform the public.[41]

In 1977 the Court and public could not have foreseen the impact of deregulation on the economic, social, and political processes. The 1980s and 1990s saw media mergers that were unprecedented in size and number.

Telecommunications Act of 1996

In 1996 Congress passed and President Clinton signed the most sweeping broadcast legislation since the Federal Communication Act of 1934. The Telecommunications Act affects broadcasting as well as telephone, cable television, and the Internet. Table 5.2 summarizes its major provisions. The impact of this legislation on society and the political process has yet to be fully felt, but it will be far reaching. Two areas are of particular significance to the relationship between the media and the political process. The first is the expanded role of the FCC in developing and enforcing the provisions of the law discussed below. The second is in the area of broadcast reform, which includes the V-chip, broadcast/cable-ownership, and television and radio ownership.

The V-Chip

Protests over violence and sex on television have led to the development of a computer chip know as the V-chip, which allows users to block violent or sexually explicit programs, designated by computer coding, from their sets. These chips are to be installed in all new television sets beginning no *sooner* than two years after enactment of the legislation, with the precise date to be determined by consultation between the FCC and the industry.

Broadcast/Cable Cross-Ownership

The act directs the FCC to eliminate restrictions on co-ownership of television networks and cable systems. The commission is advised to revise its rules, if necessary, to "ensure carriage, channel positioning and nondiscriminatory treatment of non-afflicted broadcast stations" by network-owned cable systems. The elimination of restrictions is particularly interesting in light of the initial arguments for cable television that cable would promote competition in programming and expand viewership.

Television Ownership Cap

The act eliminates the ceiling on the number of stations that may be owned by any person or company nationally, and raises the permissible audience

table 5.2
Summary of the 1996 Telecommunications Act

TELEPHONE	CABLE TV
Removes entry barriers, opening up local telephone markets to competition.	Allows local telephone companies to provide cable TV.
Requires incumbent providers to resell local services.	Removes rate regulations for cable providers on certain services.
Allows local companies to enter the long-distance market after successfully opening up the local market.	
Creates universal service rules for subsidized service to rural and low-income individuals; also gives schools and other public institutions access to advanced communication service.	

Source: The Telecommunications Act of 1996.

reached to 35 percent. The FCC is directed to determine whether to relax local ownership restrictions, although the Conference Committee of Congress noted that VHF-VHF combination in a local market should be approved only in "compelling circumstances." Judging from past FCC behavior in license renewals, there does not appear to be a likelihood of strong commission regulation in this area.

Radio Ownership Cap

The act eliminates FCC rules limiting the number of radio stations than can be owned by any person or company nationally. Locally, the number of stations one entity can own is determined by a sliding scale, depending on the size of the market. In smaller markets (fourteen or fewer stations), one can own up to five commercial radio stations (up to three FM) so long as these constitute no more than half the stations in the market. In the largest markets (forty-five or more stations), one entity can own up to eight radio stations (five of which may be FM). In addition, the FCC has the authority to waive these limits.

INTERNET & ONLINE	BROADCAST TV & RADIO
Imposes criminal penalties on anyone who knowingly transmits indecent material to minors.	Allows a single company to own TV stations that reach up to 35% of households in an area.
Imposes penalties on those who intended to harass others via the Internet.	Allows networks to own cable TV systems.
Solidifies the FCC's jurisdiction over the Internet.	Requires all new TVs to have a "V-chip". (Allows for parental blocking of information.)

These are enormous changes in the relationship between the media and political institutions. They legitimize the warning of those who are concerned about oligopolistic control of content. A flurry of mass media buyouts was spurred by the legislation. For instance, Rupert Murdoch's News Corporation purchased New World Communications' top ten U.S. stations, giving News Corp stations reaching 34.8 percent of households in America.

The media have been transformed by deregulation and the increasing number of television and radio station mergers. The largest mergers in media history resulted in part from the changes in regulatory policies. These changes contributed to the telecommunications industry's becoming the largest industry in America by the year 2000. While in theory the public owns the airwaves, in fact the airwaves are controlled by private industry. Deregulation has significantly reduced the public service expectations previously codified in law.

As we will see in the following chapters, the nature of politics has been transformed by the strong role the media, primarily television, play. The media have come to hold more power than the traditional agents of political change: political parties and organized political machines. As deregulation continues, the concentration of ownership, the focus on profit over substance, and the use of the media to promote political agendas are transforming the American political landscape in profound ways. Individuals, candidates, and institutions have all felt the impact of the media. In the chapters that follow we will address some of these changes.

summary

We have seen the historical struggle in America between freedom and regulation with regard to the mass media—a struggle that continues. At stake are free and vibrant media that perform an essential function of a democracy—monitoring the government.

Freedoms have always been balanced by regulations. The most common of these in the area of freedom of speech and communication are libel and slander laws. Throughout the nation's history, the protection of individual means of expression has been a principle that survived changes in means of communication. However, a delicate balance exists between free expression and false statements, either written (libel) or spoken (slander). The courts have given greater weight to libel in the belief that the written word has a more lasting impact.

Privileged communications traditionally include those between husband and wife, doctor and patient, and lawyer and client. Journalists have argued that their communications with those who provided them with information should also be privileged. While the courts have recognized the importance of journalist-informer relationships, they have continued to deny their communications this status. Journalists have turned to the states for protection from legal pressure to divulge their sources under "shield laws," and a number of states have enacted such laws. An area in which the media have prevailed in the courts is prior restraint. The courts have consistently ruled that only in the most extreme cases (such as national security) can the government prevent the media from carrying a story.

All media are not treated equally. Since the advent of the broadcast media in the 1920s, the government has applied different standards to broadcast than to print media. While libel and slander apply to each, additional regulations have been enacted involving broadcasting. Initially those in the new medium of radio *sought* government regulation of the airwaves, which led to creation of the Federal Communications Commission in 1934. This agency has been responsible for regulating broadcast media from licensing to overseeing content. In the 1980s the government began deregulating the media by abolishing the fairness doctrine and expanding the number and types of broadcast media that could be owned by an individual or corporation. The most significant consequence has been the growth of conglomerate ownership of multimedia. The passage of the Telecommunications Act of 1996 profoundly altered America's mass media by amending the Communications Act of 1934.

The continued struggle to find the proper balance between freedom and regulation is vital not only to the media, but also to a vibrant and healthy democracy.

Endnotes

[1]Robert F. Copple, "The Dynamics of Expression Under The State Constitution," *Journalism Quarterly*, 64(Spring 1987):106–113.

[2]Justice Potter Stewart in *New York Times* v. *United States*, 403 U.S. 713 (1971).

[3]Carl Freidrich, *Constitutional Government and Democracy*, 4th ed. (Waltham, Mass.: Blaisdell, 1968), 520–521.

[4]*New York Times* v. *Sullivan*, 376 U.S. 254 (1964).

[5]*Associated Press* v. *Walker*, 388 U.S. 130 (1967).

[6]*Gertz* v. *Robert Welch, Inc.*, 418 U.S. 323 (1974).

[7]*Ibid.*

[8]States with these statutes are Alabama, Arizona, Colorado, Florida, Georgia, Idaho, Louisiana, Mississippi, Oklahoma, South Dakota, and Texas.

[9]Mark Babineck, "Texas Jurors Reject Cattlemen's Law Suit Against Oprah Winfrey," Associated Press, February 26, 1998.

[10]*Food Lion* v. *ABC*, 116 F3d 472 (1997).

[11]Louis D. Brandeis and Samuel D. Warren, "The Right to Privacy," *Harvard Law Review*, 4(1890):193–220.

[12]*Ibid.*, 198.

[13]*Pavesich* v. *New England Life Insurance Co.*, 122 Ga. 190, 50 S.E. 68 (1905).

[14]*Doe* v. *Sherman Publishing*, 593 A. 2nd 457, R.I. (1991).

[15]*Garner* v. *Triangle Publications Inc.*, 97 F. Supp. 546, S.D.N.Y. (1951).

[16]Felicity Barringer, "In a New Atmosphere, Press Is Silent on Subpoena Flurry," *New York Times*, April 24, 1998: 1.

[17]*Branzburg* v. *Hayes*, 406 U.S. 665, 92 S.Ct., 2646, 33 L.ed. 2nd 626 (1972).

[18]*Riley* v. *City of Chester*, 612 4. 2dF. ed 708, 714, 3rd Cir. (1979).

[19]William Francois, *Mass Media Law and Regulation* (Dubuque, Iowa: William C. Brown, 1978).

[20]*Westmoreland* v. *CBS, Inc.*, 596 F.Supp. 7170, S.D.N.Y. (1984).

[21]Brandeis and Warren, *op. cit.*

[22]The court has upheld prior restraint in only one instance, that barring publication of movement of troopships during wartime.

[23]For an excellent history of *Near* v. *Minnesota*, see Fred W. Friendly's *Minnesota Rag* (New York: Vintage Books, 1981).

[24]*Near* v. *Minnesota*, 283 U.S. 697 (1931).

[25] *New York Times* v. *United States*, 403 U.S. 713 (1971).

[26] *CBS* v. *Davis*, 114 S.Ct. 912 (1994).

[27] *ACLU* v. *Reno*, 929 F Sup. 824 (1996).

[28] This included the network's ability to program affiliates' time and ownership of affiliates.

[29] *National Broadcasting Company* v. *United States*, 319 U.S. 191 (1943).

[30] *Central Florida Enterprises, Inc.* v. *FCC* (1982), cited in T. Barton Carter, Marc Franklin, and Jay Wright, *The First Amendment and the Fifth Estate: Regulation of Electric Mass Media* (Mineola, N.Y.: Foundation Press, 1986), 538.

[31] Dean E. Alger, *The Media and Politics*, 2nd ed. (Belmont, Calif.: Wadsworth Publishing Co., 1996).

[32] *Ibid.*

[33] Erwin Krasnow, Lawrence Longley, and Herbert Terry, *The Politics of Broadcast Regulation*, 3rd ed. (New York: St. Martin's Press, 1982), 223.

[34] Alger, *op. cit.*, 109.

[35] Fred W. Friendly, *The Good Guys, The Bad Guys and the First Amendment: Freedom of Speech vs. The Fairness Doctrine* (New York: Random House, 1976), 23.

[36] *Ibid.*, 24.

[37] *Red Lion Broadcasting Co.* v. *FCC*, 395 U.S. 367 (1968).

[38] Friendly, *op. cit.*, 72.

[39] *Miami Herald Publishing Company* v. *Tornillo*, 418 U.S. 241 (1974).

[40] For a legal history of access, see Dom Caristi, *Expanding Free Expression in the Marketplace: Broadcasting and the Public Forum* (New York: Quorum Books, 1992).

[41] *Miami Herald Publishing Co.* v. *Tornillio*, 1974, *op. cit.*

CHAPTER 6

The Gatekeepers and the elite

The media provide us with most of our images of the world. Because they determine what is and is not news, they are often referred to as "gatekeepers" that let in what they deem important and close off what they perceive as not newsworthy. Walter Lippmann noted this critical role in 1922 when he argued that the political world is by necessity a pseudoenvironment, created for the most part by the mass media, which gather, organize, and filter the events.[1] He explained: "The real environment is altogether too big, too complex and too fleeting for direct acquaintance. We are not equipped to deal with so much subtlety, so much variety, so many permutations and combinations. And although we have to act in that environment, we have to reconstruct it on a simpler model before we can manage with it."[2]

Lippmann recognized the power of the press to shape the events that citizens must act on. Yet for many years those responsible for gathering and reporting the news have suggested that the news is a "mirror" of society. As Edward J. Epstein noted, a former president of CBS News stated in the late 1960s, "What the media do is hold a mirror up to society and try to report it as faithfully as possible."[3] This suggests that what is presented as news has not been tainted by human judgments, values, or orientations, that journalists simply report what has occurred to the public. Journalists frequently argue that their reporting is objective because they only reflect what is occurring in society and do *not* alter events. They say their objectivity is ensured by their high levels of education and professional training.

Given the vast number and complexity of events that journalists must cover and the limitations of time, space, and resources, some selection inevitably occurs. The goal of complete objectivity is laudable, but beyond human capabilities or the structural constraints on the media. No individuals can make truly value-free judgments; they must view events from their own perspectives. Trained journalists may be more cognizant of the problem and may therefore set aside their own values more easily than the average citizen, but they cannot completely free themselves of their values.

Herbert Gans, in a study of the background and values of reporters and editors of major news organizations, identified a set of basic social and political values held by those working in these organizations. He called these "enduring values" and said they were instrumental in creating "reality judgments." In *Deciding What's News*, he states:

> When journalists must decide what is new, they must also make assumptions about the old and therefore no longer newsworthy; when they report what is wrong or abnormal, they must decide what is normal. If they favor the old or the new, and if they believe that what is normal should be normal, reality judgments then become preference statements.
>
> In any case, journalists cannot exercise news judgments without a composite of nation, society, and national and social institutions in their collective heads, and this picture is an aggregate of reality judgments.[4]

Other scholars have shown how reality judgments affect the construction of the news and the versions of reality that are presented to the public as news.[5] Stories must have meaning, and some of these meanings are developed by those presenting the story.

The idea that "straight reporting" of a story, reporting just the "facts," prevents bias and aids objectivity is also frequently heard among both those in the media and the general public, but it is also a myth. Each story has its own context. For example, a presidential address cannot be adequately reported in isolation. Where was the speech given, to what group, and to what audience response are a few important contextual properties involved in the reporting of a speech.

There are multiple pressures on journalists reporting the news. Marvin Kalb, a former CBS correspondent, noted the increasing economic pressures in television, as well as the importance of the visual image:

> If you are paying a lot of money for a picture from Iran or Somalia or wherever, that picture had to tell you something right then and there; it had immediacy, it was live. . . . And if you are looking at Somalia, as the Marines landed on the beach, it's no longer seen as important for you to hear the reporter or anchor talk about the background of tribal warfare in Africa, etc. [In effect, the news gatekeepers now say] "Forget that, tell me more about the Marines wading through the water to get to the beach."[6]

The increasing economic pressures influence the process of selecting what is news, and reality is increasingly constructed on the basis of economic incentives, not objective reporting. Journalists have recently come to invoke "fairness" as their standard, which translates into trying to achieve a balance in the reporting of a story. This acknowledgment by the media that straight reporting is not practical and objectivity is unobtainable harkens back to Lippmann's observation.

The Gatekeepers

Objectivity is not possible for those reporting the news or for their audience, as each has his or her own set of values and norms. It is therefore necessary to understand the backgrounds of those reporting and producing the news to comprehend their values and norms. Journalism professors David Weaver and G. Cleveland Wilhoit have extensively researched the demographics and orientations of newspeople.[7] Using their own data and data from other sources on journalists and the general population, they have been able to address change over time in those reporting and producing the news.

Demographics of Journalists

An issue at the core of concerns about the objectivity of the news is that those presenting the news do not represent the public as a whole philosophically or demographically. Because they do not represent the general public, the argument goes, their view of what is important and newsworthy is not the same as that of the general public. To address this concern, we shall examine several demographic factors.

Age

On average, American journalists in 1992 were older than in 1982–83, with a median age of 36 years, virtually identical to the U.S. labor force as a whole. Journalists were, however, disproportionately clustered in the 25- to 35-year and 35- to 44-year age brackets, and substantially underrepresentative of the portion of the labor force under 24 years of age. This underrepresentation is explained in large measure by the education required to be a journalist today. Print journalists were, on average, older than broadcast journalists— 39 years old, as opposed to 33.

Gender

Comparing data from three periods, 1971, 1982–83, and 1992, Weaver and Wilhoit found little increase in the overall percentage of female journalists. Between 1971 and 1982–1983 there was a 13.5 percent increase in female journalists, but in the last two periods the percentage of female journalists remained constant at 34 percent, despite the increased number of female journalism students and the emphasis on hiring women in the 1980s. One explanation for the lack of change in 1992 was the curtailment of hiring during the late 1980s because of economic downturns and corporate mergers that resulted in job displacement.[8]

The authors did find that, contrary to popular belief, female journalists most frequently worked for newsmagazines and weekly newspapers, not television networks. The percentage of news stories covered by women remains low compared with women's share of the general population. A 1996 study of the three major news networks (ABC, CBS, and NBC) found women covered only 19 percent of the stories[9] and accounted for only 14 percent of the reporters.[10] Of course, many magazines address women's issues, but the mainstream news media remain predominantly male oriented, a fact that is important in evaluating news bias, for public opinion polls continually show differences between men and women on many important social and economic issues.

Ethnicity

The Weaver and Wilhoit data indicate that ethnic minorities have increased their representation in the news-gathering process since the 1970s, although they remain a very small faction of mainstream journalism and clearly do not match their numbers in the general population. Blacks represent the largest group, followed by Hispanics, Asian-Americans, and Native Americans. The authors estimate that there are twice as many blacks as Hispanics in journalism.[11] There is a lively minority press in many parts of the county. For instance, there are nearly 200 members of the National Newspapers Publisher Association, which represents the black press, as well as a number of black radio stations. The Black Entertainment Television (BET) cable channel has its own news division. There are nearly 200 Hispanic publications, most weeklies, in addition to Univision television network, which is estimated to reach 92 percent of the Spanish-speaking population. Minority views are still not equally represented in the major media organizations, but diversity in the media has increased through the years and will continue to do so as more television channels become available and other means of communication are developed.

Religion

In the 1990s, when important news stories often revolved around religious issues and groups in society, the religious backgrounds of journalists could be important. However, Weaver and Wilhoit found no significant change in those backgrounds from 1982–83 to 1992. As Table 6.1 indicates, journalists' religious backgrounds are strikingly similar to those of the general population. The table reveals a decline in the percentage of journalists from Protestant backgrounds, but this is also true of society in general. The same pattern applies to those claiming to be brought up with no religion or those from other than traditional Protestant, Catholic, or Jewish backgrounds. Thus, journalists religiously reflect the general population quite closely.

Table 6.1
Religious Backgrounds of U.S. Journalists Compared with Entire Adult Population (Percentages in Each Group)

RELIGION	JOURNALISTS			U.S. ADULT POPULATION		
	1971[a]	1982–83[b]	1992	1972[c]	1981[d]	1992[e]
Protestant	61.5	60.5	54.4	60	59	55
Catholic	24.5	26.9	29.9	27	28	26
Jewish	6.4	5.8	5.4	2	2	1
Other or none	7.7	6.8	10.2	11	11	18
Total	101[f]	100	99.9[f]	100	100	100

[a]From Johnstone, Slawki, and Bowman, *The News People,* pp. 90, 255. Figures calculated from Table 5.9.

[b]From Weaver and Wilhoit, *The American Journalist,* p. 24.

[c]From George H. Gallup, *The Gallup Polls: Public Opinion,* Vol. 1 1972–1977 (Wilmington, Del.: Scholarly Resources, 1973, 1977): 393.

[d]From *The Gallup Polls: Public Opinion* (1987):37.

[e]Gallup Organization national telephone survey of 1,001 U.S. adults July 31–August 2, 1992. Question: What is your religious preference? Data provided by the Roper Center, University of Connecticut.

[f]Figures do not total to 100 percent due to rounding.

Source: David H. Weaver and G. Cleveland Wilhoit, *The American Journalist in the 1990s: U.S. News People at the End of an Era* (Mahwah, N.J.: Erlbaum and Associates, Inc., 1996), Table 1.9: 14.

Education

As one would expect, journalists have more formal education than the general population. Table 6.2 shows that between 1971 and 1992 there was a 22 percent increase in journalists with college degrees. Among those, 40 percent majored in journalism in 1982–83 and 1992. What are not reflected in the table are radio, television, telecommunications, and communications majors, who accounted for 15 percent of journalists in 1971 and 1992.

The typical American journalist in 1992, as revealed by Weaver and Wilhoit's data, was a white, male Protestant with a bachelor's degree from a public institution, married, 36 years old, earning $31,000 a year. He had been a journalist for twelve years, and worked for a medium-size, group-owned daily newspaper.[12] Journalists as a whole were similar to the general population in their religious beliefs, while women and ethnic minorities remained underrepresented in the mainstream media. Women were more likely to seek employment in the print media than television. In addition, as mentioned earlier, print journalists were older, on average, than television journalists.

Table 6.2
Education of Journalists

1971		1982–1983		1992	
College graduate	Journalism major	College graduate	Journalism major	College graduate	Journalism major
60%	34%	75%	40%	82%	40%

Source: David H. Weaver and G. Cleveland Wilhoit, *The American Journalist in the 1990s: U.S. News People at the End of an Era* (Mahwah, N.J.: Erlbaum and Associates, Inc., 1996): 29.

Why do demographics matter? Herbert Gans, in his study of CBS and NBC News, *Time*, and *Newsweek*, found that personal experiences and life circumstances of news personnel were middle class.[13] S. Robert Lichter, Stanley Rothman, and Linda Lichter, in their study of the "most influential media outlets" in America, found that 40 percent of journalists had professional parents, and another 40 percent described their parents as members of the business community.[14] They concluded, "Many among the media elite enjoy socially privileged upbringings."[15] They also claimed that the media elite were more secular, more civil libertarian, more tolerant of diverse opinions and lifestyles, and more supportive of government action in dealing with public problems.[16] As we have seen, Weaver and Wilhoit did not find journalists to be more secular; on the contrary, they found them to be extremely close to the general public with regard to religion. Regardless of the particular finding or the particular subgroup of journalists studied, scholars agree that one's demographic characteristics inevitably influence the way one constructs the news, either implicitly or explicitly.

Television news has produced a different economics than other forms of the mass media. Salaries of major network reporters have increased dramatically over the past decade. Today most television journalists, including reporters, editors, and producers, are upper middle class. Major network personalities are upper class financially and have become celebrities. Sam Donaldson, for example, owns a 27,000-acre ranch in New Mexico. His regular speaking fee is $30,000, and he appears frequently on the David Letterman and Jay Leno shows. Many print journalists, such as George Will, Jack Germond, William Safire, Pat Buchanan, Maureen Dowd, Cokie Roberts, Gwen Ifill, Al Hunt, and Steven Roberts, have also become celebrities through their appearances on TV news programs.

Celebrity can blur the line between journalism and performing. Mort Kondracke, of *Roll Call*, and Fred Barnes, of the *New Republic*, staged a debate at a $75-a-plate dinner for American Express Platinum Cardholders.[17] William

Schneider, CNN's political analyst, addressed the *Atlantic* magazine forum touting the new Toyota Camry. An American Express frequent flier can, with 300,000 miles, get to meet *New York Times* correspondent William Safire.

Has the high socioeconomic status of many of America's leading journalists compromised their journalistic judgment? Could it influence their criteria for determining what is newsworthy? What the upper middle and upper classes perceive as normal may not be seen the same way by the general public. For example, after President Clinton nominated Zoe Baird to be Attorney General, it was discovered that she and her husband had knowingly hired a pair of illegal immigrants as nanny and chauffeur. The Washington press treated the matter as a minor infraction. From the *Washington Post* to the *Wall Street Journal* to CNN's Capitol Gang, there was little criticism of the Bairds' behavior. But there was a vastly different reaction from the general public, as was revealed by call-in comments on talk radio programs and letters to editors. The argument that a $500,000-a-year corporate lawyer could not find a legal nanny did not convince most Americans, many of whom made clear they felt she was unfit to be the nation's top law enforcement officer. The entire episode confirmed suspicions that journalists' values affect what they see as newsworthy.

General and specific orientations of journalists

There are two types of orientations that are important in the creation of the news. The first are broad, general orientations that have developed in most journalists through the years. The second are characteristics of individual journalists, such as party identification, political ideology, or attitudes toward social issues. Herbert Gans argued that the general values of American journalists are reflected in their reporting. For example, their *ethnocentrism* is reflected in both the limited amount of news from other countries and the tendency to "judge other countries by the extent to which they live up to or imitate American practices and values."[18]

Another value of most American journalists is what Gans labeled *altruistic democracy*, the tendency to indicate "how American democracy should perform by . . . [paying] attention to deviation from the unstated ideal, evident in their stories about corruption, conflict, protest, and bureaucratic malfunctioning."[19] Gans pointed out that journalists tend to focus on formal political organizations and procedures and pay little attention to the distribution of economic resources that affect the realization of the ideal democracy. His study has even greater implications today in light of the massive numbers of media mergers, which affect what and how news is reported.

Other values found among journalists are difficult for them to challenge because of the nature of the media. One is the idea that *responsible capitalism* is the linchpin of democracy in America. Studies indicate that news media personnel are far less likely to run stories about failures or inefficiencies in business than in government.[20] Economic stories that involved business violations of law were reported in the 1980s and 1990s and received considerable attention, but they were relatively few compared with stories about government. There are three reasons for this imbalance. First, the media are businesses and depend on other businesses for various forms of support. Second, it is considerably easier to obtain information about government and its activities than it is corporations. Democratic government operates openly, unlike corporate America. Finally, ethnocentricity precludes comparison with other nations. During the debate over heath care reform in the early 1990s, the media generally did not examine how other democratic nations provided health care. During the debate over the Family Leave Act, the media did not examine family leave policies in other western nations, most of which are quite generous.

Gans also noted that the media place a high value on *individualism*. There is, he argued, a strong tendency among those in the media to focus on individuals, whether "self-made millionaires" or celebrities. This focus on individualism helps "personalize" the news and is seen as a way of increasing one's audience. Coverage of the death penalty illustrates this phenomenon. The death penalty is most frequently reported in terms of individuals who are on "death row". Rarely do the media address the abstract issues of effectiveness, cost, or alternatives. For example, does the state of Michigan, which has no death penalty, have a higher crime rate than its socioeconomically similar neighbor Illinois, which does? Most social issues are not addressed as problems to be solved, but as a series of stories involving individuals.

Another enduring journalistic value identified by Gans was what he called *moderation*. Gans argued that the media's strong orientation toward moderation affects coverage of individuals who might be considered rebels or deviants from society's norms. The media generally treated Ralph Nader and Martin Luther King, Jr., as extremists outside the American "mainstream". Similarly, Ross Perot's third-party bid for the presidency, like most such bids, received comparatively little attention.[21]

Finally, Gans claimed that journalists share a *small-town pastoralism*. Events in small towns are reported nostalgically, and the demise of such towns or their absorption by suburbs is often treated with great sentiment. This is linked to the "traditional values" theme treated so frequently in the media. Whether these values exist to the extent Gans believed is not the issue here; rather it is that values do exist within the organized media. Moreover, a strong case can be made that these values are present in today's reporting.

The second set of values that are important to understanding the way the news is covered are those that characterize individual journalists. We shall see how three such values affect how journalists view the world around them. It is frequently said that journalists are more liberal than the general population and that their presentation of the news is biased by their political orientation. To address this question we shall examine three measures of political orientation: party identification, political orientation, and voting behavior in the 1992 presidential election.

Party Identification

While candidates of both political parties have complained about being treated unfairly by the media, the current popular sentiment suggests that Republicans are more likely to suffer from a press that favors the Democratic Party. In 1995 the Media Studies Center and the Roper Center for Public Opinion surveyed Washington reporters and national newspaper editors, and compared their results with those for a sample of the general population. As Figure 6.1 shows, half of the sampled Washington-based reporters (including bureau chiefs) identified with the Democratic Party. The newspaper editors were nearly the same as the national sample in their identification with the Democratic Party: 31 percent and 34 percent, respectively. Washington reporters were much less likely to identify with the Republican Party than the public (4 percent versus 28 percent), while only 14 percent of the editors were Republicans. Both the Washington reporters and editors were more likely to identify themselves as independents than the general public. The pattern of party identification that emerges is that those reporting from the nation's capital in 1995 were more likely to identify with the Democratic Party, while those responsible for the editing of the nation's newspapers were somewhat less likely to identify with the Democratic Party than the public but only half as likely to identify with the Republican Party. Both the Washington reporters and the editors claimed identification as independents more than the public. These patterns are similar to those found earlier by Weaver and Wilhoit in their study of journalists' party affiliations.[22] While Republicans claim there is a media bias against them, the issue of bias, as we shall see, is complex. The evidence indicates that reporters identify with the Democratic Party and editors and owners identify with the Republican Party.

Political Ideology

Party identification is only one part of political orientation. Both major political parties have supporters who hold widely conflicting views. Democrats and Republicans exist along a political continuum that makes maintaining party cohesion and direction difficult, if not impossible. In 1994 the Republicans finally regained control of both houses of Congress after four decades, only to find themselves divided along ideological lines. Their divisions only intensified as they struggled to maintain control.

Just as there are significant differences in party identification between journalists and the general public, so there are similar differences in

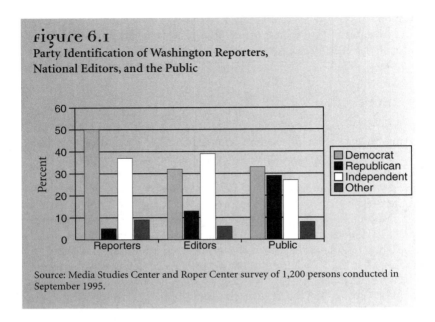

figure 6.1
Party Identification of Washington Reporters, National Editors, and the Public

Source: Media Studies Center and Roper Center survey of 1,200 persons conducted in September 1995.

self-described ideological positions. A 1995 study conducted by the Media Studies Center and Roper Center found 61 percent of Washington reporters and their bureau chiefs claimed to be liberal or liberal-leaning. The nation's newspaper editors were half as likely to have a liberal orientation, with 32 percent so describing themselves.[23] Nonetheless, this was 12 percent higher than the portion of the general public that described themselves as liberal. Among moderates there was very little difference between reporters, editors, and the public. Roughly a third of editors and the public said they were moderates, and the Washington reporters are only slightly less likely to describe themselves as moderates (30 percent). As with liberal identifiers, there was a considerable gap between the percentages of Washington reporters and the public who considered themselves conservative. Only 9 percent of Washington reporters were conservative, compared with 37 percent of the public. Editors were closer to the public's orientation, with about a quarter in this category.

These data provide strong evidence that Washington-based journalists are more Democratic and liberal than the nation's newspaper editors, and significantly more so than the general public.[24] These findings are limited and do not address the question of personal political bias in news reporting, but they raise several important questions. First, do the media have a liberal bias in their reporting of the news? Second, do they slant their coverage of policy issues in favor of a liberal perspective? Finally, are there checks on the reporting of the news?

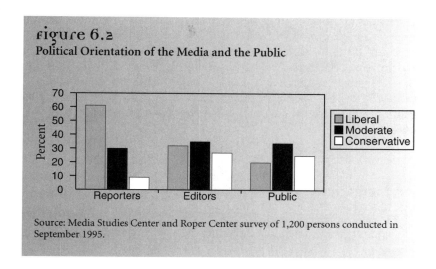

figure 6.2

Political Orientation of the Media and the Public

Source: Media Studies Center and Roper Center survey of 1,200 persons conducted in September 1995.

The cannons of the profession guide journalists. They usually strive in their news stories to be impartial and fair, to exclude their personal opinions, and to achieve a balance by including different sides to avoid bias. In addition, the fact that reporters tend to be more liberal while editors and owners are increasingly conservative can serve as an internal check on reporting. As we have seen, mergers may have a profound affect on the ultimate checks and balances in the reporting of the news.

Voting Patterns

In the 1992 presidential election, Washington reporters claimed to have voted for Clinton over Bush by a margin of 89 percent to 7 percent.[25] In contrast, only 44 percent of the general public voted for Clinton. Newspaper editors voted for Clinton over Bush by a margin of 60 percent to 22 percent, with 4 percent voting for Perot. Clearly, in the 1992 presidential election even editors, who were relatively close to the public in political orientation, were not close in voting. Gans's earlier observation may help explain some of the disparity between the editors and the public. Most editors felt that Ross Perot's candidacy had little chance of success, and their support for him was significantly less than the general population's. This may have been due to the editors' belief in moderation, something Perot did not espouse. Furthermore, all elections occur within a context. The personalities of candidates, the economic condition of the nation, and international events all play significant roles in presidential elections. But what is clear from this sample is that journalists' orientations are different from those of the general public.

The values and orientations of reporters and editors are important to an understanding of how the world we view through the media is constructed, but it is not a complete picture. For if reporters and editors controlled the flow of news in newspapers, for example, these papers should have been far more supportive of Democratic presidential candidates on their editorial pages than has been the case. As Figure 6.3 illustrates, Republican candidates for president have received substantially more newspaper endorsements than Democrats since 1932.[26] Only twice has the Democratic candidate received more endorsements than the Republican candidate during this period: Lyndon Johnson in 1964 and Bill Clinton in 1992. Republican candidates have averaged 54 percent of endorsements, compared with 19 percent for Democratic candidates. With the exception of 1984, there has been a precipitous decline in newspaper endorsements. In 1992, for example, 67 percent of the nation's newspapers endorsed neither President Bush nor Governor Clinton. What does Figure 6.3 tell us? First, newspapers are far more likely to endorse the Republican candidate for president than the Democrat. Newspaper owners are business people, and the Republican Party has strongly been associated with business interests. Second, focusing on reporters and editors may be misleading, for owners may intervene in the editorial process on important issues. Finally, newspaper endorsements are becoming less common.

factors in Reporting the News

Before we address the issue of bias in the news, it is important to understand what drives news reporting. First and foremost, reporting the news is a *business*. Newspapers, television, cable, and radio stations, and Web sites are all in the business of making a profit. There are three methods of achieving this: increasing audiences, expanding advertising, or merging with other media. Mergers increase capital, audience, and advertising markets. Lance Bennett has stated, "If there is a single most important flaw in the American news style, it is the overwhelming tendency to downplay the big social, economic, or political picture in favor of the human trials and triumphs that sit at the surface of the news."[27] Bennett identifies four factors that are important in the way American media present a story: personalized human interest, dramatization, fragmentation, and normalized interpretation.[28]

Personalized Human Interest

The media frequently attempt to appeal to their audience's emotions to hold their attention. Coverage of the deaths of Princes Diana and John F. Kennedy, Jr., illustrates the media's personalizing of human interest stories. The media attempted to portray them as "normal" people, but the coverage

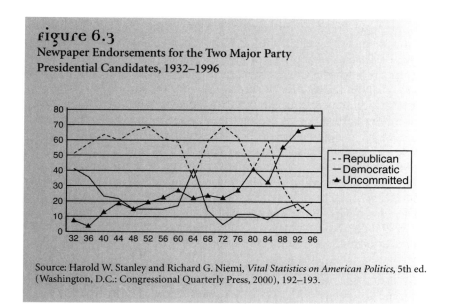

figure 6.3

Newpaper Endorsements for the Two Major Party
Presidential Candidates, 1932–1996

Source: Harold W. Stanley and Richard G. Niemi, *Vital Statistics on American Politics*, 5th ed.
(Washington, D.C.: Congressional Quarterly Press, 2000), 192–193.

was anything but normal. The public was provided with extensive coverage of Princess Diana's death and funeral, and according to Pew Research Center polls, the public claimed to have followed the story very closely.[29] The networks began live coverage of the Kennedy story as soon as news was received that Kennedy's plane was late, and reran old film clips in an effort to hold their audience's attention. Special memorial programs were developed prior to confirmation of the deaths of Kennedy and his passengers. In both cases the media's focus on human interest spurred a debate over the media's proper role. What held the audience in both cases was the emotional, personalized coverage.

Bennett argues that this approach to the news "encourages people to take an egocentric rather than a socially concerned view of political problems."[30] This personalization of the news encourages the public to focus on the personal lives of political figures and may distract attention from the critical examination of complex issues that is essential to a vital and healthy democracy.

Dramatization

In an effort to personalize the news, stories are often selected for their dramatic impact. Coverage of dramatic stories drives out coverage of larger and more important issues like social inequality, hunger, resource depletion, the environment, and political oppression. The use of the dramatic is illustrated by the media's coverage of the O.J. Simpson case. Networks interrupted their regularly scheduled programming for live coverage of the pursuit of Simpson's car before he was arrested. Later the Simpson courtroom drama unfolded daily in the media. During the six months prior to the trial, the major television networks devoted nearly fourteen hours of evening news programming to the case, exceeding the time spent on health care reform or the midterm congressional elections that returned control of the Senate and House to Republicans.[31] Once the "trial of the century" began in January 1995, it received twice as much network coverage as the president's activities. While the public complained about the extensive coverage, polls indicated that a significant segment followed the trial on a daily basis.[32]

The news describes the day's events but does not advocate policy positions. In 1968 Reuven Frank, the executive producer of NBC Evening News, proposed a formula for evening news stories:

> Every news story should, without any sacrifice of probity or responsibility, display the attributes of fiction, of drama. It should have structure and conflict, problem and denouement, rising action and falling action, a beginning, middle, and end. These are not only essentials of drama; they are essentials of narrative.[33]

Chronic conditions are reported only after they have reached unusual levels. Whether the story is a worldwide famine, epidemic, or revolution, it is presented only after the situation has become grave.

Michael Milburn and A. McGrail examined the effects of dramatic coverage of news events.[34] They hypothesized that television stories that were formatted in a dramatic manner evoked emotional responses, related the events to a more general myth or simplified schema for viewers, and thereby reduced the cognitive complexity of political events. The authors selected two stories to test their hypothesis, the trade imbalance with South Korea and an upcoming election in Chile. They selected a series of highly dramatic news stories and presented the most dramatic scenes. Subjects then watched either the dramatic or nondramatic versions and were asked to recall as much information from them as they could. In addition, they were asked to write several paragraphs about what the United States should do in the two situations. After controlling for background variables, such as the subjects' political ideologies and the levels of education of the subjects' parents, the authors found that individuals who watched the dramatic versions recalled significantly less and the cognitive complexity of their thinking was significantly lower.[35]

All media dramatize the news. Doris Graber has shown the stability in patterns of news reporting across different media.[36] As Table 6.3 shows, among similar media, differences in the types of stories reported were marginal. Among the three major networks (ABC, CBS, and NBC), coverage of government and politics accounted for the majority of news stories. Local affiliates, however, emphasized stories about crime and sports. The two

Chicago newspapers in Graber's study devoted the most space to entertainment and sports coverage.

It is not only the type of story covered that is significant, but how and where the story appears in the news report. There is abundant evidence that crime has long been overreported by the news media. Steven Chermak found that newspapers average nine cover stories a day, and daily television newscasts average four prominent stories (about one fourth the total number of stories).[37] As Clarence Page has written, "News distorts, and TV news distorts absolutely. Television makes America look like a far more violent, corrupt, oversexed and crime-ridden place than it really is, simply because it devotes so much time and hyperventilation to the subjects."[38] A study of eight local news programs found that 29.3 percent of the stories were on crime, compared with 2 percent on education and 1.2 percent on race relations.[39] According to Page and others, crime receives significant airtime because it draws audiences, which can be sold to advertisers.[40] Paul Klite, Robert Bardwell, and Jason Salzman, in a study of one hundred local television news programs in fifty-six cities across thirty-three states, found no significant differences in the content or construct of the news.[41] They found that less than half the airtime was spent reporting news, and most news stories dealt with crime. One third of the news airtime was devoted to crime stories.[42]

Fragmentation

The emphasis on personalized and dramatic stories leads to the isolation of stories and a fragmented view of the world. To hold the public's attention, news executives avoid large, complex stories. Fragmentation of the news has increased because of increased competition within and among the various media and the concentration of ownership control, and can be seen in the emergence of two all-news networks—MSNBC and FOX News. At the same time the concentration of ownership through mergers and acquisitions has resulted in less diversity of viewpoints in political coverage.

There are two recent examples of such concentration. First, NBC and the *Washington Post* Company formed an alliance for sharing news. Contributors to the alliance include NBC News, the MSNBC cable network and the Internet site, and the print and Web operations of the *Washington Post* and its sister publication, *Newsweek*.[43] Second, ABC, CBS, and FOX Television networks agreed to merge their news services into a single domestic news cooperative—Network News Service (NNS). Under this agreement NNS collects video from the networks' news-gathering divisions and local affiliates, and each network's news service can then use any of the day's material in its regular feeds to affiliates.[44]

There is a paradox in the extensiveness of coverage in the current environment. In stories like those involving O.J. Simpson, Princess Diana, and

Table 6.3
Frerquency of Mention of News Topics: June 1, 1995, to July 20, 1995 (in percentages)

NEWS TOPICS	SUN TIMES (2,777)	CHICAGO TRIBUNE (2,445)	ABC (440)
Government/politics			
National government	3.8	4.5	26.2
Elections	1.0	1.3	1.0
State government	1.0	1.5	1.5
Local government	2.2	2.4	0.4
International news	6.1	7.2	19.5
National affairs news	2.1	2.7	4.2
Local affairs news	3.5	3.7	0.0
Total	19.7	23.3	52.8
Economic issues			
Economy	1.4	1.9	3.0
Business	7.5	9.6	2.4
Labor/unemployment	1.5	1.4	3.0
Transportation/energy	2.3	2.4	2.1
Health care	1.3	1.7	7.0
Total	14.0	17.0	17.5
Social issues			
Civil rights/deprived groups	0.7	0.9	1.9
Education	1.2	1.4	0.9
Media	0.6	0.8	0.8
Religion	0.4	0.7	1.5
Abortion/contraception	0.3	0.4	2.0
Disease/Ebola virus	0.6	0.6	4.3
Other health issues	1.1	1.7	1.5
Disasters/accidents	1.7	1.2	1.2
Environment	0.9	1.0	1.1
Justice system	0.8	1.3	4.6
Individual crime	3.5	4.1	2.5
Total	11.8	14.1	22.3
Other			
Obituaries	1.8	3.5	0.0
Weather	1.3	1.8	1.3
Sports	23.6	18.7	3.0
Entertainment	28.1	22.2	4.3
Total	54.8	46.2	8.6

Source: Doris A. Graber, *Mass Media and American Politics*, 5th ed. (Washington, D.C.: Congressional Quarterly Press, 1997), 110–111.

NATIONAL TV			LOCAL TV	
CBS	NBC	ABC	CBS	NBC
(435)	(425)	(530)	(555)	(541)
24.1	23.3	7.8	8.7	6.2
2.0	1.0	1.5	1.2	1.5
2.2	0.6	1.3	1.1	0.8
0.1	0.0	3.7	1.6	2.5
17.5	19.0	7.0	4.5	6.4
7.5	9.1	2.3	3.9	6.3
0.0	0.0	9.5	8.7	8.0
53.4	53.0	33.1	29.7	31.7
5.2	5.4	0.6	0.3	0.5
1.9	1.4	2.4	1.2	1.0
1.9	2.2	0.8	0.8	0.9
1.1	2.0	1.5	1.3	2.5
6.7	5.3	3.7	4.1	3.5
16.8	16.3	9.0	7.7	8.4
2.2	1.8	0.5	1.2	1.2
1.3	1.1	2.2	0.3	0.3
2.2	2.3	2.0	1.7	1.8
0.3	0.6	0.6	1.2	1.3
1.0	0.8	0.3	0.9	0.3
3.7	3.0	2.4	1.8	1.2
1.6	0.8	1.5	2.9	1.6
3.1	3.2	2.7	4.1	6.1
1.0	1.2	0.6	1.0	1.0
4.4	3.7	2.2	1.7	0.9
2.2	1.5	13.1	12.3	7.1
23.0	20.0	28.1	29.1	22.8
0.0	0.0	0.0	0.0	0.0
2.3	2.1	6.0	7.5	7.2
1.2	4.0	18.9	19.8	20.7
4.1	5.1	5.2	6.4	9.1
7.6	11.2	30.1	33.7	37.0

John F. Kennedy, Jr., there was no fragmentation, for the media covered them around the clock, even when there was nothing new to report. However, when far more important issues of budgetary debates, government gridlock, or health care reform are involved, coverage is fragmented and inconsistent. Fragmentation works against well-developed coverage because the reporting is constantly interrupted.

Normalization

Bennett has also suggested that what passes for depth and coherence in our system of reporting is the "normalized" interpretation of otherwise threatening and confusing stories.[45] He argues that journalists seek to reassure citizens through the use of authoritative voices. When a crisis occurs, officials are swift to assure the public that things will return to normal quickly, and the public should trust them to act in their best interest. Journalists also prompt officials with questions that show the journalists' concern about the problem. Throughout the years public officials have normalized such issues as toxic wastes, breast implants, tobacco use, air pollutions, and drug use. In each instance officials have assured the public that they are aware of the problem and have acted to restore safety.

Some have argued that officials' attempts at "normalization" have led to the public's increased anger at both the media and politicians. As citizens see elected officials propose simplistic solutions to complex problems, they become more cynical about politics and government. The news media are a major contributor to this cynicism because they first solicit the simplistic solutions and then criticize the officials for providing them. Others have suggested that current presentations of the news lead to inadequate reasoning about social problems.[46] Iyengar, for instance, finds that television news rarely provides viewers with complete, coherent coverage of important issues. Instead it provides what he terms "episodic" coverage by continually emphasizing different issues to attract and maintain audiences.

These are characteristics of news presentation that are driven by the media's need to maintain audiences and sponsors. Other characteristics result from the structural constraints of space and time. A typical newspaper, for instance, has 105 column inches of front page space, and the evening news program has twenty-two minutes of airtime to present the day's events. A time breakdown for local news programs aired in Dallas, Texas, during the spring 1997 "sweeps week" is shown in Table 6.4. The four major network news stations in Dallas averaged 14.5 stories per newscast. Among the three major network affiliates (ABC, CBS, and NBC), the average was 12.6 stories, with a range from 11 to 15.[47] During this week nearly one third of the stories the four network stations aired were on violent crime.

Table 6.4
Dallas Local News Breakdown During Sweeps Week 1997

	AVERAGE NUMBER OF NEWS STORIES PER HOUR	PERCENT TIED TO VIOLENT CRIME
FOX	20	32
NBC	15	27
ABC	12	26
CBS	11	32
Average	14.5	29.2

Source: Ed Bark, "10 O'Clock News Report Card," *Dallas Morning News*, March 9, 1997:C6. Reprinted with permission of the *Dallas Morning News*.

Bias in the News

The media issue that generates the most intense public debate is that of perceived bias. All communication is selective and therefore somewhat biased. Media gatekeepers select the stories they present, while the public select the stories they prefer and filter them through their own experiences and beliefs. The question is whether the media systematically attempt to mislead the public, as Bob Dole claimed during his bid for the presidency in 1996.[48] Unfortunately, studies of bias have not resolved the debate, in part because most have been conducted during political campaigns, and therefore scrutinize bias in the context of campaign reporting. Consequently, there is little information on long-term effects of media bias. The studies of campaigns have found little or no bias in the media's presentation of campaigns, candidates, and issues.

A second difficulty in understanding bias is the lack of a common and precise definition of bias. Doris Graber concludes there is no bias by her commonly accepted definition of the term: "A number of content analyses . . . refute the charges of political bias, if bias is defined as deliberately lopsided coverage or intentional slanting of the news. These analyses show instead that most news people try to cover a balanced array of issues in a neutral manner and do include at least a few contrasting viewpoints."[49] In his seminal study of network news coverage of the 1972 presidential campaign, C. Richard Hofstetter also found no bias in the three major networks' coverage of the candidates, campaigns, or issues.

Hofstetter notes two types of bias. First, because of the competitive nature of the media, there is a need to maintain an audience and to provide information in a very small time period. The need to select and prioritize items to be aired produces what Hofstetter calls *structural bias*. This bias is most clearly seen in the similarity of news reported by the mainstream media. For instance, studies have found that at least two of the networks share lead stories on the nightly news 91 percent of the time, and the third network also covers the story but in a different news slot.[50] All three networks carry the same lead story 43 percent of the time. In her study of national and local television and local newspapers, Graber found "striking evidence that the same kinds of stories and story types . . . are reported by all news outlets."[51] This bias is not normally viewed as an overt attempt to sway the viewer or reader. However, as we noted earlier, it does set the agenda and frame the political news.

Political bias, the second type cited by Hofstetter, is more important, for it involves selecting items based on political considerations or prejudice. As we have seen, like everyone else, reporters, editors, and publishers have prejudices and preferences. The issue is to what extent they inject these prejudices and preferences into the transmission of news. When they do, the news becomes politically biased. To the extent that it can be quantified, most scholars have found little political bias in the mainstream press.

In a study of the media's coverage of the 1992 presidential campaign, Dalton, Beck, and Huckfeldt found that roughly one third of all news items presented a balanced view. That is, evaluative content favoring one candidate was matched by an equal amount of negative news (or equivalent coverage of a rival candidate) in the same story.[52] About one tenth of the items had no evaluative content, and provided simply straight factual information. Table 6.5 shows a significant difference between newspaper and television coverage. Television provided the least negative reporting, with roughly one half of television stories providing a balanced view of the candidates or no evaluative content.

The authors explain, "Most articles contained at least some evaluative content, such as whether one campaign was doing well or another was fairing poorly. In 1992 the imbalance in this reporting was clear: the newspaper coverage of the Bush campaign was predominately negative."[53] However, they view this negative coverage of Bush as a reflection of his campaign: "We attribute this largely to the content and dynamics of the campaign and less to any conscious media bias. Media coverage of the 1992 campaign primarily reflected the failures of the Bush campaign, which the media did not create."[54] There was little evidence that evaluative comments in the campaign news reflected the explicit opinions of journalists.

As the media compete increasingly for audiences and economic support, there is a tendency for them to appeal to the audience by sensationalizing the news and a greater likelihood of political bias. But one should remember that the charge of media bias has persisted since the founding of the country and will certainly continue. However, survey conducted during the 1996 presidential campaign found that most Americans believed the media were evenly balanced in their coverage and did not lean toward liberal or conservative positions.[55]

The biggest problem the modern media face is financial constraints. The need to produce more exciting stories than the competition does not promote balance, but unbalanced representation has not been traditionally viewed as bias, for there is no personal motive or intentional attempt to misinform the public. Instead, there is an effort to attract the same audience. Financial incentives become the major factor in the mass media's approach to the news.

The Media Elite

The public's discontent with the media focuses on those who report, edit, and produce the news, for these are the people they associate with the media. We have seen that these gatekeepers do not share the general population's political values or orientations. But such media observers as Michael Parenti, Edward S. Herman, Noam Chomsky, and Robert Entman have argued that to focus on reporters and editors is to focus on the "lowest link in the news manufacturing chain."[56] Parenti contends that "the media do not fail to do their jobs, rather they perform these functions all too well. Their objective is not to provide an alert, critical, and informed citizenry but the kind of people who will accept an opinion universe dominated by corporate and governmental elites, almost all of whom share the same ideological perspective about political and economic reality."[57]

Unlike the gatekeepers, who are involved in the daily presentation of the news, the media elite are the executives, owners, and members of the boards who direct the corporate side of the business. Most Americans do not know who they are or what power they wield. The ways the elite influence and control communication have not received as much attention as the roles of the gatekeepers. There are several reasons for this. First, the elite concept is contrary to the prevailing norm of social pluralism. Second, it is far more difficult to obtain information about the activities of individuals who own and control the media, rather than those who report the news. Third, there are numerous methodological problems associated with the elitist approach. Two of the most important of these are accurately determining who the elite are and accurately assessing their influence. Nonetheless, the media are indeed influenced by powerful elites. For example, when Rupert Murdoch, the owner of the FOX Network, was asked to what extent his politically conservative views influenced the editorial posture of his newspapers, he responded, "Considerably, the buck stops on my desk. My editors have input, but I make the final decisions."[58] The influence of the financially powerful elite on the political process can be seen in their actions behind the scenes, through their financial contributions to elected officials.

Table 6.5
Evaluative Content of Coverage of 1992 Presidential Campaign

	NEWSPAPER REPORTS		
	BUSH	CLINTON	PEROT
Positive	0.9%	43.4	19.1
Balanced	31.0	32.5	38.8
Negative	51.2	16.6	30.5
No Evaluative			
Content	6.8	7.5	11.6
	EDITORIAL REPORTS		
	BUSH	CLINTON	PEROT
Positive	12.9	28.1	15.5
Balanced	21.0	29.1	24.9
Negative	63.1	37.7	55.3
No Evaluative			
Content	3.6	5.1	4.4
	TELEVISION REPORTS		
	BUSH	CLINTON	PEROT
Positive	9.3	34.1	10.5
Balanced	34.5	27.8	17.8
Negative	47.2	14.7	28.0
No Evaluative			
Content	19.0	23.4	43.6

Source: Adapted from Russell J. Dalton, Paul A. Beck, and Robert Huckfeldt, Table 1, "Percent of Evaluative Content Stories in the 1992 Presidential Elections" from "Partisan Cues and the Media: Information Flows in the 1992 Presidential Election," *American Political Science Review*, 92(1):115.

The passage of the Telecommunications Act of 1996 demonstrates both the direct influence the media elite have through their contributions to political parties and candidates and the nature of their Washington connection.

Direct Influence

Nearly all segments of society are active in politics through lobbyists, citizens groups, and political action committees (PACs). What distinguishes the media elite is that they reside in all congressional districts. In addition, they have financial resources and provide a medium for elected officials to communicate with their constituents. (As we shall see later, this benefits incumbents and helps explain why the public views the institution of Congress negatively but their own representatives positively.) Furthermore, they can selectively set the national political agenda to an extent unlike any other group.

The influence of the media elite's money in politics was particularly evident in the passage of the 1996 Telecommunications Act. The debate over the bill occurred when lawmakers were looking for ways the government could cut costs and raise money. Some felt broadcasters should pay for the use of a valuable public resource, the airwaves, worth more than $70 million. Then–Senate Majority Leader Robert Dole opposed giving use of the public airwaves to the broadcasters for free; instead, he favored auctioning off the news broadcast spectrum as the act proposed. Senator Dole stated: "Here we are trying to balance the budget, cutting welfare, cutting other programs, and about to give a big handout here to the rich."[59] Despite Dole's opposition, the Telecommunications Act of 1996 was enacted, signaling the beginning of an active role in government by those who own and operate the mass media.

Over the past decade an estimated $9.5 million in political donations has been given by the four major networks—ABC, CBS, NBC, and FOX. In addition, the networks' owners—Disney, Westinghouse, General Electric, and Rupert Murdoch's News Corp.—have contributed generously to the political parties and candidates. Just counting the PACs for the four major networks and the National Association of Broadcasters (NAB), more than $6 million was contributed to candidates of both parties between 1987 and 1996. The seventy representatives of both parties who sat on the Senate and House Commerce Committees in the 104th Congress received more than $1.26 million from broadcast PACs and top executives during this period. The committee chairs received $212,000. During the first half of 1996 the NAB spent more on lobbying than such traditionally powerful lobbies as the Bank of America, Chrysler, and the National Rifle Association. These figures do not fully reflect the direct monetary contributions of the media elite, for they do not include donations through lobbies by Disney, General Electric, or Westinghouse. The pattern reflects who holds power in Washington. For instance, 60 percent of soft money contributions from the telecommunication industry during the 1997–1999 election cycle went to Republicans.[60]

Broadcasters who received billions of dollars in digital spectrum rights from the FCC as a result of the Telecommunications Act gave nearly $5 million in soft money contributions to the Republican and Democratic parties from 1991 through the first six months of 1997. They also gave to state parties. Rupert Murdoch alone gave more than $1 million to the California Republican Party.[61] Table 6.6 shows the broadcasters who received digital spectrum rights and the amounts they gave to each party.

Table 6.6
Broadcasters Receiving Digital Spectrum and Soft Money Contributions

DONOR	DEMOCRATIC PARTY	REPUBLICAN PARTY	TOTAL
Capitol Cities/ ABC Inc./Walt Disney*	$569,050	$491,450	$1,065,500
FOX Broadcasting/News Corp*	75,000	853,950	928,950
NBC/General Electric*	342,009	419,393	761,402
Viacom Int. /Paramount Communications*	418,400	122,700	541,100
CBS/Westinghouse Electric Corp.*	77,000	234,576	311,759
Newsweb Corp./Fred Eychaner	258,000	0	258,000
Gaylord Broadcasting Co. LP*	0	160,000	160,000
Univision Holdings/ A. Jerrold Perenchio	5,000	155,000	160,000
National Association of Broadcasters	79,450	54,200	133,650
Silver King Communications/ Home Shopping Network*	95,500	7,000	102,500
Argyle Television Inc./ Edward Blake Byrne	78,450	0	78,450
Telemundo Group/Leon D. Black	60,000	0	60,000
Tribune Broadcasting	59,300	0	59,300
Paxson Communications Inc.*	20,000	25,000	45,000
Grant Broadcasting Inc.*	40,000	0	40,000
Hubbard Broadcasting Inc.*	25,000	6,500	31,500
Chris-Craft Industries/ BHC Communications*	0	27,000	27,000
Granite Broadcasting Corp.	27,000	0	27,000
Meredith Corp.	0	15,000	15,000
Florida Association of Broadcasters	0	10,500	10,500
Total	$2,229,159	$2,582,452	$4,816,611

*Denotes contributions from broadcast subsidiaries and/or executives.

Source: Common Cause news release, "Return on Investment: The Hidden Story of Soft Money, Corporate Welfare and the 1997 Budget & Tax Deal," November 15, 1997.

A basic function of the media is to monitor government on behalf of its citizens. Government waste and mismanagement have been prime targets of their reporting. In recent years the media have reported on such misuse of funds as $600 toilet seats and $7,000 coffeepots purchased by the government for various government agencies. Two of the network news programs include regularly scheduled segments on waste in government and corporate welfare: ABC's *It's Your Money* and NBC's *Fleecing America*, yet there have been no reports of how broadcast money is used to influence government policy.

The Washington Connection

The media elite not only contribute money, but also hire spokespersons who have direct connections with those they are lobbying. Table 6.7 shows only some of those who were actively involved with lobbying over the telecommunication bill in 1996 and their previous positions of power. The list includes some of the most well-connected individuals in Washington, with a well-tuned understanding of how the process works, which individuals are most influential, and how best to manipulate the process.

There are four characteristics of this Washington connection that make it noteworthy. The first is the enormous growth of the telecommunications industry. The second is the fact that these industries have moved from remaining aloof toward the federal government to lavishing attention on government officials by actively lobbying and writing campaign checks. The third is that representatives of the industry often receive red carpet treatment once reserved for Hollywood stars. Finally, many benefactors work across party lines to get things done on issues they consider nonpartisan and nonideological.[62] As a result, Republicans and Democrats cooperate in this area to pass industry-supported legislation.

The Washington connection extended directly into the 1996 election of the president. At the Democratic National Convention in Chicago, the Tribune Company, which also owns the Chicago Cubs baseball team, held a party for delegates at Wrigley Field. The Disney Corporation held a Chicago Blues House Party for the California delegates, CBS provided a brunch, and NBC a luncheon. The Republicans received similar treatment at their San Diego convention. While reports of parties are commonplace on the nightly news during conventions, the media's wining and dining of candidates and delegates is unreported by their news organizations.

A number of other groups lobby on media issues, some of which are very powerful, like the American Medical Association, Parent-Teacher Association, and the National Organization of Women. There are also citizens' groups organized specifically for the purpose of monitoring and pursuing media issues. These include Accuracy in Media, the Coalition for

Table 6.7
Media Lobbyists and the Washington Connection

NAME AND FORMER POSITION	LOBBYING ASSOCIATION
Henry Cisneros Former secretary of HUD	President and CEO of Univision
Edward Fitts College roommate of Senate Majority Leader Trent Lott and member of his leadership PAC	Lobbyist for Griffin and Rogers
Haley Barbour Former chairman of the National Republican Party	Lobbyist for Griffin and Rogers
Tom Korologos Long-time GOP advisor and senior convention advisor to Senator Bob Dole	Lobbyist for Timmons and Co.
George Mitchell Former Democratic majority leader	Lobbyist for Verner, Liipfest, Bernhard, McPherson, and Hand
Lloyd Bentsen Former Democratic senator from Texas, former secretary of the treasury, and vice presidential candidate	Lobbyist for Verner, Liipfest, Bernhard, McPherson, and Hand
Ann Richards Former Democratic governor of Texas	Lobbyist for Verner, Liipfest, Bernhard, McPherson, and Hand
Berl Bernhard Ran Edmund Muskie's campaigns	Lobbyist for Verner, Liipfest, Bernhard, McPherson, and Hand
Lawrence Sidman Chief counsel and staff director of House Telecommunications Subcommittee	Lobbyist for Verner, Liipfest, Bernhard, McPherson, and Hand

Common Cause news release, "Channeling Influence—Working Washington's Special-Interest Money System," April 2, 1997.

Better Television, Citizens for the American Way, the National Black Media Coalition, and the National Latino Media Coalition. The media elite were able to defeat efforts to provide public funds for citizens' lobbying groups. Thus, while numerous groups are involved in media lobbying, the power resides primarily with those in the media elite.

summary

Studies of media gatekeepers have focused on two areas—demographics and political orientations. Those who bring the news to us are predominantly white, male, Protestant, and holders of bachelor's degrees from public institutions. Women and ethnic minorities are underrepresented. The religious backgrounds of the gatekeepers are reflective of the general population. In terms of political orientation, those who present the news differ to varying degrees from the general population. In addition, there are differences between Washington-based reporters, editors, and owners, and it is highly probable that reporters not from the nation's capital likely differ from those based in Washington.

The structure of the news is important, for the media provide citizens with their view of the world. There are two conflicting objectives in this process. One is the social responsibility of the media to inform and educate the public about candidates, policies, and major issues. The second is the financial need to compete within an increasingly competitive market. Since the media are in business to make money, this objective prevails. The news is structured to attract and hold the audience's interest. Consequently, stories of human interest and drama are given higher priority.

The issue of bias in reporting was also examined. The public has always been concerned with the question of media bias. Hofstetter has pointed out two types of bias. Political bias is an overt effort to mislead, and structural bias reflects the constraints placed on a medium by space or time limitations. Most studies have failed to find evidence of systematic political bias in coverage; more often the bias is in the public's interpretation of the news.

Since the media are businesses, it is not surprising that those who own them differ substantially from those who write and produce the news. The owners apply direct influence on the political system through lobbying, campaign contributions, and social engagements with political figures. While this has always been the case, as the diversity of the media has been reduced through mergers and acquisitions, the role of the media elite has become more significant and, some would argue, destructive to the democratic process.

ENDNOTES

[1]Walter Lippmann, *Public Opinion* (New York: The Macmillan Co., 1922).

[2]*Ibid.*, 16.

[3]Edward J. Epstein, *News From No Where* (New York: Vintage Press, 1974), 13–14.

[4]Herbert Gans, *Deciding What's News* (New York: Vintage Press, 1980), 201.

[5]Gaye Tuchman, *Making News: A Study in the Construction of Reality* (New York: The Free Press, 1978); W. Lance Bennett, *News: The Politics of Illusion*, 3rd ed. (White Plains, N.Y.: Longman Publishers, 1996).

[6]Dean E. Alger, *The Media and Politics*, 2nd ed. (Belmont, Calif.: Wadsworth Publishing Co., 1996), 126.

[7]David Weaver and G. Cleveland Wilhoit, *The American Journalist in the 1990s: U.S. News People at the End of an Era* (Mahwah, N.J.: Lawrence Erlbaum and Associates, 1996).

[8]*Ibid.*

[9]"Newscasts Really Deliver the Males," *Dallas Morning News*, July 23, 1997:5C.

[10]*Ibid.*

[11]David H. Weaver and G. Cleveland Wilhoit, *The American Journalist: A Portrait of U.S. News People and Their Work*, 2nd ed. (Bloomington, Ind.: Indiana University Press, 1991), 3–5.

[12]Weaver and Wilhoit, *op. cit.*, 1996, 232.

[13]Gans, *op. cit.*

[14]S. Robert Lichter, Stanley Rothman, and Linda Lichter, *The Media Elite: America's New Powerbrokers* (Bethesda, Md: Adler and Miller, 1986), 22.

[15]*Ibid.*, 22.

[16]*Ibid.*, Chapter 3.

[17]Howard Kutz, "When the Press Outclasses the Public," *Columbia Journalism Review*, 32(May/June 1994):32.

[18]Gans, *op. cit.*, 42.

[19]*Ibid.*, 43.

[20]*Ibid.*, 46.

[21]Marion R. Just, Ann N. Crigler, Dean E. Alger, Timothy E. Cook, Montague Kern, and Darrell West, *Crosstalk: Citizens, Candidates, and the Media in a Presidential Campaign* (Chicago: University of Chicago Press, 1996), 115.

[22]Weaver and Wilhoit, 1996, *op. cit.*

[23]Media Studies Center and Roper Center survey, September 1995.

[24]*Ibid.*

[25]*Ibid.*

[26]Harold Stanley and Richard Nieme, *Vital Statistics on American Politics* (Washington, D.C.: Congressional Quarterly Press, 2000), 192–193.

[27]Bennett, *op. cit.*, 39.

[28]*Ibid.*, 39–42.

[29]Pew Research Center press release, "Attention to Personal Tragedy and Major Celebrity Stories," January 9, 1999.

[30]Bennett, *op. cit.*, 39.

[31]"1994—The Year in Review," *Media Monitor*, 9(Jan./Feb. 1995):9.

[32]"Did O.J. Do It?" *Times Mirror* Center for the People and the Press news release, April 6, 1995.

[33]Epstein, *op. cit.*, 4.

[34]Michael Milburn and A. McGrail, "The Effects of the Dramatic Presentation of News Events on Individual's Cognitive Complexity," paper presented at the Annual Meeting of the International Society of Political Psychology, Washington, D.C., June 12, 1990.

[35] *Ibid.*

[36] Doris A. Graber, *Mass Media and American Politics*, 5th ed. (Washington, D.C.: Congressional Quarterly Press, 1997):110–111.

[37] Steven Chermak, *Victims in the News: Crime and the American News Media* (Boulder, Col.: Westview Press, 1995), 13.

[38] Clarence Page, "It's No Wonder We All Want to Take a Break from News," *Dallas Morning News*, July 20, 1997:5J.

[39] *Ibid.*

[40] *Ibid.*

[41] Paul Klite, Robert A. Bardwell, and Jason Salzman, "Local TV News: Getting Away with Murder," *Press/Politics*, 2(Spring 1997):102–112.

[42] *Ibid.*

[43] *New York Times* wire service, "Two Media Giants Form Newsgathering Alliance," *Dallas Morning News*, November 18, 1999:2D.

[44] The Associated Press, "3 TV Networks Announce News-Coverage Cooperation," December 21, 1999.

[45] Bennett, *op. cit.*, 41.

[46] Shanto Iyengar, *Is Anyone Responsible? How Television Frames Political Issues* (Chicago: University of Chicago Press, 1992).

[47] Ed Bark, "Time Trials," *Dallas Morning News*, March 6, 1997:C4.

[48] Bob Dole was not the first candidate to argue that the media were biased. President Bush in 1992 and Michael Dukakis in 1988 both had harsh words for the way the media covered them and their campaigns.

[49] Doris A. Graber, *Mass Media and American Politics*, 5th ed. (Washington, D.C.: Congressional Quarterly Press, 1996), 127.

[50] Joe S. Foote and Michael E. Steele, "Degree of Conformity in Lead Stories in Early Evening TV Newscasts," *Journalism Quarterly*, 63(Spring 1986):19–23.

[51] Graber, *op. cit.*, 109.

[52] Russell J. Dalton, Paul A. Beck, and Robert Huckfeldt, "Partisan Cues and the Media: Information Flows in the 1992 Presidential Election," *American Political Science Review*, 92(March 1998):115.

[53] *Ibid.*

[54] *Ibid.*, p. 123.

[55] Kenneth Dautrich and Jennifer Necci Dineen, "Media Bias: What Journalists and the Public Say About It," *The Public Perspective*, 7(Oct./Nov. 1996):12.

[56] Michael Parenti, *Inventing Reality: The Politics of News Media*, 2nd ed. (New York: St. Martin's Press, 1993), 7; Edward S. Herman and Noam Chomsky, *Manufacturing Consent: The Political Economy of the Mass Media* (New York: Pantheon Books, 1988); Robert M. Entman, *Democracy Without Citizens: Media and the Decay of American Politics* (New York: Oxford University Press, 1989).

[57] Parenti, *op. cit.*, 8.

[58] Walter Laqueur, "Foreign News Coverage: From Bad to Worse," *Washington Journalism Quarterly*, 14(June 1983):34.

[59]Common Cause press release, "Channeling Influence—Working Washington's Special-Interest Money System," April 2, 1997.

[60]Common Cause, "Soft Money Donors from the Telecommunications Industry for the 1997–1999 Election Cycle," *www.commoncause.org/laudromat/result.html,* January 8, 2000.

[61]Common Cause, Press Release, "Return on Investment," November 15, 1997.

[62]Lizette Alvarez, "The Courtship of Washington and the High-Tech Industry," *New York Times,* December 16, 1999:1.

CHAPTER 7

The Mass Media and political Behavior

We have examined the relationship of the mass media to the political process in the broad social context. We have explored the evolution of the media, their role in a democracy, the ways they are studied, the ways government has reacted to changes brought about by their evolution, and the characteristics of those who produce the news. We now shift our attention to the media's effects on the political behavior of individuals and institutions.

Former Speaker of the House Tip O'Neill frequently said, "All politics is local," referring to the important role of local parties and other organizations in determining the outcome of political issues, whether electing certain candidates or increasing the number of garbage collections. He meant that the most important factor in determining political outcomes is the citizen's perception of the local political process. But "all politics is local" has an alternative meaning. According to a 1997 survey, a majority of Americans claimed to have received their political information from local television news—*not* political parties, local organizations, or national newscasts. We shall explore four main areas of direct media involvement in the political process: political advertising, election coverage, political talk radio, and the use of public opinion polls.

The public's knowledge of candidates seeking public office has become increasingly dependent on how the candidates are presented by the media. Media advertising serves as the candidates' initial contact with citizens. A candidate may choose to stress personal traits or connections and may emphasize certain issues, but if the campaign is wisely planned, his or her advisors will project a message receptive to the voters. Candidates often adopt messages that proved effective in other campaigns. In 1997 the New Jersey race for governor was very close, even with a popular incumbent governor, Christine Todd Whitman. Governor Whitman made an issue out of lowering the state's gasoline tax. Her ultimately successful campaign was determined by an issue on which the voters had not demanded action. Other candidates seeking office soon adopted this issue. For example, in 1998 George W. Bush made it an issue in the Texas governor's race. In both races television ads were developed around the candidates' support of lower taxes.

Today's media technology gives candidates important tools for developing a popular image. Public opinion polls, focus groups, media consultants, and political consultants are all part of the modern campaign. They help candidates identify "hot" issues and then exploit them in media advertisements. If there is no existing hot issue, one can be manufactured and used in campaign advertisements, as in New Jersey. Issues that the public had not previously perceived as important suddenly become vital to the campaign. In bringing these issues to the public's attention, candidates are often able to set the policy agenda, and it may not represent the primary concerns of the public.

It is important to remember that the information that reaches the public is never a full and complete record of significant events and developments in the world. Rather, it is highly selective and simplified. The presentations of the news, for instance, are *short, simple,* and *highly thematic,* and subsequent political behavior influenced by these limitations. Political advertisements represent a controlled form of information that citizens interpret and then act upon. Behavior in the form of voting or abstaining is thought by scholars to be a consequence of this form of political communication.

political advertising

Whether by slogan, song, partisan newspaper, pamphlets, banners, or billboards, political messages have always been directed toward the masses. What has changed has been their form and their increasing ease in reaching mass audiences. The transformation in methods of political advertisement is directly related to technological change. Each new technology—cylinder press, telegraph, radio, television, or the Internet—has quickly been embraced by politicians.

The influence of radio and television on candidates' communications with the electorate has been significant. Each new technology has increased the sophistication of political communications. Radio and television introduced the candidates to an expanded audience. However, as the novelty wore off, new methods of attracting and maintaining an audience were needed. Initially radio stations broadcast candidates' complete speeches. However, these were soon replaced with shorter excerpts of speeches and the introduction of "entertainment" in the form of songs and skits to hold the audience's attention. The same pattern occurred with television. Visuals, songs, and "sound bites" are today the core of televised campaigns. Political advertisement has become critical to electoral success. A by-product of the media's role has been the increased cost associated with running for public office. The techniques used in political advertisements are the same as those found in other forms of marketing, and they are closely intertwined. What differentiates the two is the product.

There are several reasons why the study of political advertising is important to understanding the link between the media and the political process. It addresses the lingering question of the influence of the media over the citizen, as well as the question of how political advertisements affect democracy. It shows how political advertisements are complex and multidimensional: the message, the context, the visuals, and the strategies. It also shows how political advertisements contribute to the increasing cost of political campaigns. It raises the question of whether advertising money is an effective allocation of funds. Do political advertisements, for instance, have different effects on voters than nonvoters? It highlights the paradox of a public that is increasingly mistrustful of the media yet still dependent on them as the primary source for information about candidates and campaigns. It raises the question of what messages are accurately provided. Finally, there is no other area that illustrates the transition of American politics from a party-centered to a media-centered activity better than political advertisements.

Studies of political advertisements have produced often-conflicting findings. Some have found that most voters receive their information about politics and candidates from spot advertisements. They therefore argue that television advertisements influence election outcomes by providing voters with critical information. Others argue that television advertisements have little direct influence, that their influence is not possible to identify in elections, and, at most, advertisements reinforce voters' predispositions.

Lynda Lee Kaid addressed the question of the effect of visual imagery in television political ads. Through the use of experimental designs with student and adult populations during campaign and noncampaign periods, she found that visuals had a significant impact on voter behavior.[1] Specifically, she found "the presence of technological manipulation in television spots can affect voter judgments about candidates. The presence of such distortions has the effect sought by their producers: the distortions significantly increase the evaluation and vote likelihood of the sponsoring candidate and decrease the evaluations and vote likelihood of the opposition."[2]

While political advertisements may not be new, they dominate today's politics to an extent unprecedented in American political history. Advertisements consume more attention, time, and money than any other aspect of modern campaigning. As a result, citizens are inundated by millions of dollars' of advertisements during the course of a campaign. The political ad is synonymous with campaigns. Advances in media technology, the increasing sophistication of the ads, the increased size of political districts in terms of both geographic area and population, and the decline of American political parties have conferred on the media increased power and influence.

The purpose of the advertisements is straightforward—to convey information that will evoke positive feelings about the candidates. Both information and feelings can be positive or negative. Political advertisements have moved from defining candidates and their positions on issues to defining their opponents as well.[3] They allow candidates to control the content and therefore enhance their appeal. However, political advertising occurs in the larger context of the campaign. The way voters respond to advertisements is influenced by long-held predispositions about issues, personalities, and political parties.

Each of the two major political parties in the United States has traditionally been perceived by the public as handling some issues better than others. For instance, the public has generally considered Democrats more able than Republicans to deal with unemployment and civil rights problems. Conversely, the Republicans are perceived as better able to handle crime and maintain a strong military. These preconceptions serve as significant "filters" for political advertisements and help media consultants develop advertising that is appropriate to their candidate and party. For example, in the mid-1990s the Republican Party became associated with "family values," an ill-defined but influential concept.

While political advertisements have always been a part of American politics, the evolution of media technologies has changed the nature of campaigns. Since the first televised political commercial in 1952, the use and sophistication of today's political advertisements have expanded greatly. For example, televised political commercials have been presented in a variety of formats and lengths. Presidential campaign ads range in length from one hour to the more common sixty- and thirty-second spots, though recent campaigns have generally relied on short ads. Patrick Devlin's study of the allocation of time in presidential advertisements over the past four decades reveals interesting changes in the pattern of usage. During the 1950s and 1960s, sixty-second spots were most commonly used by candidates. In the 1970s, ads increased in length to 260 seconds, while during the 1980s, the thirty-second spot dominated. The 1992 presidential campaign produced a wide variety of time allocations. President Clinton used several fifteen-second spots during his campaign, and Perot's thirty-minute spot on various problems was watched by an estimated 30 million viewers.[4]

Political advertisements have been shown to be an effective means of communication. Viewers have high rates of recall of political advertisements; one study found a recall rate of nearly 80 percent for political advertisements, compared with 22 percent for other advertisements.[5] Two explanations for the high recall rate for political advertisements are the facts that elections occur in unique contexts and political advertisements are newer and shorter than other advertisements.

The content of presidential campaign advertising has been the subject of important research. Recently Darrell West, in his book *Air Wars*, analyzed prominent presidential advertisements since 1952.[6] Figure 7.1 summarizes the percentage of advertisements allotted to domestic issues, international affairs, and personal character in presidential advertising during the period.

figure 7.1
Contents of Prominent Presidential Campaign Ads, 1952–1996

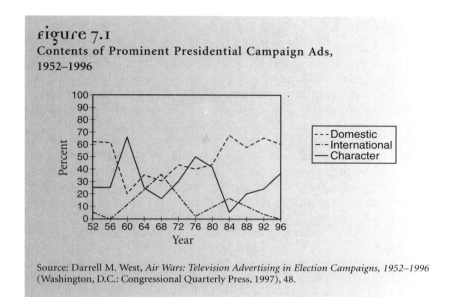

Source: Darrell M. West, *Air Wars: Television Advertising in Election Campaigns, 1952–1996* (Washington, D.C.: Congressional Quarterly Press, 1997), 48.

Since 1984 there has been an increase in personal character ads, but they have not reached the levels found in the presidential campaigns of 1960, 1976, or 1980. In the 1960 campaign between John Kennedy and Richard Nixon, the principle focus of the political ads was on leadership and experience. In the 1976 race, in which Jimmy Carter defeated Gerald Ford, the focus was on trustworthiness and honesty—concerns that naturally arose following Watergate. Four years later, when Ronald Reagan defeated incumbent Jimmy Carter, the issue was competence. The Carter administration came under heavy criticism for its handling of the economy. While it initially received high approval ratings for its handling of the Iran hostage situation, the administration's inability to resolve the crisis became a negative by November. Domestic issues have generally dominated the content of prominent presidential advertisements with three exceptions. In 1960 and 1976, ads focused on character, as noted above, but the most notable exception occurred during the 1968 election, when the Vietnam War divided the nation as well as the Democratic Party.

Political advertisements allow candidates to transmit carefully designed, short, thematic, and strategic messages. Television is the principal medium for candidates, replacing political parties, local organizations, and newspapers. Two aspects of media advertising, primarily television, have helped transform the modern political landscape. The first is the financial cost associated with the modern political campaign, and the second, and equally important, is the social cost.

Financial Cost

While political advertising has been a part of the American political process since its inception, its increased use and sophistication are altering the process. Political ads have greatly increased the financial cost of running for public office. Television advertisements alone represent the largest expenditure of most campaigns.[7] This increasing cost has led some providers of financial support to seek special treatment once their candidates are elected. The 1997 Senate and House hearing on foreign campaign contributions established that both parties were involved in soliciting money from foreign individuals and organizations. The loss of the citizen's control raises questions about the viability of democracy. Senator McCain and former Senator Bradley made this a central issue in their efforts to obtain their parties' presidential nominations in 2000. They and others have argued that democracy's viability depends on citizens' participation and confidence in the process. The expense of running for public office has become so great that fewer individuals can now seek office, and those who do must rely on large contributions, making them susceptible to outside influence in their decision-making processes. The record amount of campaign contributions raised by Governor George W. Bush indicates that the financial cost of campaigning may be reducing the average citizen's voice in government. As larger amounts of money are essential for a successful bid for major public office, the average contributor's voice is muted.

In the presidential election of 1996, the two major parties aired 1,397 hours, or 58 days, of commercials for their candidates.[8] The sheer number of advertisements may increase voter disenchantment, cynicism, and apathy. The American use of political ads has also been exported to other nations. In Russia, for instance, Boris Yeltzin relied heavily on American media consultants in his 1997 election, as did Great Britain's Tony Blair in the same year and Israel's Ehud Barak in 1999.

Figure 7.2 shows the percentage of presidential campaign budgets spent on television and radio advertisements since 1952. Since 1960 the percentage of campaign funds spent on television and radio advertisements has risen dramatically, with the exception of the 1972 campaign. In 1972 Richard Nixon was seeking reelection against the Democratic nominee, George McGovern, whom much of the public, including many in his own party, perceived as being too far to the left. Because Nixon had such a commanding lead, he could reduce campaign expenditures. The figures for 1992 do not include the expenditures of Ross Perot, the Reform Party's candidate. As an independent candidate, Perot had no restrictions on spending limits, and the total amount he spent on the campaign is still a matter of speculation. Since 1972 over one half of presidential campaign budgets for both parties have been used for radio and television advertisements, with television receiving the larger portion. The amount spent on television and radio time in presidential campaigns has increased dramatically from $3.575 million

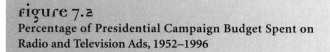

figure 7.2
**Percentage of Presidential Campaign Budget Spent on
Radio and Television Ads, 1952–1996**

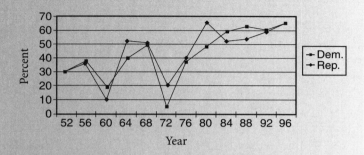

Source: 1952–1992 adapted from Darrell M. West, *Air Wars: Television Advertising in Election Campaigns, 1952–1992* (Washington, D.C.: Congressional Quarterly Press, 1993), Figure 1-2:8; 1996 from Max Frankel, "Money: Soft and Hard," *New York Times Magazine,* October 26, 1997, p. 28.

in 1952 to $400 million in 1996. In 1994 congressional incumbents spent $50 million on television and radio ads, or 40 percent of their total budgets. These figures represent not only substantial investments in the media, but great faith in the media's ability to persuade the public. According to one study, in 1992 television advertising accounted for 42 percent of the money spent on Senate races and 27 percent on House races.[9]

Aside from the direct cost of purchasing airtime, there is the cost involved in hiring media consultants. This cost was estimated at $165 million for congressional candidates in 1992. It is important to remember that the bulk of the money spent on political advertisements is for "one-sided conversations" between incumbents and voters. Incumbents of both political parties outspend their challengers in general, particularly on television advertisements. One by-product of heavy media advertisement has been the increased cost of running for public office. In 1976 congressional advertising expenditures were $98 million, compared with $621 million in 1994.

The 1996 presidential campaign introduced a new mode of communication—free television spots. After Rupert Murdoch announced that his FOX Network would donate airtime to the major party candidates, CBS, CNN, NBC, and PBS also donated airtime to allow President Clinton and Senator Dole to address viewers in recorded mini-speeches ranging in length from one to two and a half minutes. Each candidate was given four to six free spots, depending on the network. Some networks asked the candidates to answer particular questions, and all required them to talk directly to the camera. In August the Federal Communication Commission exempted this free time from the equal-time requirement of section 315(a) of the Communications Act of 1934. An analysis of the free spots indicated that the candidates used them predominantly (45 percent) to draw comparisons between themselves and their opponents.[10]

The cost of political advertisements became an issue in the 2000 presidential race. Attempts at campaign finance reform have not succeeded, in large part because those empowered to make the necessary changes, congressional incumbents, are themselves recipients of large political contributions. The result is the escalating cost of political campaigns in America and the increasing entrenchment of those in office.

Social Costs

The increasing financial costs of political advertising have led to a variety of social costs, including increased voter cynicism and apathy and a reduced choice of candidates, making politics a game played by the financial elite at the expense of the general public. Political advertisements have been associated with a number of outcomes, including increased political knowledge, agenda setting, positive candidate orientation, and polarization.[11] Political advertisements increase voters' political knowledge by providing information on issues and exposure to the candidates. From the candidates' perspective, advertisements allow them, rather than their opponents or the media, to set the political agenda. They pick the issues they view as important and communicate their positions. Since few citizens have the opportunity to meet candidates directly, advertisements are an effective way for candidates to present a positive image of themselves to the public. Political advertisements are also used to focus on differences between candidates. In the 2000 presidential primaries, one of Senator McCain's issues was his opposition to the excessive fund-raising required in presidential campaigning, while Governor Bush argued that it was a sign of a healthy political system. Vice President Gore and former Senator Bradley used advertisements to highlight the differences in their proposed health care plans.

The debate over the transmission of political knowledge through political advertisements gained increased attention with the publication of Thomas Patterson and Robert McClure's *The Unseeing Eye*.[12] In this study of the 1972 presidential election, the authors concluded that voters received more information from political advertisements than they did from watching the nightly news.

A more recent study by Craig Brians and Martin Wattenberg using data from the 1992 presidential campaign found that "recalling political ads is more significantly associated with knowledge of candidates' issue position than reading the newspaper or watching political news on television."[13] More specifically, they found that

- "although many political analysts denigrate political ads, and negative political ads in particular, . . . they likely contribute to accurate information about issues, as well as active use of issues in candidate evaluations,"
- there is "support for previous empirical research finding a weak association between television news watching and political knowledge,"
- "attention to newspaper political coverage fails to improve one's knowledge of a candidate's stands over viewing TV news," and
- "consistent newspaper readers fare no better than the most attentive TV watchers in issue-based candidate evaluations."[14]

One study found that political advertising conveys candidate issue positions more accurately than televised debates in experimental situations.[15] However, another study reported that one third of viewers did not recall anything from political advertisements they reported watching.[16] Nonetheless, the authors found evidence of increased knowledge from political ads, and concluded that involvement in the political process had the largest impact on recall and that issue information was recalled as frequently as image items.[17]

Since political campaigns have become increasingly campaigns of "managed" visibility, understanding the role of advertisements in the process is important to understanding the political process itself. While the debate over the effectiveness of political advertisements in transmitting knowledge about issues and candidates continues, the impact of political advertisements on the way political issues are communicated to voters is no longer debated because of their critical role in modern campaigns.

The effectiveness of a political advertisement is judged by the success of the advertisement's candidate at the polls. However, while those responsible for ads for successful candidates would argue that they produced the winner, in reality there are many factors that determine how a person votes, including voters' party affiliation, candidates' personalities, issues, and the social context of the election. In 1996 the Media Studies Center survey of voters found that voters placed advertisements at the bottom of the list of sources of information,[18] with only 5 percent claiming they learned a lot from political ads. The CBS News/*New York Times* survey found only 11 percent reported presidential ads had helped them decide how to vote in 1996.[19]

The connection between the political advertisement is not normally as direct as advertisers would lead us to think. For instance, Kathleen Hall Jamieson's study of the 1988 presidential campaign revealed valuable insights into what was perceived to be the "critical" ad of the campaign— George Bush's "revolving door ad."[20] Also known as the "Willie Horton ad," it showed a black person walking through the gates of a prison and then a mug shot of the actual black felon who was charged with rape after his release from prison through a state program. At the time, forty-five states offered furlough programs, which released inmates from prison for a limited time to see how they handled freedom. In 1976 Governor Dukakis had vetoed a ban on furloughs for first-degree murderers. The implied message of the ad was that Dukakis was soft on crime.

As Jamieson points out, the ad's effectiveness was enhanced by the majority culture's underlying fears about black men raping white women and by news stories that sensationalized Horton's past. Bush did not have to mention Horton by name to link Dukakis to his crime. The Horton ad shows how ads can lead the media in their coverage of a story. Although Horton's given name was William and court records cited him as William, after the ad referred to him as Willie, the press began using "Willie" in its references to the case. Furthermore, the media adopted the vocabulary of the Bush ad, and words like "torture," "terrorize," "weekend passes," and "revolving door" soon found their way into reports on the case.

To dismiss the importance of advertisements, however, would be to gravely misread the political landscape, for they provide information and help voters identify candidates. Their role in campaigns is undeniable, but their precise impact is in question.

Negative Advertisements

Early studies of voting behavior emphasized that voter turnout increased with the "level of political stimulation to which the electorate is subjected."[21] However, today this assertion is challenged on a number of grounds. First, the nature of political campaigns has changed considerably. The most notable change has been the injection of television into the political process. Today candidates are rewarded more for their image and rhetorical skills than their substantive positions. Second, political organizations, which traditionally organized and ran campaigns, have been weakened by the direct media appeals of the candidates. Third, campaigns have become increasingly negative, personal, and often ugly in tone and focus. A study by the *National Journal* of campaigns in 1988 and 1990 found that advertisements attacking opponents had become the norm.[22] When observers of the American political process compile a list of the most heinous sins in campaigning today, negative campaigning and attack advertisements are near the top of the list.

Pippa Norris notes three characteristics of modern campaigns. The first is the fragmentation of audiences and outlets, with the shift from network television toward more diverse news sources, including talk radio, local television news, and newer media like the Internet. The second is a "tabloidization" of the news caused by fierce commercial pressures. Finally is the development of permanent campaigns that rely on continual feedback from polls, focus groups, and electronic town meetings.[23]

Whether negative advertisements increase political participation is unclear. William Mayer has suggested this is due in part to the way negative advertisements are defined in the popular press and academic studies.[24] He argues that negative campaigns and advertising are good for society, serving three important functions for the political process. First, they provide valuable general information needed to make a choice. Mayer notes that all positive positions must first stem from reasons why other positions are incorrect or inappropriate. Second, they reveal information about candidates' character, their strengths and weaknesses. Finally, negative advertisements keep candidates "a bit more" honest.[25]

Other research on negative advertisements does not permit a clear and concise conclusion about their impact. For instance, Gina Garramone and her colleagues, using student participants and fictitious candidates, found that exposure to negative advertisements did not depress measures of political participation.[26] However, Basil, Schooler, and Reeves found that negative advertisements reduced positive attitudes toward both candidates in a race, and thereby reduced political involvement.[27] A third study, by Thorson, Christ, and Caywood, reported no differences in voting intentions between college students exposed to positive and negative advertisements.[28]

Stephen Ansolabehere and his colleagues used an experimental design to study three California elections: the 1990 California gubernatorial race, the 1992 California Senate races, and the 1993 Los Angeles mayoral race.[29] They concluded, "Taken together, our studies demonstrate that attack advertising extracts a toll on electoral participation. In the experiments, voting intention dropped by 2.5 percent when participants were shown an attack advertisement and increased 2.5 percent when they were shown a positive advertisement."[30] This study and their later work produced the negativity-demobilization hypothesis, according to which negative advertisements are responsible for significantly depressing turnout.[31] Furthermore, negative advertisements were found to have the strongest effect on political independents, whose lack of attachment to the political process was reinforced by the ads' negative tone. These findings led the authors to conclude, "Campaign advertising has contributed significantly to the disappearance of the nonpartisan vote and the polarization of elections."[32] In addition, they found that "negative advertising breeds distrust of the electoral system and pessimism about the value of an individual's own voice."[33] The authors concluded that negative advertising poses a serious threat to democracy.[34]

Jon Hale, Jeffrey Fox, and Rick Farmer examined negative advertisements in senatorial campaigns in the period 1984–1994 to determine who used them and how they were used.[35] Analysis of 420 advertisements randomly selected during this period found that challengers in large states most frequently used negative advertisements.[36] The major conclusion of the research was that the context of a campaign is critical in determining the extent of negative advertising.

If the findings in these three studies are correct, they raise serious questions about the relationship between negative ads, campaigns, and electoral turnout. However, these findings have been challenged. Steven Finkel and John Geer argue that, rather than reducing participation, negative advertising stimulates the electorate into action.[37] They contend that negative advertisements convey a significant amount of policy and retrospective information to voters, and more knowledgeable voters are most likely to use the ads. Second, these ads are given more weight than positive ads in the political process and provide voters with more discriminating information, which in turn assists them in the selection process. Finally, these advertisements produce stronger emotional and affective responses than positive ads.[38] The authors analyzed ads sixty seconds in length or shorter in nine presidential elections from 1960 through 1992 to determine the tone, or negative/positive nature, of each ad. They then compared the national turnout with the tone of the ads. They found that "attack advertising does not influence either turnout rates or individual self-reported votes. Similarly, we find no demobilized effect for negative advertisements among independent voters."[39]

Presidential campaigns are not as negative as the news media portray them to be, according to a study by Kathleen Hall Jamieson. Jamieson analyzed the content of candidates' speeches, ads, and debate performances from the 1960, 1980, 1988, and 1992 presidential elections. Figure 7.3 shows that news coverage of the campaigns was considerably more negative than the candidates themselves. Approximately one third of statements from the candidates' campaigns about their opponents were negative over the four elections studied, while two thirds of news coverage focused on negative comments. This led Jamieson to conclude that reporters searching for the perfect "sound bite", or continuous speech segment, are apt to take statements out of context, for they have found that short negative sound bites attract attention. Journalists have also been accused of relying on sound bites because they are easily obtained and do not require reporters to spend time researching a story. As a result of the twenty-four-hour news cycle, reporters have increasingly relied on shared information and public opinion polls as sources for their stories.

This pattern of negativism in reporting also could be found in the 1996 presidential election campaign. An analysis of campaign coverage on the three major television networks (ABC, CBS, and NBC) performed by the Markle Presidential Watch found it was primarily negative. The study found that nearly two out of three television news evaluations of candidates were negative.[40]

The networks also help to shape campaigns. In 1968 the average network news sound bite for presidential candidates was 42.3 seconds. In more than one in five instances networks permitted candidates to appear unedited for a minute or more. By 1988 the average sound bite had shrunk to 9.8 seconds and none were 60 seconds or longer, and in 1996 it was only 8.4 seconds. The consequence of this shift is obvious. Such short excerpts, edited to emphasize the dramatic, do not permit candidates to convey their remarks in a meaningful context. Through their use of short, provocative sound bites,

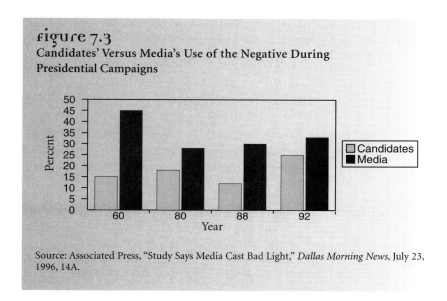

figure 7.3
Candidates' Versus Media's Use of the Negative During
Presidential Campaigns

Source: Associated Press, "Study Says Media Cast Bad Light," *Dallas Morning News*, July 23, 1996, 14A.

the media increasingly shape the public's understanding of politics. In turn, candidates and consultants plan each day to provide the media with sound bites that will likely be picked up and aired on the nightly news at the expense of substantive comments.

While there are still positive campaign ads, the vast majority have been structured in a manner to place an opponent, an institution, or government itself in a negative light. Because television appeals to emotions and intensifies what is being communicated through visuals, the impact of negative television advertisements on the social structure is enormous. As two consultants have written, "The problem with positive [ads] is that they have to run it again and again and again to make it stick. With negative [ads], the poll numbers will move in three or four days."[41]

Since the political system of electing public officials rewards only those who win, it is not surprising that political advertisements focus on winning and rarely address the broader questions of governing. Fred Wertheimer notes, "If winning on election day means undermining your own credibility or damaging your ability to govern or breeding public distrust and cynicism or turning large segments of the public away from voting, so be it. Thus we end up with the perverse result that many politicians use TV advertising in their campaigns in ways that ultimately do as much damage to their own credibility as they do to their opponents."[42] Thus, the paradox that winning the election has the effect of making it more difficult to govern. The politics of the 1990s has clearly demonstrated this paradox. The declining rate of voter participation is perhaps the ultimate effect of the emphasis on winning. With fewer citizens participating in the process, the ideal of representative democracy is seriously damaged because the relatively few who are active have disproportionate power.

The media's coverage of elections

Elections are citizens' ways of controlling and influencing governmental policy. How the media choose to cover elections is critical because voters depend on them for information to make choices and form positions. This is increasingly the case as citizens' attachment to political parties has declined.

The media's role in the coverage of presidential elections has been the focus of increased inquiry and debate. A consistent theme among those reviewing that coverage is the question of whether the media provide sufficient information to allow citizens to make intelligent choices at the polls. Since the 1970s the one constant theme to emerge has been that the media are more concerned with the "horserace" aspect of the campaign than they are with substance. The media focus on campaign events and hoopla at the expense of issues and qualifications. As the nature of coverage has changed, so have the expectations of the candidates. They, too, have been involved in the "game" that surrounds the campaigns, with increased emphasis on photo ops and sound bites.

Patterns of Campaign Coverage

In his book *The Mass Media Election*, Thomas Patterson analyzed coverage of the 1976 presidential election campaigns by nine media outlets—the three major television networks (ABC, CBS and NBC), *Time* and *Newsweek* magazines, and four daily newspapers. He concluded that, in contrast to the conclusions in Lazarsfeld et al.'s studies of presidential elections,[43] policy and leadership were not the focus of coverage but rather the race itself and the candidates' style and image. In the media he studied, Patterson found that between 51 percent and 58 percent of all campaign coverage was about "the game—who was winning or losing, strategy, logistics, and appearances. Only a quarter to one third of the media's coverage involved the substance of the election."[44] He added, "These figures underestimate the news media's emphasis on the game because they represent all campaign stories."[45] If one selected those stories that appeared at the top of the news, even greater emphasis on the game would appear. Among the outlets studied, the *Los Angeles Times* paid the most attention to substance.

Michael J. Robinson and Margaret Sheehan examined the 1980 presidential election coverage of CBS and compared it with that of the UPI wire service. They used two measures in their analysis. First they asked "if the story is in plurality an 'issue piece'—is most of it about policy issues?"[46]

Second, since they believed that most stories "meld" the issues into the events of the day, they also did a sentence-by-sentence measure to ascertain the amount of policy coverage during the campaign by these two media. They found that "59 percent of the full-fledged presidential campaign news on CBS failed to contain even one issue sentence. On UPI, 55 percent of the news items made not a single meaningful reference to any one of the ninety-odd policy issues we identified during the course of Campaign '80.'"[47] They found that 20 percent of CBS stories and 18 percent of UPI stories emphasized policy issues.[48] The impact on the voter is potentially greater than these figures suggest, since many modest-size newspapers rely on the UPI wire service for their campaign coverage. The authors found that "at every level, in every phase, during each and every month CBS and UPI allocated more news space to competition between candidates than to any other aspect of the campaign."[49] They concluded that the "horserace" approach permeated the coverage of the campaign and the candidates in the 1980 presidential election.[50] Michael J. Robinson, in another study, found that in 788 presidential campaign stories CBS reporters made only six explicit evaluations of the candidates' competence and they drew no conclusions regarding the candidates' policy positions.[51]

A similar pattern of news coverage was discovered in the 1988 presidential election. Data from the four networks and PBS, nine newspapers, and three leading newsmagazines indicated that the media placed more emphasis on the horserace and "candidate conflict" than on policy issues or candidate qualifications.[52]

By 1992 the media vowed to improve its performance after coming under heavy criticism. They were accused of not paying attention to the issues important to voters, of not presenting adequate information concerning differences between candidates, of relying on polls too often in their coverage, and of being driven by the profit motive, which resulted in sensationalized coverage of the candidates.

However, three studies of the 1992 election found that the horserace remained the dominant theme of campaign coverage. Thomas Patterson's *Out of Order* reviews how campaigns have been covered through the years and includes his content analysis of the front page of the *New York Times* from the 1960 election through 1992. Patterson found that twice as many front page stories in the paper focused on the "game" in 1992 than in 1960. He also cited data from the Center for Media Studies and Public Affairs showing that 35 percent of network news coverage directly concerned the horse-race aspect and another 33 percent focused on polls and other strategic matters.[53] This represented an increase of 8 percent in horserace coverage over 1988, and a decrease of 7 percent on policy issue coverage compared with 1988.[54]

Matthew Kerbel, in a study of the 1992 election, examined the coverage of ABC and CNN and found that horserace stories were the primary type of story reported.[55] CNN was more likely to present the campaign in the light of a horserace, with nearly 50 percent of its stories falling into this category, compared with 37 percent for ABC. ABC had more policy stories than CNN, 31 percent compared with 27 percent, respectively.[56] There was, however, an increase in policy coverage in 1992 from previous elections, with the issue of the economy accounting for nearly half of issue stories.

In a comprehensive exploration of the 1992 election, Marion Just and her colleagues examined the campaign from January 1992 through election day. They collected data from four communities—Los Angeles, Boston, Winston-Salem, and Fargo/Moorhead,[57] and found strong evidence of horserace journalism and focus on economic issues. Their study indicated that this pattern held in all three media—network newscasts, local television, and newspapers. Local television was most likely to report issues in the month of May, when a little over 20 percent of local television news concerned the campaign and focused on issues. The authors' findings disputed the contention that there is a news media monolith but confirmed "the continuing unwillingness of the journalist—in any medium—to spend much time focusing on issues as the *main* topic of their reports."[58]

Doris Graber, in reviewing the 1996 presidential campaign, reported several positive aspects of the media's coverage. First, she found a concerted effort to place complex issues into a meaningful context. Second, there was an increased effort to feature comments from ordinary citizens and a movement away from political elites. Finally, greater length was given to policy issue stories.[59] However, on the negative side, old familiar themes resurfaced. First, the campaign remained framed as a horserace. Second, there was undue negativity in the reports. Third, there was insufficient coverage of foreign affairs and congressional races. Finally, there was an overreliance on public opinion polls in newscasts.[60]

Matthew Kerbel and Marc Ross's study of the media's coverage of the 1996 presidential election confirmed Graber's assessment that the horserace theme dominated reporting.[61] They found that there were over twice as many stories on the horserace as on any other aspect of the campaign. Issues accounted for only 17 percent of the stories, compared with 64 percent that depicted the campaign as a horserace.[62] This is particularly striking when nearly every poll had President Clinton leading Senator Dole by a sizable margin from the beginning of the campaign.

Coverage of the 1998 midterm elections on the three networks (ABC, CBS, and NBC) from Labor Day through the election dropped 73 percent from coverage of the 1994 midterm elections.[63] In 1998 no single race attracted ten or more stories; in contrast, in the 1994 midterm election six races produced more than twenty stories apiece. Despite the lack of attention paid to the 1998 midterm elections, analysis of the three networks' coverage indicated somewhat more substantive stories than in 1994. In 1998 28 percent of candidates' sound bites referred to policy stands on issues or performance in office, compared with 22 percent in 1994.[64]

However, in 1998 most coverage was devoted to calling the races, and the networks' ability to do so accurately was not impressive. Republican candidates were portrayed as probable winners 68 percent of the time. Even during the last week of October, they were considered probable winners by 81 percent of those assessing their prospects. The election resulted in the Democrats gaining five seats in House of Representative and a standoff in the Senate, despite the fact that there were more Democratic senators up for reelection, which normally makes maintaining or gaining seats very difficult. The outcome made for a historic voting year, for the president's party did not lose seats, which is the normal pattern.

Horserace reporting also dominated the 2000 presidential primary coverage, with Governor Bush and Vice President Gore quickly perceived as the leading candidates for their parties' nominations. By June 1999 a *Dallas Morning News* headline read, "Poll Says Bush Is Front-runner for the Presidency."[65] The same nationwide poll indicated that 75 percent of those surveyed did not know the governor's positions on most issues. However, after months of soft coverage helped turn former Senator Bill Bradley and Senator John McCain into serious challengers, reporters began emphasizing in the weeks prior to the Iowa caucuses and the New Hampshire primary that these contests were do-or-die for Bradley and McCain.

The media had an interest in making the 2000 presidential campaign dramatic, and they used horserace journalism to provide the dynamics. But this increased public interest in the campaign only marginally, if at all. One reason why the public did not share the journalists' interest in the campaign during 1999 was that the major networks' evening newscasts devoted only about half the amount of airtime to the presidential campaign that they did in 1995. According to the Center for the Media and Public Affairs, the three major networks (ABC, CBS, and NBC) had less coverage during the first two weeks of the 2000 campaign than during the first two weeks of the 1996 campaign.[66] According to the Center, during the first two weeks of 2000 there were fifty-three stories totaling one hour and thirty-one minutes, compared with eighty-eight stories totaling two hours and forty-five minutes during the first two weeks of 1996. Despite the fact that the presidential campaign of 2000 started earlier than that of 1996, it failed to generate the same intensity of media coverage in the early weeks.

The media's coverage of the 2000 New Hampshire presidential primary demonstrated three important patterns of coverage. First, it reaffirmed the dominance of horserace journalism as the media once again focused on who was winning and losing. In the Democratic race their attention focused on how well Bradley was running against Gore, in the Republican race on how well McCain was running against Bush. The other Republican candidates—Steve Forbes, Alan Keyes, and Gary Bauer—received little attention. The networks competed to see who could first predict the winners, and commentators dropped hints throughout the day about the likely outcome. This resulted in some correspondents' declaring victors while the polls remained open.[67] For example, when FOX News interviewed former New York Senator Alfonso D'Amato at 4:15 p.m., he stated, "I think he's (McCain) going to surprise people and win by 8 to 12 percent." Judy Woodruff of CNN betrayed a twinge of guilt over the breathless pace of declaring winners before all votes had been cast. She announced about twenty minutes after CNN had called the Republican race that "there are still some New Hampshire voters making their way to the polls" and went on to say, "This election isn't over yet."[68] Second, cable news networks emerged as the primary source of political news. For example, CNN, MSNBC, and FOX News all covered the primary very closely, even in the face of the Alaskan Airline crash that claimed the lives of eighty-five persons, while ABC, CBS, and NBC did not commit as much time to campaign coverage. Finally, the coverage had an immediate impact on Senator John McCain's candidacy, not only because he won the primary, but also because his campaign raised over $1 million over the Internet in the next two days.

Winners Versus Declared Winners

With only three exceptions, prior to 1968 the presidential candidate who led in the initial Gallup poll, even if the poll was conducted three years prior to the elections, had an unobstructed path to his party's nomination. This led James Beniger to propose "Beniger's law" in *Public Opinion Quarterly*, which held that the front-runner, no matter how many polls before the election that status was achieved, would almost certainly become the nominee.[69]

This "law" has been broken more often since 1968. Michael J. Robinson has argued that the change is due to the role of television in the election process. Television helps produce quicker dissatisfaction, new faces look better and old faces worse, and the selection of delegates becomes increasingly tied to the primaries.[70] These changes have produced a less committed electorate that in later primaries tend to support the winner of the New Hampshire primary.

Robinson argues that since 1968 television networks have had an inordinate impact on the fate of candidates. He cites two cases in which the media declared a person the winner of the New Hampshire primary when that person had technically lost. In 1968 Eugene McCarthy *lost* the primary to President Lyndon Johnson, by 7.7 percent but was *declared* the winner by the major networks because of his strong showing against the incumbent president. In 1972 George McGovern *lost* to then front runner Edmund Muskie by 9.3 percent but was *declared* the winner based primarily on the contention that Muskie was a native of nearby Maine and, according to the networks, should have won by a larger margin.

In 1976 Jimmy Carter's victory in New Hampshire placed his picture on the cover of *Time* and *Newsweek* magazines and made this little-known governor from Georgia instantly recognizable to the nation. At the same time Ronald Reagan lost the New Hampshire primary to incumbent President Ford by only .8 percent and was declared the *loser*. Robinson's thesis is that

Table 7.1
Media Coverage of 1984 Presidential Primary Campaigns
January to June 1984

STATE	STATE PRIMARY STORIES AS PERCENTAGE OF TOTAL PRIMARY CAMPAIGN COVERAGE	STATE POPULATION AS PERCENTAGE OF TOTAL U.S. POPULATION
New Hampshire	19.2	.4
Iowa	12.8	2.5
New York	11.1	7.5
California	6.9	10.8
Pennsylvania	5.5	5.0
New Jersey	5.0	3.2
Illinois	4.1	4.9
All other states	35.4	65.7

Source: William C. Adams, "As New Hampshire Goes . . .," in Gary R. Orren and Nelson Polsby, *Media and Momentum* (Chatham, N.J.: Chatham House Publishers, Inc., 1987), 45.

New Hampshire is critical to a candidate's success and the media's reporting of this event has altered reality.

The significance of New Hampshire can be seen in the strategy that John McCain employed in 2000. He chose not to contest the Iowa caucuses and to concentrate instead on New Hampshire. This allowed him to improve his standing in the New Hampshire polls. With his improved poll ratings came increased media attention as well as increased donations.

Table 7.1 shows the disproportionate media coverage of the New Hampshire primary in the presidential campaign of 1984. Nearly one fifth of the stories involving the primary campaign in 1984 came from New Hampshire, whose population represented .4 percent of the nation's total population. One third of all stories reported focused on two state primaries—New Hampshire and Iowa. The combined population of these states is less than 4 percent of the nation's total.[71]

In their study of the media's coverage in the 1992 New Hampshire primary, Stephen Farnsworth and S. Robert Lichter found that "network news coverage affected poll standings in the 1992 New Hampshire Democratic Primary. The impact was felt most strongly with respect to the relatively insignificant (but more frequently discussed) matter of horse-race standings rather than through substantive issues like a candidate's character, capacity to govern, or policy agenda."[72] The authors argue that Democratic voters in the 1992 New Hampshire primary "simply paid more attention to the game of politics, who was ahead and who was behind, when they made their decision in 1992 about whom they favored."[73] The media's use of polls provided the context in which New Hampshire voters made their decisions.

Beginning in 1976, candidates' strategies began to profoundly change as a result of the influence of New Hampshire. Primary candidates began to focus on the Iowa caucuses to develop "momentum" before entering New Hampshire. Jimmy Carter in 1976 was among the first to use the Iowa caucuses as a springboard to national recognition. He spent considerable time in Iowa, where he had the opportunity to meet personally with many voters. He also made himself available to the local media and then the national media. Since then, candidates have flocked to Iowa to gain the media's attention and develop a national exposure they hope will benefit them in the primaries.

By June 1998, two years before the presidential election of 2000, Senator Bob Smith of New Hampshire, a longshot for the Republican nomination, had spent twenty-seven days in Iowa. Lamar Alexander, the former governor of Tennessee and another Republican candidate, had spent twenty-six days. According to Hugh Winebrenner, who has followed the Iowa caucuses over the years, 1998 represented the heaviest early campaigning ever.[74] The importance of Iowa and New Hampshire has increased through the years. How the media interpret the results is critical to a successful run for the presidency. However, these states are not as socially or economically diverse as the general population. They are predominantly Republican in presidential voting and conservative on social issues. Therefore, the media's heavy coverage of events in these two states gives a boost to early winners chosen by nonrepresentative populations. Political observers suspect that Governor Bush's commanding lead in the polls and fund raising may make the Iowa caucus and the New Hampshire primary less important in the 2000 campaign.

Voters Versus Nonvoters

The relationship between voters and nonvoters has been the focus of much research.[75] Among the many questions about the impact of the media on voting, two stand out. First, do the media have an impact on how individuals cast their votes? Second, does increased media involvement lead to greater political participation? The answer to the first question appears to be that any impact is indirect. The media do set the political agenda and cast elections in terms of winners, losers, and gainers. With regard to the second question, one of the most consistent observations over the past four decades has been the declining voter turnout. While the media's coverage of the elections has increased, voting turnout has steadily decreased.

Table 7.2
Voters' and Nonvoters' Use of the Media in the 1996 Presidential Campaign

USE	VOTERS	NONVOTERS
Watched a program about the election	81%	58.7%
Listened to a political talk radio program	42.5	24
Read about the campaign in a magazine	39	15
Paid attention to newspaper reports	99	88

Source: Interuniversity Consortium for Political and Social Research, American National Election Studies, 1996, University of Michigan.

A basic tenet of democracy is that participants should hypothetically be better informed than nonparticipants. Table 7.2 demonstrates the difference in media usage between voters and nonvoters in the 1996 presidential election.[76] Voters were more likely than nonvoters to consult all forms of media during the 1996 campaign. This finding is consistent with voting studies conducted through the years. Among those who claimed to have voted, 81 percent said they watched a campaign program on television while 43 percent listened to a political talk radio program. The number of voters and nonvoters who claimed to have read about the campaign in a magazine dropped sharply, to 39 percent and 15 percent, respectively. The findings for newspaper reading are high for both voters and nonvoters. Nonvoters claimed to have paid more attention to newspaper reports about the campaign than to any other medium.[77]

Today's media diversity and the willingness of candidates to use nontraditional outlets like Leno, Letterman, MTV, and the Internet make evaluating media usage increasingly difficult for both voters and nonvoters. The growing public disenchantment with the traditional political parties provides opportunities for well-known but nontraditional candidates, such as Jesse Ventura.

political talk radio

Journalists, pundits, and politicians declared talk radio "the new force" in American politics in 1992. Candidates appeared on programs hosted by Rush Limbaugh, Larry King, and Don Imus, thus linking their names to entertainment personalities as well as to politics. There is substantial anecdotal evidence to support the claims of a "new" force in politics. Richard Davis notes that after 1992 the following events occurred:

- In September 1993 the White House invited talk radio hosts to broadcast from the south lawn. One hundred twenty-four hosts accepted the invitation. President Clinton expressed hope that "this will be the first of a number of opportunities" for talk show hosts to be briefed by the administration.
- Nine talk radio hosts ran for statewide or local office during the 1994 elections. Although most were unsuccessful, their positions gave them instant recognition. At the same time, unsuccessful candidates like former National Security Council staff member Oliver North, former New York governor Mario Cuomo, former New York mayor Ed Koch, and former California governor and presidential candidate Jerry Brown moved from elected officials to talk radio hosts.
- Talk radio hosts were credited with mobilizing young male Republican voters in the 1994 midterm elections, which saw both houses of Congress come under Republican control for the first time in forty years.
- The Republican Speaker of the House, Newt Gingrich, allowed talk radio hosts to broadcast from the basement of the Capitol. The Republican freshmen of the 104th Congress made Rush Limbaugh an honorary member of the House.[78]

Richard Silverman and Edwin Diamond have claimed that the 1992 presidential election signaled the complete collapse of the boundary between news and entertainment. They perceive the culprits as those ever-popular TV talk shows, where politicians' remarks go unchecked and half-truths are banished by hosts in the process of "informing" the public.[79] "In a time of electronic populism," they explain, "the television 'reality' was the [1992] campaign reality."[80] Whether these events represent a new and powerful force in American politics has been the subject of debate among scholars, pundits, and the public.

Four intertwined factors have increased the importance of political talk radio over the past three decades. First was the use of "antigovernment" attacks by candidates beginning in the late 1960s. This theme became increasingly important for candidates, the media, and the public. It served not only to mobilize voters, but also to circumvent the "traditional" channels of power—the political parties. To reach prospective voters, candidates increasingly sought the "free media" as vehicles for their messages, which were critical of the very institutions they sought to represent. George Wallace's 1968 presidential campaign was built on his theme of "sending them a message." Second, the lines between the mainstream media and political talk broadcasting (radio and television) have become increasingly blurred. Mainstream media (network news and major newspapers) once claimed to be governed by the ideal of objectivity and generally deplored those who did not meet that standard. The "downsizing" of news staffs at all the major networks has resulted in what one author calls "marketeers" who try to hold audiences through the mass appeal of "infotainment."[81] Third was the decision in 1987 to discard the FCC's "fairness doctrine." This decision reduced the accountability of stations for the content of their broadcasts and initiated a rapid expansion of radio talk programs. Finally, the economics of broadcasting led to increased use of talk programming. As costs and competition increased, talk radio programs became an inexpensive way of attracting new and larger audiences. The result was an explosive growth in talk shows.

The talk radio format first emerged in the 1920s. Radio programs such as "Town Meeting of the Air," the "People's Platform," and the "American Forum of the Air" were all popular programs that involved "talking" to America. Beginning in 1926 Father Charles Coughlin broadcast his sermons from his Royal Oak, Michigan, church and became one of the first major radio voices in American politics. His sermons combining appeals for social justice and patriotism soon made him the voice of America's underclass. Father Coughlin had an estimated audience during the 1930s of 10 million listeners, and he received more than 80,000 letters a week. In one national poll in 1933 he was voted the "most useful citizen of the United States."[82] He was rabidly anti–New Deal and anti-Communist, but it was his support of the fascist regimes of Hitler and Mussolini and his anti-Semitism that ultimately led to his withdrawal from radio.[83]

While radio during that era has been correctly associated with significant changes in American politics and with the development of new types of candidates and campaigns, ones that called for shorter speeches given by people whose voices were appealing over the radio, it was not interactive, the distinguishing trademark of talk radio today. While local talk radio had developed the "open mike" format much earlier, it was not until the 1970s that the first nationally syndicated "open mike" show was produced, hosted by Larry King. As a result, this medium began to achieve more attention.

Several distinctions should be made about talk radio. The first is the difference between general talk radio and *political* talk radio. The latter refers to programs that specifically address political and social issues, rather than occasionally discussing them. The second is the difference between "closed mike" programs, where a host has total control of the content and no outside opinions are voiced, and "open mike" programs, which are based on exchanges of opinions between callers and hosts. Finally, there is a difference between local political talk radio, where the audience is small and local, and syndicated political talk radio. While the former is important in today's mediated politics, it is syndicated political talk radio that garners the most attention from national politicians, pundits, scholars, and advertisers. The reason for this attention is that they are perceived to have more impact on the political process because of their audience size, the number of cities carrying them, their economic impact, and the frequent celebrity status of their hosts.

Certain elements are common to all forms of political talk radio. It has close ties to the commercial side of broadcasting. While all media are concerned with commercial success, larger news organizations have traditionally provided a buffer between entertainment and news and a tradition of objectivity not found in political talk radio. Political talk radio frequently strays from traditional news coverage to focus on personalities and events that are easily recognized by listeners. The programs emphasize entertainment over information. Finally, these programs take positions deliberately designed to provoke their audiences.[84]

The impact of political talk radio on the political process continues to be the focus of debate and research. Proponents of political talk radio argue that it makes an important contribution to the democratic process by stimulating debate, increasing political communication, and helping to define political issues.[85] Opponents argue that political talk radio exaggerates the opinions of small minorities, breeds cynicism and distrust, transforms the trivial into the substantial, is ideological and unbalanced, and appeals to socially isolated listeners.[86] Exposure to political talk radio can be perceived along a continuum. At one end are those who are very familiar with the media personalities and programs, and listen regularly. Some research suggests that these listeners engage in what has been termed "parasocial interactions," interactions in which the listener personalizes the relationship with the media personality, perhaps referring to him or her by first name.[87] At the opposite end of the continuum are listeners who view the personalities as entertaining and engaging "oddities."

Regardless of where one falls along the continuum, research indicates that changes in one's political orientation occur over time through the process of indirect learning. Sustained exposure to repeated messages is often associated with modest changes in perceptions.[88] These messages also have a powerful effect on listeners' agenda setting, framing, priming, incidental learning, political mobilization, and construction of reality.[89] Political talk radio, therefore, has both direct and indirect effects. The first occur among those who listen regularly and take some type of action based on what they hear. The second occur when topics on the programs make their way to the mainstream media.

Over the past few decades there has been episodic research on political talk radio. The research falls into three general categories. First are those studies that focus on what is said and how it is presented.[90] Second are studies that examine those who call in to these programs.[91] Third are studies that compare those who listen and those who do not.[92]

Diana Owen's study of talk radio sought to empirically test the notion that talk radio generated negative attitudes toward President Clinton and his policies.[93] She found that "the listening public is less positively disposed toward President Clinton than people who rely on television and/or newspapers for news."[94] She further stated that, compared with television or newspaper reports, talk radio was unabashedly partisan. Owen concluded that talk radio, beyond being negative toward President Clinton, may be a way for people to validate their already negative opinions of government.

If political talk radio is to have an effect on the political process, one would expect that those engaged in political talk radio would be more involved in the political system through traditional means of participation such as elections. C. Richard Hofstetter and Christopher Gianos, in a study of San Diego area residents, classified respondents as nonlisteners, listeners and talkers, and listeners, actors, and callers.[95] Individuals in these three groups were then examined in terms of their social-psychological dimension and their political participation and attention to political coverage in the media. They found that those who listened to political talk radio were more likely to believe that they could have an effect on government than nonlisteners and were more likely to participate in the political process.

One view of political talk radio participants is that they are generally highly partisan, highly ideological, and highly cynical. However, Hofstetter and Gianos found these traits to be higher among nonlisteners than listeners. Examination of these groups along the social psychological dimension also revealed a mixed pattern. Those who listened to political talk radio had greater faith in people and scored lower on authoritarianism and higher on individualism. Nonlisteners scored higher on self-estrangement, normlessness, cultural estrangement, social equality, and an ability to restrain their personal values when interacting with others. Thus, a comparison of listeners and nonlisteners of political talk radio along the social psychological dimension revealed a mixed pattern, but listeners were *not* more partisan, ideological, or cynical.

The authors then explored the three groups' relationships to political activity and attention to politics. They found that those who engaged in political talk radio programs voted more, talked about issues more, signed more petitions, and generally were more engaged in the political process. However, they were also more likely to agree with law breakers and to be more politically conservative. While this is but one study, it does suggest the complex role political talk radio plays in American politics.

In another study Hofstetter found that "ideologically charged talk show hosts may increase ideology and partisan sensitivity, possibly by priming, and political talk activity may stimulate political participation and attention to political events. Political talk radio may function as a form of civic entertainment, subscribed to by more politically attentive publics and thereby constituting a distinct mode of political participation."[96]

David Barker, in a study of Rush Limbaugh listeners using data from the National Election Studies, concluded that "listening to the Rush Limbaugh program appears to increase the individual political efficacy of conservative and moderate listeners, thus spurring them to action."[97] David Jones examined the question of how like-minded the audience of talk radio shows were to the host. Using data from the 1996 National Election Study, he found that members of the Rush Limbaugh audience were remarkably like-minded on issues that were emphasized on the program. He pointed out that listeners who shared the host's view on low-salient issues cast doubt on the possibility that the program's messages are a source of the listeners' free market orientation.[98] Even when compared with other conservatives and controlling for other factors, Limbaugh listeners were more supportive of free-market solutions to economic problems, more optimistic about the effects of tax cuts, and more opposed to government efforts to protect the environment.[99]

Stephen Bennett, using *Times Mirror*/Pew Research Center data from May 1993 to September 1996, found that frequent listeners were better informed and more politically active than nonlisteners. These findings were also true when key demographic variables and exposure to other forms of media were taken into account. He concluded that talk radio programs are beneficial to democracy.[100] These and other studies examining the impact of political talk radio indicate a strong relationship between listening to talk radio and being involved in the political process.

David Campbell examined whether talk radio programs represent a solution to the decline in civic engagement.[101] He found that listeners to political talk radio were more likely than the general public to believe political matters are simple enough for them to understand, and that they can have a say in how the government is run. They knew more about politics than nonlisteners, and were politically more active. Does this mean that political talk radio is a solution to declining civil engagement? The author answers this by stating, "If the perceived benefit is the expression, raw though it may be, of public opinion, then talk radio is unquestionably a solution, although one limited to 'cut-and-dried' issues only. But if the end is less the opinions expressed than the social ties built as a by-product of groups formed to express and mediate public opinion, then the virtual engagement facilitated by talk radio can be correctly labeled a problem."[102]

Kenneth Dautrich and Thomas Hartley, in their analysis of voters' use of political talk radio in the 1996 presidential election, conclude, "As a whole, we found that talk radio listeners were more likely to use a wide variety of news media. Analyzing talk radio listeners in this way is misleading, how-ever, because some talk radio listeners used elite media while others did not."[103] An important contribution of their research was their dividing of political talk radio listeners into two groups: elite—those who used a broad variety of elite news media (*NewsHour*, Sunday morning political talk shows, C-SPAN, *Inside Politics*, and National Public Radio) and non-elite—those who did not, and then comparing the two groups. They found that those who used elite media and listened to talk radio were "no more attracted to television news (81 percent vs. 79 percent) or newspapers (63 percent vs. 67 percent) than those who did not listen to talk radio."[104] However, those who did not use elite media and listened to talk radio were a little less likely to watch television news (59 percent vs. 67 percent) and less likely to read newspapers (49 percent vs. 55 percent).[105] The study found evidence that talk radio listeners may be less likely to use some type of mainstream media, that they prefer news in an easily accessible and entertaining format, and that listeners to political talk radio should not be viewed as a monolithic group.[106] The studies of political talk radio demonstrate that there are many reasons one may choose to listen, ranging from obtaining information, seeking and interacting parasocially to evaluating alternative views, sharpening alternatives, or simply entertaining oneself.

The Role of public opinion

The media and public opinion have always been intertwined. As we have seen, the media affect the public's perception of issues in many ways. There is little doubt about their role as agenda-setters, framers, or primers. In addition, today's media have become increasingly involved in the process of gathering and interpreting the public's attitudes through their use of public opinion polls. The pervasiveness of polls in the media is shown by their widespread use in major news stories. In 1995 and 1996 public opinion polls served as an integral part of nearly one third of the stories in the three leading newsmagazines, *Newsweek, Time,* and *U.S. News & World Report.*[107]

Using a variety of methods, several scholars have concluded that "the political information environment" exerts great influence on public opinion.[108] President Clinton's support fell 7 percentage points in the days immediately following the emergence of the Monica Lewinsky story, when the media coverage was basically negative.[109] As the media's coverage became more balanced, the president's approval ratings rose,[110] demonstrating the relationship that exists between the way the media presents information and the public's perceptions.

Surveys have always intrigued journalists. Scientific sampling was not invented until 1932, but in 1886 an independent Chicago paper, the *Reporter,* sent postcard ballots to all Chicago voters and from the response predicted McKinley would get 57.95 percent of the Chicago's vote. He received 57.91 percent. After polling became a staple in the social sciences, the media reported poll results on a regular basis.

More recently, Jack Holley, in a sample of national newspapers in 1989, found that nearly 40 percent of daily newspapers sponsored or conducted polls.[111] The Roper Center's survey of news coverage during the 1980 election found the seven major news organizations conducted 122 separate polls, and in 1988 eight organizations conducted 259 polls.[112] Initially the media used election polls to attract an audience and predict a winner. Today, however, polls are used in the reporting of issues other than campaigns. One study examined 296 stories that included polls in their coverage of public policy issues between 1994 and 1997.[113] The authors concluded that the inclusion of polls resulted in "shallow and myopic reports that track the political strategy of insiders rather than conveying substantive information on the public's preferences."[114]

Journalists increasingly rely on polls to shape the stories they use to inform the public. This reliance on polls is visible in all media; however, since television is so pervasive, its use of polls is of particular concern. In a study of the Gallup/CNN/*USA Today* tracking polls during the 1992 presidential election, June Woong Rhee found "tracking polls are a technique that enables news organizations to create 'news.' In turn, poll-driven horse-race stories invite journalists to cover election campaigns in a strategy-oriented manner."[115]

Television is a medium that relies on pictures, color, and sound bites to titillate and hold its audience's attention. Public opinion polls serve this medium particularly well, for they represent snapshots in time. News organizations' use of polls has increased dramatically over the past four decades, raising increasing concern about their negative effect on both the media and the political process. Many believe the networks' reliance on polls is excessive.[116] Television news has traditionally reported the results obtained by national polling organizations like Gallup, Harris, and Roper, but in 1967 CBS News established the first network polling organization and entered directly into the polling enterprise. In 1975 yet another new development occurred when television and print media, CBS and the *New York Times*, entered into a partnership on polling. NBC and the Associated Press wire service and then NBC and the *Wall Street Journal* soon followed. In the early 1980s ABC joined up with the *Washington Post*, and CNN with *Time* magazine.

The advantages of the joint print/broadcast polling partnership are several. First, it spreads the costs of the surveys. The polling cost for a presidential election cycle is about $12 million. Second, each organization brings different skills to polling. The print media offer in-depth analysis of public opinion polls by national correspondents widely recognized by the industry and the public for their expertise, while the broadcast media can reach large audiences and present polls in highly visual and appealing ways. Finally, print often lends prestige to a poll, and extends its news value by reporting the results in greater detail than is possible via television, and by keeping the results before the public for a longer period of time. But such joint efforts also raise serious questions. First, the final poll is the product of a collaborative effort between polling editors and reporters to decide which questions should be kept and which discarded. This increases the agenda setting, framing, and priming functions of the media. Second, the information influences the way elections are reported. Because the media have fairly reliable information on voter preferences well in advance of the election, this information changes the way the election is reported in the days leading up to the election and on election night. In the 1996 presidential election, Kathleen Frankovic notes, "the major television news organizations had enough information about the expected outcome to plot their election night broadcast, half hour by half hour."[117]

Between 1968 and 1976 the networks experimented with sampling methodology for exit polls. After the 1988 election, the three broadcast networks and CNN began talks about merging their election day operations. Since the midterm elections of 1990, Voter Research and Surveys (later Voter News Service, or VNS) has been the major source of information about election day voting behavior for nearly all broadcast and print media. Besides the Associated Press and the member television networks, many national and local newspapers and local television stations also purchase election day poll results from VNS.

Currently VNS exit poll questionnaires are designed by a committee of representatives from ABC News, the Associated Press, CBS News, CNN, FOX News, and NBC News, along with survey specialists from VNS. The effect of the collaborative effort is that what the major news organizations consider important become poll questions and later the news agenda. In 1996 VNS included as important issues Medicare, Social Security, crime, and drug abuse, thus helping to set the issue agenda. Exit poll information is used to "call" the election and then to "explain" the reasons for the outcome. The whole question of media polling raises serious ethical questions.

Critics of media polling point to several detrimental effects of the media's use of polls. They charge that candidates and the media are more concerned with electability than with the merits of the candidates or issues. Further, they contend that opinion polls divert attention from important issues to candidates' levels of popularity. The critics argue that the reporting of poll results can directly affect the outcome. Voters may choose not to vote because the polls indicate that their candidate either cannot win or will win and does not need their vote. Finally, critics argue that election night polls (exit polls) depress voter turnout by making it seem that the outcome is settled even before the voting ends. The existence of this last phenomenon was debated extensively during the 1980s. Studies of the impact of the exit polls have varying results, but the general consensus is that at least at the margins—in close races—election results are affected.

Do polls Have an Effect?

Polls do have an effect, but only in modest and often offsetting ways. Harrison Hickman has identified six factors that affect the impact of media polls. First is the citizen's "orientation" toward the election. If the election outcome is perceived to be important, the polls become more influential. Second, if the information is not available in other forms, the "saliency" of the media's polls becomes an important factor in the citizen's decision-making process. Third, if the citizen feels an "urgent" need to make a decision, the polls presented in the media have more impact. Fourth, polls have the greatest impact on those who have low "commitment" toward a candidate or party. These individuals do not have the normal anchoring of party or candidate loyalty to guide their decision. Fifth, when citizens have a "predisposition" toward a candidate, the polls also perform a major role in tracking their candidate's progress. Finally, the degree of "trust" the citizen places in the poll will affect its utility. The greater the trust, the greater the person's acceptance of the polls.[118]

Presidential campaigns are about winning, and polls represent a fast method of assessment. In addition, the manner in which campaigns are reported provides the drama associated with these and other elections. W. Lance Bennett and others have shown that those who produce the news steer coverage toward events, not social policies.[119] The questions of who is ahead and who is gaining are important to the media, candidates, and voters because they provide the drama of an election. By contributing to the priming process, or "the standard by which people make political judgments," opinion surveys perform an important role in media coverage of elections. Polls also lend credibility to news stories by virtue of their "scientific" orientation, their use of scientific methods to gather data. Most important, network polls have an "echo effect" because they are reported many more times by local stations, radio stations, and newspapers. Darrell West has also documented the "echo effect" in his study of political ads.[120] The media's reporting of public opinion polls clearly has an agenda-setting and framing function, and may have a priming one as well.

There are at least four reasons why poll results are so important to media producers: they simplify the complexities of campaigns, personalize the campaign, make reporting easier (for reporters can obtain the latest results and then craft a story around their interpretation), and create excitement and drama.

Public opinion polls carried by network news programs provide drama in presidential campaign reporting. It is difficult to measure with any precision the effect of repeated polls on the viewer, but recent evidence suggests that exposure to network television news produces several strong effects.[121] However, there is unobstructed evidence that polls have significantly altered how campaigns are reported. With three straightforward measures of public opinion polls in network newscasts, the emerging role of polls in campaign reporting is evident. These measures include the number of polls reported, the time allotted to stories that contain the polls, and the salience of polls in the newscast.

Table 7.3 indicates that the networks dramatically increased the number of polls reported between September 1 and election day over a period of twenty-eight years. During the 1968 campaign combined airtime assigned to public opinion polls by the three networks (ABC, CBS, and NBC) was less than one hour. In 1996 the three major networks aired thirty-two polls during the campaign, the third fewest during the period. However, the polls accounted for over two hours of airtime, compared with thirty-one polls and under fifty minutes in 1968. What Table 7.3 indicates is that the number of polls aired is less important than the stories' placement in the newscast or the time allotted to them. For instance, in 1984, when the networks aired the fewest polls, they accounted for two and one half hours of airtime. In both 1984 and 1996 incumbent presidents ran well ahead of their opponents from the beginning of the campaign—no drama to report. There were no major issues confronting either incumbent, yet polling stories were

Table 7.3
Network News Use of Polls (September 1 Through Election Day)

YEAR	NUMBER	TOTAL TIME	HOURS/MINUTES/ SECONDS	AVERAGE (SECONDS)	AVERAGE STORY PLACEMENT
1968	31	2,420	:40:20	8.06	4.1
1972	37	3,860	1:04:20	104.32	6.0
1976	36	4,970	1:22:50	138.05	4.9
1980	53	16,030	4:27:10	302.45	3.8
1984	27	8,800	2:26:40	325.95	2.7
1988	58	14,610	3:46:00	251.89	2.8
1992	51	17,410	4:50:10	341.37	1.7
1996	32	7,610	2:13:10	237.81	1.9

Source: Television News Index and Archive, Vanderbilt University, 1968–1996.

among the first three stories in the newscasts. Finally, in 1996 one network dominated poll reporting, ABC, which was responsible for over half the 32 polls aired by the networks. ABC "tracking polls" provided poll information on a daily basis. Also since 1980 the average placement of stories involving presidential polls has moved up to third. In the 1992 and 1996 elections, such stories moved into the second position. In another trend, since the 1980s there has been a decrease in poll reporting in years in which the outcome of the election was in little doubt, such as 1984 and 1996.

The use of public opinion polls conducted by the media raises serious questions. When the media conduct polls, they are *creating* news, or what Daniel Boorstin has called "pseudo news."[122] They frame the questions, interpret the responses, and then report the results as news. While we have focused on television's use of polls, reliance on polling also characterizes newspapers, magazines, and radio. The danger many see is that the media no longer can view the events of government from a detached position, for they are now part of the process. Moreover, as we saw earlier, the concentration of ownership exacerbates the issue. A *Washington Post* survey in 1996 found that voters preferred fewer or no polls (62 percent) in the reporting of the campaign.[123] Lawrence Jacobs and Robert Shapiro found that polls reported by the media in 1996 overwhelmingly focused on the horserace element of the campaign, not on issues of substance.[124] Regardless of the public's desires, the use of public opinion polls in campaign reporting has become intertwined with regular stories of the campaign and there are no signs that this will change. Stephanie Larson, in a study of television's use of public opinion polls in the 1996 presidential election, found that polls were used chiefly to report the campaign horserace and to introduce campaign strategy reports.[125] Her comparison of reported television polls to people-on-the-street interviews indicated the polls were not reflective of the concerns of people.

summary

Throughout American history, the media have been closely intertwined with the political process. In this chapter we have explored the media's role in the political process by focusing on four areas: advertisements, campaign reporting, political talk radio, and public opinion.

Political advertisements have two notable results. Financially, the cost of modern campaigns and the prominence of the media in campaigns, particularly television, have made seeking public office affordable to only a few. In addition, the types and frequency of advertisements extract a social cost in the form of cynicism, mistrust, and lower participation in the political process. Each of these has potentially serious implications not only for the political process, but for democracy itself.

How the media report campaigns may not alter the outcome of elections, but they do set the agenda and context of campaigns. There is strong evidence that the horserace theme (who's winning, who's gaining, and who's losing) dominates the reporting, not the issues.

There is a long-held belief that voters obtain more information from more diverse sources than nonvoters. Perhaps this was the case when the number of media was limited and campaigns were organized by local party organizations. Today, however, this common thesis is challenged in part by the low involvement and high cynicism about the political process. The media are themselves changing, with greater diversity in number and type, yet despite these changes there is greater homogeneity of content. Competition for audiences and sponsors continues to drive the content of most media reporting, and politics is no exception.

The development of political talk radio in the 1990s has received a great deal of attention from scholars, pundits, and the public. While some conclusions are tentative at best, others appear to withstand a variety of tests. Those who listen to political talk radio are not a monolithic group, and their reasons for listening vary from information seeking and parasocial interaction to evaluating alternatives and finding entertainment. Recent studies have shown that those who rely on talk radio at the expense of other elite media are more influenced by the ease of accessibility and entertainment. The long-term question is whether these programs are healthy in an age of "mediated" democracy.

Finally, we examined the media's use of public opinion polls. Reflecting society, the media are exposed to and use public opinion polls as an integral part of their political reporting. The cost of polling helped to forge the Voter News Service in the 1990s, which allowed users to develop the questions and then access the results. But the use of opinion polls has raised serious questions about their proper use. For example, does the heavy reliance on polls create news and thereby give today's media an excessive role in the political process? The reliance on polls by journalists molds the campaign reporting around the polls' results at the expense of other issues.

The media have always played a role in the political process, but what is different today is the nature of this role and the techniques used. As we enter the 21st century, both will continue to evolve.

Endnotes

[1]Lynda Lee Kaid, "Measuring the Effects of Distorted Political Ads," paper presented at the American Political Science Association Annual Meeting, Atlanta, Georgia, September 2–5, 1999.

[2]*Ibid.*, 17–18.

[3]Patrick Devlin, "Political Commercials in American Presidential Elections," in Lynda Lee Kaid and Christina Holtz-Bacha, eds., *Political Advertising in Western Democracies: Parties and Candidates on Television* (Thousand Oaks, Calif.: Sage Publishing, 1995), 186–205.

[4]*Ibid.*, 191.

[5]N. O'Shaughnessy, *The Phenomenon of Political Marketing* (New York: St. Martin's Press, 1990).

[6]Darrell M. West, *Air Wars: Television Advertising in Election Campaigns, 1952–1996* (Washington, D.C.: Congressional Quarterly Press, 1997).

[7]Darrell M. West, *Air Wars: Television Advertising in Election Campaigns, 1952–1992* (Washington, D.C.: Congressional Quarterly Press, 1993), 7.

[8]*New York Times*, November 13, 1996:A13.This does not include Ross Perot's advertisements or those of any of the other "minor" political party candidates.

[9]Dwight Morris and Murielle E. Gamache, *Handbook of Congressional Spending: Money in the 1992 Congressional Races* (Washington, D.C.: Congressional Quarterly Press, 1994).

[10]Christopher Adasiewicz, Douglas Rivlin, Jeffery Stanger, and Eric Zimmer, "Free Television for Presidential Candidates: The 1996 Experiment," *Political Communications*, Special Electronic Issue, 1998:3.

[11]Charles Atkins and Gary Heald, "Effects of Political Advertising," *Public Opinion Quarterly*, 40(1976):216–228.

[12]Thomas Patterson and Robert McClure, *The Unseeing Eye: The Myth of Television's Power in National Elections* (New York: Putnam, 1976).

[13]Craig L. Brains and Martin P. Wattenberg, "Campaign Issue Knowledge and Salience: Comparing Reception from TV Commercials, TV News, and Newspapers," *American Journal of Political Science*, 40(February 1996):185.

[14]*Ibid.*

[15]Marion Just, Ann Crigler, and Lori Wallach, "Thirty Seconds or Thirty Minutes: What Viewers Learn from Spot Advertisements and Candidate Debates," *Journal of Communication,* 40(1990):120–155.

[16]Ronald Faber and M. Claire Story, "Recall of Information from Political Advertising," *Journal of Advertising,* 13(1984):39–44.

[17]*Ibid.*

[18]Reported in the *Providence Journal,* "Hype Swells as First Presidential Debate Approaches," September 29, 1996: A7.

[19]Richard Berke, "Should Dole Risk Tough Image? Poll Says He Already Has One," *New York Times,* October 16, 1996:A1.

[20]Kathleen Hall Jamieson, "Context and the Creation of Meaning in the Advertising of the 1988 Presidential Campaign," *American Behavioral Science,* 32 (1989):415–424.

[21]Angus Campbell *et al., Elections and the Political Order* (New York: John Wiley and Sons, 1966); Samuel Patterson and Gregory Caldeira, "Getting Out the Vote: Participation in Gubernatorial Campaigns," *American Political Science Review,* 77(1983):675–689.

[22]Jerry Hagstrom and Robert Guskind, "In the Gutter," *National Journal,* 24(October 31,1992):2477–2482.

[23]Pippa Norris, "Introduction: The Rise of Postmodern Political Communications?" in Pippa Norris, ed., *Politics and the Press: The News Media and Their Influences* (Boulder, Col.: Lynne Rienner Publishers, 1997), 6.

[24]William G. Mayer, "In Defense of Negative Campaigning," *Political Science Quarterly,* 111(1996):443.

[25]*Ibid.*

[26]Gina M. Garramone, Charles Atkins, Bruce Pinkleton, and Richard Cole, "Effects of Negative Political Advertising on the Political Process," *Journal of Broadcast and Electronic Media,* 29(1985):147–159.

[27]Michael Basil, Caroline Schooler, and Byron Reeves, "Positive and Negative Political Advertising: Effectiveness of Advertisements and Perception of Candidates," in Frank Biocca, ed., *Television and Political Advertising* (Mahwah, N.J.: Lawrence Erlbaum Associates, 1991), 245–262.

[28]Esther Thorson, William Christ, and Clarke Caywood, "Effects of Issue-Image Strategies, Attack and Support Appeals, Music and Visual Content in Political Commercials," *Journal of Broadcast and Electronic Media,* 35(1991):465–486.

[29]Stephen Ansolabehere, Shanto Iyengar, Adam Simon, and Nicholas Valentino, "Does Attack Advertising Demobilize the Electorate?" *American Political Science Review,* 88(December 1994):829–838.

[30]*Ibid.,* 835.

[31]Stephen Ansolabehere and Shanto Iyengar, *Going Negative: How Attack Ads Shrink and Polarize the Electorate* (New York: The Free Press, 1995).

[32]*Ibid.,* 145.

[33]*Ibid.,* 113.

[34]*Ibid.*

[35]Jon Hale, Jeffrey Fox, and Rick Farmer, "Negative Advertisements in U.S. Senate Campaigns: The Influence of Campaign Contests," *Social Science Quarterly*, 77(June 1996):329–343.

[36]*Ibid.*

[37]Steven E. Finkel and John G. Geer, "A Spot Check: Cast Doubt on the Demobilizing Effect of Attack Advertising," *American Journal of Political Science*, 42(April 1998):573–595.

[38]*Ibid.*, 573.

[39]*Ibid.*

[40]The Center for Media and Public Policy, "The Markle Presidential Election Watch," February 29, 1996:1.

[41]Barbara Salmore and Stephen Salmore, *Candidates, Parties, and Campaigns: Electoral Politics in America* (Washington, D.C.: Congressional Quarterly Press, 1989):159.

[42]Fred Wertheimer, "TV Ad Wars: How to Cut Advertising Cost in Political Campaigns," *Press/Politics*, 2(Summer 1997):96.

[43]Paul Lazarsfeld, Bernard Berelson, and Hazel Gaudet, *The People's Choice* (New York: Columbia University Press, 1948). This study of Erie County, Ohio, voters found that policy and leadership were the primary focus of the media coverage.

[44]Thomas E. Patterson, *The Mass Media Election* (New York: Praeger, 1980), 24.

[45]*Ibid.*, 25.

[46]Michael J. Robinson and Margaret A. Sheehan, *Over the Wire and On TV: CBS and UPI in Campaign '80* (New York: Russell Sage Foundation, 1983), 145.

[47]*Ibid*, 146.

[48]*Ibid.*

[49]*Ibid.*, 148.

[50]*Ibid.*

[51]Michael J. Robinson, "A Statesmen Is a Dead Politician: Candidate Images on Network News," in Elie Able, ed., *What's News* (San Francisco, Calif.: The Institute for Contemporary Studies, 1981), 160–161.

[52]Bruce Buchanan, *Electing a President* (Austin, Texas: University of Texas Press, 1991).

[53]Thomas E. Patterson, *Out of Order* (New York: Alfred E. Knopf, 1993), 73.

[54]*Ibid.*

[55]Matthew R. Kerbel, *Edited for Television: CNN, ABC and the 1992 Presidential Campaign* (Boulder, Col.: Westview Press, 1994).

[56]*Ibid.*, 23–24.

[57]Marion Just, Ann Crigler, Dean Alger, Timothy Cook, Montague Kern, and Darrell West, *Crosstalk: Citizens, Candidates and the Media in a Presidential Campaign* (Chicago: University of Chicago Press, 1996).

[58]*Ibid.*, 119.

[59]Doris A. Graber, "Whither Televised Election News? Lessons from the 1996 Campaign," *Press/Politics*, 3(Spring 1998):112–120.

[60]*Ibid.*

[61]Matthew Kerbel and Marc Ross, "Television News Frames and Informed Political Choice," paper presented at the American Political Science Association Meeting, Boston, Mass., September 3–6, 1998.

[62]*Ibid.*, 28.

[63]"The Invisible Election: TV Coverage of the 1998 Midterm Elections," *Media Monitor*, 12(Nov./Dec. 1998):1.

[64]*Ibid.*

[65]*Dallas Morning News*, "Polls Say Bush Is Front-runner for the Presidency," July 25, 1999:1.

[66]Jeremy Torobin, "The Invisible Campaign," Center for Media and Public Affairs press release, January 14, 2000.

[67]Peter Marks, "Before Voting Ended, TV Dropped Hints," *New York Times*, February 2, 2000:A16.

[68]*Ibid.*

[69]James Beniger, "Winning the Presidential Nomination," *Public Opinion Quarterly*, 40(Spring 1976):22–38.

[70]Michael J. Robinson, "TV's Newest Program: The Presidential Nominating Game," *Public Opinion*, 1(May/June 1976):41–46.

[71]William C. Adams, "As New Hampshire Goes . . . ," in Gary R. Orren and Nelson Polsby, eds., *Media and Momentum* (Chatham, N.J.: Chatham House Publishers, Inc., 1987), 45.

[72]Stephen J. Farnsworth and S. Robert Lichter, "No Small-Town Poll: Public Attention to Network Coverage of the 1992 New Hampshire Primary," *Press/Politics*, 4(Summer 1999):57.

[73]*Ibid.*, 58.

[74]Carl P. Leubsdorf, "Iowa Gala-Goers Can't Forget Who's Missing," *Dallas Morning News*, June 18, 1998:31A.

[75]Kurt Lang and Gladys Engel Lang, *Voting and NonVoting* (Waltham, Mass.: Blaisdell Publishing Company, 1968.)

[76]There has been a history of "over-reporting" on the question of voting during the years. The 1996 data from the American National Elections Studies is no exception to the rule. Thus, the inferences drawn for those claiming to have voted should be viewed with caution.

[77]There, too, the social pressures to have claimed to have followed the campaign through the newspapers may account for these high numbers and readers should use these figures with caution.

[78]Richard Davis, "Understanding Broadcast Political Talk," *Political Communication*, 14(July–September, 1997):323–324.

[79]Robert Silverman and Edwin Diamond, *White House to Your House: Media and Politics in Virtual America* (Cambridge, Mass.: MIT Press, 1995).

[80]*Ibid.*

[81]Penn Kimball, *Downsizing the News: Network Cutbacks in the Nation's Capital* (Washington, D.C.: The Woodrow Wilson Center Press, 1994).

[82]Charles Tull, Jr., *Father Coughlin and the New Deal* (Syracuse, New York: University of Syracuse Press, 1965); Alan Brinkley, *Voices of Protest: Huey Long, Father Coughlin, and the Great Depression* (New York: Alfred A. Knopf, 1982); and Warren, *op. cit.*

[83]Donald Warren, *Charles Coughlin: The Father of Hate Radio* (New York: The Free Press, 1996).

[84]Al Brumley, "Conservatively Speaking," *Dallas Morning News*, April 7, 1996:1C.

[85]John Crittenden, "Democratic Functions of the Open Mike Radio Forum," *Public Opinion Quarterly*, 35(1971):200-210; C. Richard Hofstetter et al., "Political Talk Radio: A Stereotype Reconsidered," *Political Research Quarterly*, 108(1993):467–479.

[86]Robert Avery and Donald Ellis, "Talk Radio as an Interpersonal Phenomenon," in Gary Gumpert and Robert Catheart, eds., *Inter/Media: Interpersonal Communications in a Media World* (New York: Oxford Press, 1979):108–115; Jeffery Bierig and John Dimmick, "The Late Night Radio Talk Show as Interpersonal Communications," *Journalism Quarterly*, 56(Spring 1979):92–96.

[87]Richard Houlberg, "Local TV News Audiences and the Para-Social Interaction," *Journal of Broadcasting*, 28(1984):423–429.

[88]Cliff Zukin, "Mass Communications and Public Opinion," in Dan Nimmo and Keith Sanders, eds., *Handbook of Political Communication* (Beverly Hills, Calif.: Sage Publications, Inc., 1991), 244–261.

[89]Steven Ansolabehere, Robert Behr, and Shanto Iyengar, *The Media Game: American Politics in the Television Age* (New York: Macmillan Publishing Company, 1993); D. Weaver, "What Voters Learn About the Media," *Annals of the American Academy of Political and Social Sciences*, 546(1996):34–47; B. Hollander, "Talk Radio: Predictors of Use and Effects on Attitudes About Government," *Journalism and Mass Communication Quarterly*, 73(1996):102–113.

[90]John Crittenden, *op. cit.*; R.K. Avery and D. Ellis, "Patterns of Communication on Talk Radio," *Journal of Broadcasting*, 22(1978):5–17; R. Murray and A. Vedlitz, "Race, Socioeconomic Status, and Voting in Large Southern Cities," *Journal of Politics*, 39(1987):1064–1072.

[91]C.B. Armstrong and A.M. Rubin, "Talk Radio as Interpersonal Communications," *Journal of Communication*, 39(1989):84–94; H. Tramer and L. Jeffres, "Talk Radio-Forum and Companion," *Journal of Broadcasting*, 27(1983):287–300; J. Bierig and J. Dimmick, "The Late Night Radio Talk Show as Interpersonal Communication," *Journalism Quarterly*, 56(1979):92–96; and J. Turow, "Talk Show Radio as Interpersonal Communication," *Journal of Broadcasting*, 18(1974):171–179.

[92]C.R. Hofstetter, M. Donovan, M. Klauber, A. Cole, C. Huie, and T. Yuasa, "Political Talk Radio: A Stereotype Reconsidered," *Political Research Quarterly*, 47(1994):467–479; C.R. Hofstetter and C. Gianos, "Political Talk Radio: Actions Speak Louder Than Words," *Journal of Broadcasting and Electronic Media*, 41(1997):501–515; and S. Surlin, "Uses of Jamaican Talk Radio," *Journal of Broadcasting and Electronic Media*, 30(1986):459–466.

[93]Diana Owen, "Talk Radio and Evaluations of President Clinton," *Political Communication*, 14(July–September 1997):333–353.

[94]*Ibid.*, 348.

[95]Hofstetter and Gianos, *op. cit.*

[96]C. Richard Hofstetter, "Political Talk Radio, Situational Involvement, and Political Mobilization," *Social Science Quarterly*, 79(June 1998):273.

[97]David C. Barker, "The Talk Radio Community: Nontraditional Social Networks and Political Participation," *Social Science Quarterly*, 79(June 1998):269.

[98]David Jones, "Talk Radio: A Safe Haven for the Like-Minded?" paper presented at the Southern Political Science Association Annual Meeting, Atlanta, Georgia, October 28–31, 1998.

[99]*Ibid.*, 9.

[100]Stephen Earl Bennett, "Political Talk Radio's Relationships With Democratic Citizenship," *American Review of Politics*, 19(Spring 1998):17–29.

[101]David E. Campbell, "Declining Civic Engagement: Is Talk Radio Part of the Problem or the Solution?" paper presented at the American Political Science Association Annual Meeting, Boston, Mass., September 3–6, 1998.

[102]*Ibid.*, 13.

[103] Kenneth Dautrich and Thomas H. Hartley, *How the News Media Fail American Voters: Causes, Consequences, & Remedies* (New York: Columbia University Press, 1999), 39.

[104]*Ibid.*

[105]*Ibid.*

[106]*Ibid.*, 40.

[107]Herbert Asher, *Polling and the Public* (Washington, D.C.: Congressional Quarterly Press, 1998), 3.

[108]Marion Just, Ann Crigler, Dean Alger, Timothy Cook, Montague Kern, and Darrell West, *Crosswalk: Citizens, Candidates and the Media in a Presidential Campaign* (Chicago: University of Chicago Press, 1996), 89.

[109]John Zaller, "Monica Lewinsky's Contribution to Political Science," *PS*, 31(June 1998):184.

[110]*Ibid.*

[111]Jack K. Holley, "The Press and Political Polling," in Paul Lavrakas and Jack K. Holley, eds., *Polling and Presidential Election Coverage* (Thousand Oaks, Calif.: Sage Publications, 1991), 215–237.

[112]Everett Ladd and John Benson, "The Growth of News Polls in American Polls," in Thomas E. Mann and Gary R. Orren, eds., *Media and Polls in American Politics* (Washington, D.C.: Brookings Institute, 1992), 19–31.

[113]Lawrence Jacobs and Robert Shapiro, cited in Richard Morin, "Public Policy Surveys: Lite and Less Filling," *Washington Post Weekly Edition*, November 10, 1997:35.

[114]*Ibid.*

[115]June Woong Rhee, "How Polls Drive Campaign Coverage: The Gallup/CNN/*USA Today* Tracking Poll and *USA Today*'s Coverage of the 1992 Presidential Campaign," *Political Communication*, 13(April–June 1996):213–229.

[116]Jack W. Germond, "The Impact of Polling on Journalism," in Albert H. Cantril, ed., *Polling on the Issues* (Washington, D.C.: Seven Locks Press, 1980):20–27.

[117]Kathleen Frankovic, "How Polling Becomes the News: Communicating the Counting of Public Opinion," *Political Communications* (Special Electronic Issue 1998):6.

[118]Harrison Hickman, "Public Polls and Election Participation," in Paul J. Lavrakas and Jack K. Holley, eds., *Polling and Presidential Election Coverage* (Thousand Oaks, Calif.: Sage Publications, 1991), 100–133.

[119]See W. Lance Bennett, *News: The Politics of Illusion*, 3rd ed. (New York: Longman Publishers, 1996); Herbert Gans, *Deciding What's News* (New York: Pantheon, 1979); and E. Jay Epstein, *News From Nowhere* (New York: Random House, 1973).

[120]Darrell West, *op. cit.*, 1997.

[121]Larry Bartels, "Messages Received: The Political Impact of Media Exposure," *American Political Science Review*, 87(June 1992):267–285.

[122]Daniel J. Boorstin, *The Image: A Guide to Pseudo-Events in America* (New York: Vintage Books, 1992).

[123]Robert Blendon, John Young, Mooyann Brodie, Richard Morin, Drew Altman, and Mario Brossard, "Did the Media Leave the Voters Uninformed in the 1996 Election?" *Press/Politics*, 3(Spring 1998):126.

[124]Lawrence Jacobs and Robert Shapiro, *The Annenberg Public Policy Center Poll Watch: The 1996 Presidential Elections* (Philadelphia: University of Pennsylvania Press, 1996).

[125]Stephanie Greco Larson, "Public Opinion in Television Election News: Beyond the Polls," *Political Communication*, 16(April–June 1999):133–146.

CHAPTER 8

The presidency and the media

The media's role in transforming American politics is nowhere more conspicuous than in its coverage of the presidency. Presidents do not directly communicate to the American public on a day-to-day basis. The media provide citizens with most of what they know about the president, his policies, and their consequences. They interpret and analyze presidential activities—they are the "channels of power" of the political system. The media are positioned between the president and the public, which places them in a position to shape the president's agenda. Consequently, if they portray the president in a positive light, he will face fewer obstacles in obtaining public support and success in public policy. If, on the other hand, their coverage is negative, the president's task will be more difficult. For this reason, presidents go to great lengths to court the media in an effort to be portrayed positively. Their efforts include coordinating news releases with media deadlines, holding press conferences, and providing a wide range of other services, from formal briefings, interviews, photo opportunities, background sessions, travel accommodations, daily handouts, and technical computer support. Factors that have contributed to the growing power of the media include the decline of the party system, the changing primary and electoral process, the ease of obtaining information for both the media and the public, personalization of coverage, and the media's affection for the dramatic.

The Evolving Relationship Between the Media and the White House

Three factors contribute to making the White House beat what is today one of the most coveted journalistic positions.[1] First is the continual coverage of specific presidential events, like deaths and trips, that dates to the pre–Civil War period. Second is the growth in newspapers and the rise of the public's interest in the presidency. Finally there is the organized response by presidents and their aides to the demands of the media for information and access.[2] Martha Kumar points out that the presidency was a larger-than-life personal drama during the period from 1861 to the turn of the century.[3] There were two wars, three assassinations, a presidential impeachment, the death of a first lady, assorted scandals, the marriage of a president, and the birth of a president's child. It was also during this period that many precedents were established. Reporters maintained an around-the-clock watch over President Garfield from the time he became ill until his death. The press first traveled with a president in 1891, when President Harrison traveled to California accompanied by two reporters. President Andrew Johnson had frequent conversations with John "Mack" McCullagh of the Cincinnati *Commercial* during his impeachment. Finally, it was during this period that regular press coverage of White House events began and the media were provided space within the White House. The White House today includes a large network of communication personnel whose task it is to present the president and his policies in the most positive light. As we will see, there has been a change in the relationship between the office of the president and the media in recent years.

modern presidents and the media

Modern presidents have used the media to help them create "personality cults."[4] The first modern president to effectively use the media in this manner was Franklin Roosevelt. Through his radio "fireside" chats, he was able to bring a new personal dimension to the presidency. By encouraging citizens to view the nation's future as dependent on his personal success, he strengthened the relationship between the media and the executive branch. The cult of presidential personality owes its existence primarily to the media, as they are the major source of communications between the president and other governmental decision makers and the public.

Other branches of government do not receive the same intense coverage. Congress, because of its size and diversity, makes it difficult to focus on dramatic personalities. The Supreme Court, while small, has a tradition of aloofness, making it very difficult to cover in a personalized and dramatic manner. The bureaucracy is too large for dramatic media coverage.

As noted above, presidents attempt to use the media to their advantage, even while they have complained about how the media mistreat them. Timothy Cook notes, "Presidents not only spend more and more time and energy in order to give speeches, but their activities and those of the executive branch as a whole are increasingly geared toward the 'line of the day' charted out by the Office of Communications."[5] Leon Panetta, President Clinton's former chief of staff, reported that what was important was "to create a focus for the President each day. . . .What was the event, what was the message that we wanted to get across that day that fit the agenda that he was trying to implement on the Hill? And so part of the discussion in the morning was what is that focus today, how do we want to get the message out, is the event properly prepared, are the releases done, have we done all of the background work, is the statement done for the President?"[6]

While all relationships between the media and political institutions are symbiotic, the relationship with the president is particularly so. The nature of the office itself leads the media and the public to look to the president for guidance and information. When the nation is faced with major events—wars, depressions, domestic unrest, scandals, and national disasters—it is the president who speaks to and for the nation. This focus on the presidency has increased in recent decades. Political scientist Theodore Lowi, drawing on a report on political parties and the American system by leading American political scientists, has pointed out the consequences of changes in the American political process:

> A system that vests such responsibility in the president can work well enough as long as the program has been democratically formulated within the president's party. However, when there is no party support for a broad program, the president has no choice but to work up a program of his own and then secure the necessary popular support. Here, according to the committee, are the implications of that way of operating: "*In effect this concept of the presidency disposes of the party system by making the president reach directly for the support of a majority of voters. It favors a president who exploits skillfully the arts of demagoguery . . . and who does not mind turning into the embodiment of personal government.*"[7]

These factors have led Lowi to term the modern American presidency a "plebscitory presidency."[8] Television brings the president into visual contact with the citizens, resulting in an attachment to the president like that for no other public official or symbol of government.

Fred I. Greenstein has isolated five "psychological functions of the presidency."[9] First, the president stimulates perceptions of government and politics by serving as the "main cognitive handle" for the citizens. Second, the president provides "an outlet for emotional expression" through public interest in his and his family's private and public lives. This is an area that serves the media particularly well, for it adds "personalization" and drama to the office. Third, the president is a symbol of unity. President Clinton performed this function in his responses to the Oklahoma City bombing, the TWA crash that was initially believed to be an act of terrorism, and the burning of black churches in the South. Fourth, the president provides citizens with a "vicarious means of taking political action." For example, presidents often ask citizens for guidance.[10] Finally, the president serves as a symbol of social stability, providing citizens with a sense of security.

At the same time that increasing numbers of journalists have been covering the White House, new technological advances have been facilitating instant coverage of the president. This immediate coverage has caused public perceptions to be formed more by the media than the White House. The media's coverage of the president has also become increasingly negative. Studies using content analysis have discovered a consistently heavier concentration of unflattering presidential news, more than during the three decades from the 1950s to the 1970s. Figure 8.1 shows that Presidents Bush and Clinton garnered mostly negative coverage during their first three years in office. By analyzing every sentence in the three network newscasts, Samuel Kernell found that in only four quarters during the Bush and Clinton administrations' first three years did positive reporting exceed negative.[11] As Figures 8.2 and 8.3 show, on both domestic and foreign issues, the negative coverage of President Clinton's policies exceeded the positive. The increasingly negative presentation of the president through the years, evidenced in Figure 8.1, has caused many to blame the media for the decline in political activity, from working in campaigns to turning out to vote. The amount of time the president is actually heard during telecasts has diminished, and has been replaced by commentary by correspondents, anchors, and experts.

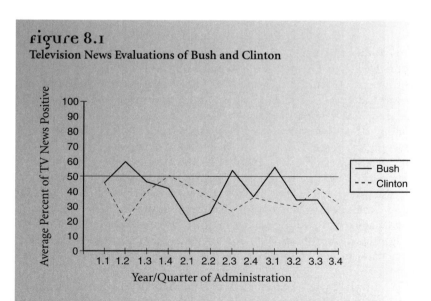

figure 8.1
Television News Evaluations of Bush and Clinton

Source: Ratings based on content analysis of sound bites on ABC, NBC, and CBS evening news programs provided by the Center for Media and Public Affairs, Washington, D.C.

Note: Clinton data are from his first term.

Source: Samuel Kernell, *Going Public*, 3rd ed. (Washington, D.C.: Congressional Quarterly Press, 1997): 95.

figure 8.2
How the Nightly News Presented President Clinton's Domestic Policies (January 20, 1993 to June 20, 1994)

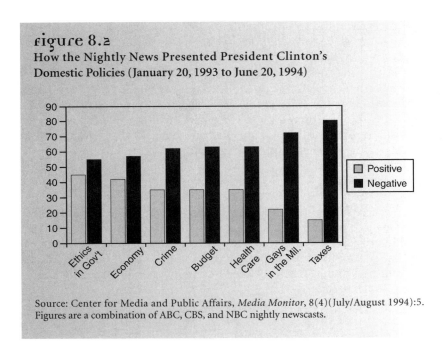

Source: Center for Media and Public Affairs, *Media Monitor*, 8(4)(July/August 1994):5. Figures are a combination of ABC, CBS, and NBC nightly newscasts.

To counter the increased power of the mainstream media, presidents have sought alternative methods for communicating with the public. They make more prime time appearances (talk show appearances, personal interviews, and addresses to the nation) and spend more time outside the White House addressing specialized groups like trade associations, college graduating classes, and advocacy groups. These non-Washington exposures serve several purposes. They remove the president from the increasingly negative environment of the Washington-based media and allow him to communicate through local media, which are generally more positive. Going public also gives the president and his staff more control over both the content and context of his addresses. Presidents and their staffs spend a great deal of time working on the smallest details for presidential appearances, from lighting, backdrops, and camera angles to personal artifacts that serve as visual background—family portraits, books, or busts of Lincoln, Truman, or Kennedy.

No administration was more skillful in this respect than the Reagan administration, which succeeded in avoiding the negative coverage that plagued preceding and succeeding administrations. As one Reagan official stated, "You get only forty to eighty seconds on a given night on the network news, and unless you can find a visual that explains your message, you can't make it stick."[12] President Reagan had the advantage of having worked in print, radio, movies, and television, which put him at ease in

Figure 8.3

How the Nightly News Presented President Clinton's Foreign Policies (January 20, 1993 to June 20, 1994)

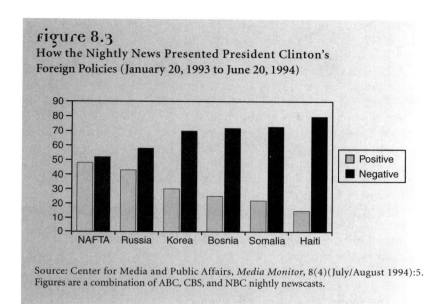

Source: Center for Media and Public Affairs, *Media Monitor*, 8(4)(July/August 1994):5. Figures are a combination of ABC, CBS, and NBC nightly newscasts.

front of cameras and microphones and helped him project the image of an amiable, nice guy. Reagan was termed the "Great Communicator" primarily for his mastery of television.

The reward for the administration was generally positive coverage for the president, despite several facts that would have normally received negative coverage. First, Reagan violated the norms of modern presidential behavior by working from only 9:00 a.m. to 5:00 p.m., taking naps, watching nightly television, and leaving details to subordinates. Second, most Americans disagreed with the president's policies on many major issues, such as aid to the Nicaraguan contras, reductions in domestic programs, and opposition to gun control and abortion. Third, Reagan governed over a major economic recession in 1981–1982, the withdrawal of American troops from Lebanon, the selling of weapons to Iran and misleading Congress about the sales, and a number of other scandals. And he was perceived as moving the nation in a more conservative direction when indications are that the nation was actually more conservative during the late 1970s than it was during his tenure as president. Despite all this, Reagan managed to elude major media attacks, which earned him the title of the "Teflon president."[13]

As noted above, neither the Bush nor the Clinton administrations were as successful in projecting positive images. The media's initial portrayals of the Clinton administration were negative. Within the first week of Clinton's first inaugural, NBC's Lisa Meyers reported, "From up close, the Clinton Administration looked like the Not-Ready-for Prime-Time Players," Fred

Barnes said the Clinton administration "hit the ground back-pedaling," Tim Russett on NBC's *Meet the Press* reported, "The president is stumbling," and Mark Shields labeled the new president "incredibly inept."[14] Clearly the traditional "honeymoon" period, during which the media gave new presidents and their administrations time to adjust to their new political environment, was not observed.

There are several reasons for this more negative coverage. The media itself has generally been more competitive, more cynical, and more combative toward politicians since Watergate. This scandal arguably changed the reporting process, as reporters focused more on the conflict and sensationalism associated with "big stories" and less on the political process. Presidents have added to the difficulty by establishing a special unit in the White House, the Office of Communication, that is dedicated to seeing that their view of daily events is presented by the media. This attempt to control the news has made many journalists more aggressive, for they know they are being furnished information that is one-sided at best. The final factor is the growth of such new media as the Internet and talk radio, which frequently lack accountability for their content or accuracy.

Colin Seymour-Ure argues the technological advances have enabled the president to communicate to the nation and the world from any location. Modern presidents have great flexibility in deciding how, under what circumstances, and where they will communicate.[15] The ability to choose among multiple locations for communicating with the public is not all positive, according to Seymour-Ure. While President Clinton's appearances on MTV, talk shows, and town meetings engaged more citizens in direct communication, they also led to confusion about the presidency, as formal distinctions between the presidency and other offices have been eroded.

shifting priorities

Prior to the 1980s, most Americans received their political information from the three major television networks, ABC, CBS, and NBC. This oligopoly proved beneficial for both politicians and the media. In their study of the impact of cable on presidential coverage, Matthew Baum and Samuel Kernell found that during the era of network dominance, presidents had greater access to television.[16] Their requests for prime time to address the nation were almost always granted. There was no drawback for the networks because all carried the broadcasts and viewers and sponsors had few alternatives. However, as cable became more affordable and accessible, the competition for viewers and sponsors altered this situation. In the 1980s the networks allotted significantly less television time for presidential addresses. During the Clinton administration, the networks began rotating coverage of some presidential appearances. As a result, only fourteen of the president's twenty prime-time addresses and news conferences were carried by all three networks.[17]

In the 2000 presidential campaign some members of the media claimed that "Clinton fatigue" had infected American politics, making Vice President Gore unelectable. They argued that the public wanted a change in leadership, but not necessarily in policies. Vice President Gore was saddled by President Clinton's affair with Monica Lewinsky and subsequent impeachment, his decision to grant clemency to Puerto Rican terrorists, and all the negative images associated with the president while receiving virtually no credit for successes in the economy. Some believe the perception stems from the media's desire for a new, exciting story. Richard Berke noted, "The ferment about fatigue may be overblown, stirred up by a restless press and pundits longing to begin the millennium with a fresh presidential story line, instead of what has seemed the inevitable faceoff between Mr. Gore and Gov. George W. Bush of Texas."[18]

In any case, the phenomenon of fatigue was too weak for pollsters to measure with confidence. Polls showed only slight evidence of "Clinton fatigue," with the president maintaining high personal approval ratings. The perception may be due in part to the shifting nature of presidential news coverage. With the advent of continual news on television and the Internet, President Clinton has been more "in the face" of Americans than any other president in history, a trend that will likely continue. This may help explain the low public involvement in the political process. While the president is more in the public's eye, the public also has more television programming options. If voters are turned off by politics, it may well be because they have tuned politics out.

presidential new conferences

Presidents have traditionally used the formal news conference to control the political agenda, as well as to create a positive impression among White House correspondents. The White House beat was very prestigious, making household names of many journalists. The first live televised presidential news conference, held by President Kennedy in January 1961, was attended by 418 correspondents. However, the relationship between the White House and the correspondents who cover it has been diluted in recent years. Members of the Clinton administration decided from the beginning to avoid the Washington press corps and traditional news conferences, partly as a result of what it had perceived as unfair coverage during the campaign. It was two months before the new president held a formal news conference. In addition, the administration barred reporters from previously accessible areas in the White House. Clinton asked reporters at the Radio and Television Correspondents Dinner, "You know why I can stiff you on the press conference? Because Larry King liberated me by giving me access to the American people directly."[19]

The Washington press corps saw Clinton's refusal to hold a formal press conference as calculated affront. Through the use of other outlets, including the Internet, satellite hook-ups with local television stations, and nationally televised speeches, the president answered hundreds of questions in the first few weeks—more than Bush, Reagan, or Carter at that stage—while breaking the Washington press corps monopoly on presidential news coverage.[20] The move away from presidential press conferences, however, did not start with Clinton. Their number had declined sharply since the days of President Franklin Roosevelt. For example, President Reagan, the "Great Communicator," held only twenty-seven press conferences.

Jarol Manheim tested the existence of the "honeymoon period" as indicated by presidential press conferences.[21] As mentioned above, it had been commonly believed that during the first months of a new administration the media were less confrontational and allowed new presidents to settle into office. Manheim compared all news conferences held within the first two months of the administrations of Presidents Kennedy, Johnson, Nixon, and Ford with 150 randomly selected ones. He found that more hostile questions were asked by journalists during the honeymoon period than during later news conferences. He also found, however, that fewer "political"

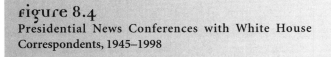

figure 8.4
Presidential News Conferences with White House Correspondents, 1945–1998

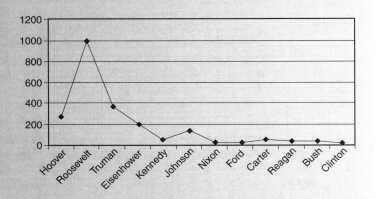

Source: Harold W. Stanley and Richard G. Niemi, *Vital Statistics on American Politics 1999–2000* (Washington, D.C.: Congressional Quarterly Press, 2000), 170. Through December 31, 1998.

questions were asked during the honeymoon period than in the post-honeymoon period (20 percent to 33 percent). In addition, reporters were more willing to following the president's lead at news conferences during the honeymoon period than during the post-honeymoon period. Manheim concluded that the honeymoon period was one of "testing" and "overcompensation" for hostile questions.[22]

If there was ever a honeymoon period between journalists and new administrations, that appears to no longer be the case. In part this is a defense against the president's increased control of the political agenda, as well as changes in journalistic standards. Today the media emphasize failures over successes and drama over substance. In 1993, when asked why his approval ratings had dropped 15 percentage points in only two months, President Clinton replied, "I bet not five percent of the American people know that we passed a budget . . . and it passed at the most rapid point of any budget in seventeen years. I bet not one in twenty American voters knows that because . . . success and the lack of discord are not as noteworthy as failure."[23] President Clinton's statement reflects his perception (and other presidents have made the same observation) that media do not report substance because it is normally not dramatic.

Drama and sensationalism in the coverage of the Monica Lewinsky Affair

Three factors eventually led to President Clinton's apologizing to the nation for his behavior in the Monica Lewinsky affair. The first was the president's behavior itself. The second was the media's methods in reporting. Finally there were preexisting unforgiving political divisions. The exact role each played in the final outcome is a question that will require the passage of time to determine.

The Lewinsky case shows how the news media report events. According to the Committee of Concerned Journalists, a watchdog group run by former *Los Angeles Times* media critic Tom Rosenstiel, the *Washington Post* went far beyond the *New York Times* in the use of single unnamed sources. The *Post* named sources only 16 percent of the time, compared with 53 percent for the *New York Times*. Furthermore, the *Post* relied on single anonymous sources in 26 percent of its attributions, compared with 8 percent for the *New York Times*.[24]

As described above, the news media have become increasingly reliant on visual and controversial news. In the process, some charge that the media overreact. The Lewinsky story dominated the news for several months, decreasing coverage of other important stories. For example, in the first two weeks after the Lewinsky story broke, stories that received less coverage included the pope's historic visit to Cuba, the showdown with Iraq over weapons inspections, federal budget negotiations, abortion clinic bombings, and the president's State of the Union address. Still other stories received virtually no coverage. The combined coverage of non-Lewinsky stories was reduced in both number of stories and minutes aired. There were 188 stories dealing with Monica Lewinsky, compared with 148 for all other stories during the period of January 21 to February 3, 1998. The Lewinsky story received twice as much airtime as all other stories combined,[25] nearly six times the time given the Iraq showdown and nearly eight times that given for the pope's visit to Cuba. As Table 8.1 indicates, in the first two weeks of the story, it occupied over one half of the news hole on the three major networks. In the first week alone it occupied 67 percent of the available news hole on the three networks.

Table 8.1
First Two Weeks of Network Coverage of Monica Lewinsky Story Compared with Other Stories (in Order of Minutes)

TOPIC	NUMBER OF STORIES	PERCENT OF TOTAL STORIES	AIRTIME (MINUTES)	PERCENT OF TOTAL AIRTIME
Clinton/Lewinsky	188	56	371.6	62
Iraq showdown	43	13	60.9	10
Pope's visit to Cuba	28	8.5	48	8
Karla Faye Tucker execution	17	5	29.1	5
El Nino	20	6	25.2	4
State of the Union Address	13	4	23.7	4
Abortion clinic bombings	10	3	11.3	2
Federal budget negotiations	6	2	11.3	2
Super Bowl	6	2	9	2
Unabomber trial	5	1.4	4.7	1

Source: Adapted from Center for Media and Public Affairs, "Scandal Watch," *www.cmpa.com*, June 3, 1998. Period covers January 21, 1998 to February 3, 1998.

Between January 21 and March 31, 1998, the three major networks allocated an average of forty stories a week, nearly seventy-three hours and one fifth of the news hole, to the Lewinsky story. The story had several implications. First, during the first weeks after the story broke, most of the news was negative. Second, the first two weeks accounted for 62 percent of all stories between January 21 and March 31, 1998. Further, these stories comprised one half of the airtime and nearly one third of the news holes available on the three networks, pushing other newsworthy events out of the telecasts.

Ms. Lewinsky's interview with Barbara Walters after the president's trial was a major moneymaker for ABC. The network charged $800,000 for a thirty-second commercial—five times the normal cost.[26] The interview furthered the debate over the blurring of lines between "news" and "entertainment," resulting in the production of what some refer to as "infotainment."

Furthermore, the three major networks were consumed with other Clinton scandals in 1996 and 1997. Those scandals were among the top ten stories in both years, and averaged 5 percent of stories aired on the network newscasts. The Lewinsky story was linked to those other scandals and did lead ultimately to the impeachment of the president, but the extensive coverage still raises several questions. Are the media so drawn to the dramatic that other issues do not receive adequate coverage? Are the media controlling the presidential-media relationship? Does media coverage reflect the real world of politics? Should the story have so dominated the news that it cast a negative light not only on President Clinton but on the presidency as well?

The clinton impeachment and Trial

The actual impeachment and trial of President Clinton raise more issues. Surveys indicate that the impeachment and trial neither engaged the public nor changed their minds about Clinton's performance as president. Less than one third of the public claimed to have paid very close attention to the Senate trial and only 15 percent said they watched much of the live coverage.[27] By a two-to-one margin, the public said they wanted the president to remain in office, and 76 percent felt the trial was too partisan.[28]

Faced with the choice of airing the hearings versus soap operas, the major broadcast networks passed up gavel-to-gavel coverage. Bob Murray, a senior vice president of ABC News and a veteran of twenty-three years with ABC, stated he "could not have imagined a year ago that broadcast networks could choose to largely ignore long airings of a House impeachment and a Senate trial and opt for highlighted coverage."[29] The cable channels—CNN, MSNBC, and FOX News—did carry gavel-to-gavel coverage, in addition to airing special nightly programs. Yet CNN's audience for the historic event did not match that for the Persian Gulf War, the

O.J. Simpson trial, or the Supreme Court confirmation hearings of Clarence Thomas.

The three major network news programs operate under different parameters than other media for they are parts of large conglomerates—General Electric, Disney, and Viacom. This allows them more discretion in programming, for short-term economic losses can be absorbed more easily. However, they have chosen to decrease their news operations, opting instead for more entertainment programming. In addition, the Internet provides other outlets for individuals to follow important stories. The growth of the Internet and the merging of representatives of different technologies, like AOL and Time Warner, offers new, instant access to political news. The question yet to be answered is whether the public will use this new medium as a source of political information.

The white House press corps

In theory, press conferences provide a conduit for accurate information from the president to the public. In reality, presidents have been disenchanted with them as a means of communication because they have become increasingly confrontational. For example, after President Clinton commented on hate crimes in a 1997 press conference at George Washington University in November, the first comment directed to him by a member of the audience was, "You murdered Vince Foster and it's not a hate crime."[30] Such confrontations have led presidents to seek other means of communicating with the American people.

The White House was once the most prestigious news assignment, but it has become less so in recent years. Over 1,700 members of the media are currently accredited to cover the White House, but only about sixty to seventy do so on a regular basis. Another hundred or so check in from time to time, depending on the news. Those who cover the White House have considerable experience and substantial reputations. They represent prestigious media outlets: the major daily newspapers, a number of large newspaper chains, television networks, newsmagazines, and the wire services.

Frequently a reporter who has covered a presidential candidate during the campaign is assigned to the White House when that candidate is elected. For example, Ed Bradley covered Jimmy Carter for CBS and Bill Plante covered Ronald Reagan for CBS. Often top correspondents from the president's home state are assigned if they are available. Dan Rather, a Texan, covered the White House for CBS during the Johnson presidency.

White House reporters gather most news from the president's press secretary's daily briefings and from news releases prepared by the press office. They also obtain information from members of the White House staff. Presidential interviews are relatively rare, but members of the White House press corps attend all presidential speeches and regularly travel with the president.

The senior White House wire service reporter, for many years Helen Thomas of UPI, opens presidential news conferences, asks the first question, and closes them with the traditional "Thank you, Mr. President." The members of the White House press corps form the core of the 500 or so reporters who regularly attend presidential news conferences.

Members of the White House press corps frequently complain that most of the information they receive comes from the press secretary. In addition, unlike their predecessors, the reporters today are not free to roam the White House. The Clinton White House was particularly skillful at controlling information, particularly through the use of "quick response." Whenever an unfavorable news story broke, the White House press section immediately responded with its own "spin" on the event. Another complaint of the corps is that much of the news they receive is inconsequential. During the Reagan administration the corps complained that they did not have enough contact with the president and that when he did communicate with them, it took the form of "on the run" answers to questions. This, they argued, gave them no opportunity to get in-depth responses.

Some have criticized the White House press corps for being too easily intimidated by the White House. Timothy Crouse first raised this charge during the Nixon administration[31] and the charge has been repeated with nearly every administration since. The media received a great deal of criticism over this issue during the Reagan administration, which was noted for its ability to defuse media criticism and gained a large measure of deference from them.[32] This was attributed to the president's naturally cheerful personality, which became the focus of many stories. The "Teflon president" was assigned some mystical capacity to remain untarnished by negative political events. But Michael Parenti notes, "In fact the press itself was acting as his 'Teflon shields' by treating him almost reverentially and being unwilling to direct criticism at him for the policies and scandals of his administration."[33] However, the media did criticize the dismantling of decades of domestic social policy, tax cuts that benefited the wealthiest in society, and growth of nation's largest deficit in history, all of which occurred during the Reagan administration.

Other administrations also benefited from periods of a generally favorable press. The Bush administration's handling of the press corps during the Gulf War was particularly efficient. Few reporters questioned the administration's version of the events leading up to the nation's military involvement. Likewise, the Clinton administration was generally able to place a favorable "spin" on media stories.

Despite occasional complaints, when a president makes a major international trip, the press has been more than willing to accompany him. When President Nixon made his historic visit to China in 1972, eighty-seven members of the press accompanied him. Three years later, when President Ford traveled to China, 150 media personnel covered the trip. In 1984, when President Reagan traveled to China, 260 members of the media accompanied him. Five years later, 200 reporters covered President Bush's trip to China. Finally, on President Clinton's June 1998 trip there were 350 members of the media. The media have averaged nearly 40 percent of the entire delegations traveling to China with presidents.

presidential agenda setting

The Office of White House Communications

As presidents became more disenchanted with press conferences, they searched for other means of getting their messages out. In 1968 President Nixon, motivated by his longtime distrust and fear of the media and the federal bureaucracy and his long history of unpleasant experiences with them, created the first White House Office of Communications and appointed his long-time friend, George Klein, as head. Second, the Nixon White House was divided into two groups, the supporters of H.R. Haldeman and those who sided with George Klein and Robert Finch. Both groups had long and strong ties to Nixon but different views of what would best serve the president. The new office was a means of keeping the two camps separate by providing Klein and his supporters an important position within the White House while at the same time making Haldeman, a representative of the more aggressive faction, chief of staff. Third, the office allowed the Nixon White House to establish direct access to local media and to avoid, or at least minimize, contact with the traditional Washington and New York media centers.[34]

By the time of Nixon's resignation, the Office of Communications had developed three distinguishable roles. First, it served as the liaison with non-Washington-based media, thereby decreasing the role of the Washington media. Second, it served as a means of coordinating the flow of information from the executive office and thus gained more control over the news agenda. Finally, it served as a political tool for generating public support for administration initiatives. The office was tested during the aftermath of the Watergate break-in. It had to handle the initial story, develop a public position for the administration, and ultimately decide how to portray the president and his administration during the Watergate hearings. One side effect of the scandal was that the media became increasingly hostile toward the presidency and the White House.

All succeeding administrations have had an office of communications. In two brief periods, in the Ford and the Carter administrations, the press office became the center of communications, but in each instance the White House Communication Office was eventually reactivated. The exact organizational scheme has changed not only between administrations but also within them. During the Bush administration the office had five major components: media relations, public affairs, speech writing, research, and public liaison. The Clinton White House structured the office to include the press office, media affairs, planning, research, foreign affairs, news analysis, policy coordination, and speech writing.[35] The office reflects the personality of the president, the comfort he feels with the media, and the nature of the times. However, it has consistently handled such duties as mailings, briefings, contacts with regional media, and serving as a liaison with public affairs officers of other departments and key agencies within the executive branch. About twenty persons have held the title of director since the office's origins.

Public Relations

The ability of the president to structure his message has drastically changed with advances in technology and social science and market research. Modern presidents employ "focus groups," small numbers of people who react to proposed messages to gauge their likely reception prior to their delivery. After the groups react, the president and his staff may rework a message to capitalize on positive feedback from the group and avoid the negative responses. Presidents have increasingly used in-house polling to determine the public's feeling on various issues. This information is then used to refine the president's position.

These techniques help ensure the president's messages will contain material that is short and thematic and embodies the most effective "sound bite" for the evening news. Visuals have become very important because they are easier to remember and leave a more lasting impression than words. Presidents have always been in the business of "selling" their policies, but today's methods are so subtle that the public is frequently unaware of them. This has led John Maltese, in his book *Spin Control*, to conclude, "Style is substituted for substance. Complicated issues are transformed into simple slogans and slick sound-bites. . . .Timid, self-interested policymakers . . . shy away from responsibility for their own actions and delude themselves and their constituents with their own symbolic spectacle."[36]

The presidency offers a unique insight into the changing relations between government officials and the media. The combination of advances in technology, increasingly adversarial relations, and a public that receives the majority of its information about politics from television have all helped change the relationship between the media and the presidency. However, as noted earlier, each needs the other, and that fact alone explains their evolution.

summary

No institution captures the public's and media's attention more than the presidency. Modern presidents have used the media to draw closer to the public, whether through Franklin D. Roosevelt's use of the radio in "fireside chats" or by "going public," a technique first used by Jimmy Carter that involves communicating directly with the public and thereby controlling the context of the communication. However, the mass media's reporting of the president has become increasingly negative. Both Presidents Bush and Clinton received more negative stories than positive.

The declining use of formal presidential news conferences is due in part to other media outlets that give presidents more control and greater exposure. The increase in cable television has drastically expanded viewer choice. A more visible change has been the declining coverage of the presidency by the mainstream media that began in the 1980s and continues today.

The media's reliance on drama and sensationalism has affected the presidency. The Monica Lewinsky affair tarnished both the presidency and the media, and led the nation through prolonged turmoil. The story had all the drama and sensationalism of a soap opera, and the media devoted a disproportionate amount of their time to reporting it, blurring the lines between news and entertainment. However, some journalists became concerned over the way the story was reported as traditional reporting standards were dismissed. As important as the story may have been, its initial disclosure distracted the media's attention from other important events.

The White House press has a long history of reporting on events associated with the president, his policies, and his family. As Washington reporters have found themselves competing with other media representatives, they have become more hostile in their questioning of presidents. Nevertheless, increasing numbers of reporters accompany the president on his foreign travels.

Finally, presidents attempt to control the news and set the public agenda through formal structures, such as the White House Office of Communication, as well as through the use of sophisticated public relations techniques. Presidential messages are shaped by the many public relations assets available to the president.

Endnotes

[1]Martha Joynt Kumar, "The White House Beat at the Century Mark," *Press/Politics*, 2(Summer 1997):10–30.

[2]*Ibid.*

[3]*Ibid.*

[4]Thomas Dye, Harmon Ziegler, and S. Robert Lichter, *American Politics in the Media Age*, 4th ed. (Pacific Grove, Calif.: Brooks/Cole Publishing Co., 1992), 223.

[5]Timothy E. Cook, *Governing with the News* (Chicago: University of Chicago Press, 1998), 122.

[6]Barbara Pfetsch, "Government News Management," in Doris Graber, Denis McQuail, and Pippa Norris, eds., *The Politics of News* (Washington, D.C.: Congressional Quarterly Press, 1998), 79.

[7]Theodore Lowi, *The Personal President* (Ithaca, N.Y.: Cornell University Press, 1985), 69–70.

[8]*Ibid.*

[9]Fred I. Greenstein, "The Psychological Functions of the Presidency for Citizens," in Elmer E. Cornwall, ed., *The American Presidency: Vital Center* (Glenview, Ill.: Scott, Foresman, 1966), 30–36.

[10]*Ibid.*

[11]Samuel Kernell, *Going Public*, 3rd ed. (Washington, D.C.: Congressional Quarterly Press, 1997), 95.

[12]Donald T. Regan, *For the Record: From Wall Street to Washington* (San Diego: Harcourt Brace Jovanovich, 1988), 247.

[13]For a more detailed account of the media's treatment of the Reagan presidency, see Mark Hertstgaad, *On Bended Knee: The Press and the Reagan Presidency* (New York: Farrar, Straus & Giroux, 1988).

[14]Paul C. Light, *A Delicate Balance*, 2nd ed. (New York: Worth Publishers, 1999), 175.

[15]Colin Seymour-Ure, "Location, Location, Location: The Importance of Place in Executive Communication," *Press/Politics*, 2(Spring 1997):28.

[16]Matthew A. Baum and Samuel Kernell, "Has Cable Ended the Golden Age of Presidential Television?" *American Political Science Review*, 93(March 1999):99–114.

[17]*Ibid.*, 107.

[18]Richard L. Berke, "You May or May Not Have Clinton Fatigue," *New York Times*, Sept. 26, 1999;4:6.

[19]Howard Kurtz, *Media Circus* (New York: Times Books, 1994), 308.

[20]*Ibid.*

[21]Jarol B. Manheim, "The Honeymoon's Over: The News Conference and the Development of Presidential Style," *Journal of Politics*, 41(1979):55–74.

[22]*Ibid.*

[23]President Clinton press conference, May 7, 1993, Washington, D.C.

[24]John B. Judis, "Below the Beltway: Irresponsible Elites," Washington, D.C., March 5, 1998, espn.org/prospect/38/38/judifs.html.

[25]Center for Media and Public Policy press release, "Scandal Watch," *www.cmpa.com*, June 30, 1998.

[26]"1998 Year in Review," *Media Monitor*, 13(January/February 1999).

[27]The Pew Research Center for the People & the Press Poll, "Senate Trial: Little Viewership, Little Impact," January 21, 1999, 1.

[28]*Ibid.*

[29]Tim Jones, "TV Faces the Yawn of History," *Chicago Tribune*, August 4, 1999;3:1.

[30]Speech at George Washington University, November 10, 1997. For nonattributed question, see White House Office of Press Secretary release, November 10, 1997.

[31]Timothy Crouse, *The Boys on the Bus* (New York: Ballantine Books, 1972).

[32]David L. Paletz, *The Media in American Politics* (New York: Longman, 1999), 245.

[33]Michael Parenti, *Inventing Reality*, 2nd ed. (New York: St. Martin's Press, 1993), 14.

[34]For a detailed description of the development of White House news control, see John Anthony Maltese, *Spin Control*, 2nd ed. (Chapel Hill: The University of North Carolina Press, 1994).

[35]*Ibid.*, 253.

[36]*Ibid.*, 6.

congress and the media

Although the framers of the Constitution envisioned Congress as the dominant institution of national government, that position has gradually been usurped by the executive branch. Two factors have contributed heavily to this shift. First, a variety of events that required a single voice to speak to and on behalf of the nation directed the nation's attention to the presidency. These included the Great Depression, World Wars I and II, the Korean and Vietnam Wars, the civil rights movement, the Watergate, Iran-contra, Kosovo, the Whitewater scandals and the impeachment and trial of President Clinton, and countless natural disasters. In each case either the public turned to the president for leadership or the president was the center of national media attention. Second, as more Americans turned to the electronic media (particularly television) for information, those holding or seeking the office of president were the first to successfully employ television and, as a consequence, to develop a national following. Congress found itself struggling to regain not only political power but also the media's and the public's attention.

There are also institutional obstacles to extensive media coverage of Congress. First, congressional activity can be boring and complex, bound as it is by rules and procedures. Second, there are 435 members in the House of Representatives and 100 members in the Senate, resulting in many conflicting voices on various policies. Third, today's media are less prepared to cover the intricacies of congressional activities because of the rapid pace of communication, which places heavy emphasis on the latest-breaking news story. One consequence is that fewer reporters cover Congress in the depth and detail that was once the norm. Today's congressional reporters do not enjoy the same personal relationships with members as those in past decades. For all these reasons, Congress receives less media attention than the presidency.

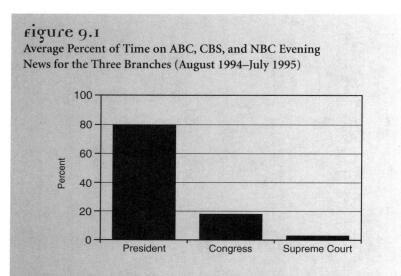

figure 9.1
Average Percent of Time on ABC, CBS, and NBC Evening
News for the Three Branches (August 1994–July 1995)

Source: Adapted from Doris A. Graber, *Mass Media and American Politics*, 5th ed.
(Washington, D.C.: Congressional Quarterly Press, 1997), Table 9-2:272.

congressional coverage

Is the media's coverage of Congress inadequate? The answer depends on one's perspective. Doris Graber compared the three major television networks' coverage of Congress from August 1994 through July 1995 with that for the president and the Supreme Court.[1] She studied the placement, timing, and numbers of stories, and found the White House dominated nightly newscasts (Figure 9.1). While the media's selection and coverage of issues that involved both Congress and the president were similar, there were significant differences in the numbers of stories and the times allotted to them. The total percent of the stories focusing on the president was 80 percent, compared to 17 percent for Congress. This translates into four times as many presidential stories as congressional.[2] Thus, Congress competes for the leftovers after the president has received prime-time network coverage.

However, these figures can be misleading, since local media furnish most congressional coverage. Members of Congress are acutely aware of the need for local exposure. They have local offices and make numerous appearances before community groups, which are carried by the local media, usually newspapers or radio stations. While these media do not provide the wide exposure of national or regional media, they help members of the Congress relate to their local constituents in a positive manner.

figure 9.2
Confidence in Congress, 1971–96

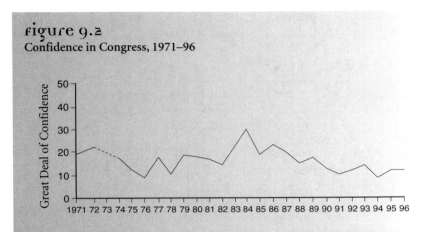

Source: John R. Hibbing and Elizabeth Theiss-Morse, "The Media's Role in Public Negativism Toward Congress: Distinguishing Between Emotional Reactions and Cognitive Evaluations," *American Journal of Political Science*, 42(April 1998): 484. Reprinted by permission of the University of Wisconsin Press.

As Figure 9.2 indicates, the public's confidence in Congress has undergone significant decline since 1986. However, while citizens do not place great confidence in Congress as an institution, they do have confidence in their own representatives, invariably giving them higher ratings than Congress as a whole. One reason for this is the effect of local media exposure for representatives, who usually receive very positive coverage. Therefore, the media's impact on Congress must be viewed at two levels. At the national level, members of Congress receive much less exposure than the president and that exposure is frequently negative. At the local level, newspapers, local television stations, and local cable networks and radio stations present a more complete and positive image.

One indication of the importance assigned to Congress by the media is the fact that there are over 7,000 members in the congressional press corps. This translates into seventy members of the press corps for each senator and sixteen for each representative. There are four press galleries on Capitol Hill for the daily publications, periodicals, photographers, and radio and television. Given these numbers, it would seem that Congress has more than enough paths for exposure.

However, the coverage of Congress follows a pattern that has evolved in media coverage of other aspects of politics—substance is secondary to the "game." As in election coverage, the focus is on winners and losers at the expense of issues and positions. Coverage of the congressional process generally focuses who is winning and who is losing political battles, not on the substance of the issues being debated. Representative David Obey (Democrat from Wisconsin) elaborated on this point at a conference on the media and Congress in 1981. He argued that the Democrats' complaints about the economic assumptions and arithmetic underlying the Reagan administration's spending and tax-cut program received inadequate media coverage. "The focus was on who was winning and losing politically," he complained, "not on the details."[3] As a result, the Reagan program passed, leading to an unprecedented tripling of the deficit in the 1980s, which became a major political issue in 1990s.

In addition to reporting the "game" rather than the substance, a number of studies have shown that the media have become increasingly negative in their reporting on Congress. Mark Rozell, in a content analysis of three major weekly newsmagazines and three national newspapers, concluded that "negativity and superficial congressional coverage is nothing new but in recent years the extent and tone have become more severe, more disturbing. . . . Many reports resort to humiliating caricature."[4] In addition, he found that "influential editorialists and columnists had nothing positive to say about the institution."[5] Charles Tidmarch and John Pitney confirmed this pattern of coverage in their analysis of ten major daily newspapers. They concluded that congressional coverage stressed perceived breaches of trust that only served to "harden the image of Congress as a defective institution."[6] Robert Lichter and Daniel Amundson, in their study of television's coverage between 1972 and 1992, found that stories about Congress and policy matters declined nearly 20 percent, while stories about congressional scandals increased 400 percent.[7] They also found that nine out of ten stories were critical of Congress. In a survey, Kimberly Coursen Parker found radio talk show hosts gave Congress the lowest rating of any of the mass media.[8]

What is the effect of the media's coverage on the public's perception of Congress? John R. Hibbing and Elizabeth Theiss-Morse addressed this question in their study of the media and Congress.[9] Drawing on a random survey of 1,400 national respondents, the authors set out to test their thesis that the media affect people's emotional reactions toward Congress but not their cognitive evaluations. The distinction is important, for it helps explain the public's negative perceptions. The authors contend that there is a difference between attitudes toward the collective membership of Congress and Congress as a body with a history, buildings, and a constitutional role in government, and that these distinctions have been blurred in analyses of the public's perception of the institution. The key issue is whether people differ in their cognitive and emotional evaluations of the Congress. A cognitive judgment is more likely to be thoughtful and deliberate, while emotional responses are instinctive reactions "from the gut." Studies have shown that there is greater consistency between attitudes and behavior when people make judgments based on emotions than when they make judgments based on cognitions.[10]

The Hibbing and Theiss-Morse study concluded that people who primarily obtained their news from television or radio were not any more or less likely to evaluate Congress negatively than people who primarily obtained their information from newspapers, that people exposed to a great deal of news did not evaluate Congress more negatively than those who pay little attention to the news did, and that a primary reliance on television and especially radio for news and generally heavy exposure to the news generated significantly more negative *emotions* toward Congress than newspaper use and low exposure to the news.[11]

congress in transition

Richard Fenno, in his famous work of representatives' "home style" in their districts, concluded that House members have two careers, one at home and the other in Washington.[12] Members seek to establish a strong image in Washington to transfer it back home. They seek to avoid blame for congressional actions that are unpopular at home, and to win publicity and power for themselves at the expense of the institution and public policy. This makes it more difficult for parties to maintain harmony among their members and get legislation passed.

When the cost of inaction by Congress is perceived to be greater than the cost of action, the media are important to legislation. In this environment the media can perform a strategic role in three ways. First, they can draw attention to the inaction and thereby apply pressure on Congress to take action. Second, they can concentrate attention on those opposing congressional action while providing the public with a policy alternative to inaction. Third, they can protect members from the potentially negative consequences of their vote. Douglas Arnold, in *The Logic of Congressional Action*, developed the concept of "traceability."[13] He argued that members are more inclined to anticipate public reaction when a particular policy or political result can be traced back to their action or vote. Members then must decide to vote with public opinion in their district or to protect themselves through the use of parliamentary maneuvers. The media are critical to a member's "traceability" on issues. If members believe their positions on an issue have not been exposed by the media, then those positions are "untraceable." One of the most important functions of media coverage of Congress is providing the public with information on how members acted (voted for or against, abstained, or not present) on various issues.

The media's double-edged sword can be seen in the story of Newt Gingrich and the 104th Congress. Republicans regained control of Congress in 1994 with the aid of their "Contract with America," a set of policies that were given catchy titles based in part on focus groups and opinion polls. The media helped Gingrich focus attention on the contract and maintain unity among Republican members of Congress. The available evidence suggests that the contract did not have much impact on individual congressional campaigns and that most Americans were unfamiliar with it, but it did provide the media with a shorthand in its reporting of the 1994 election.

However, the media soon became a problem for Gingrich. By relying on the media's attention in the 1994 elections, he became a media personality. His image was frequently pitted against that of President Clinton and his popularity in the public opinion polls soon dropped. Gingrich's negatives became a key factor in the elections of 1996 and 1998. When the White House and Congress were deadlocked over a budget bill, it was Gingrich and congressional Republicans who received the blame from those surveyed.

chan9in9 folkways: members and the media

The return of Republican control of the House and the Senate after forty years hastened a change in the behavior of members of Congress. Congress had long had institutional norms that members adhered to. Writing about the traditions that governed members of the House of Representatives, Charles Clapp noted that "traditions and folklore . . . serve to impress on them the virtues of being patient and not being troublesome. They operate to restrain a freshman from exercising his impulse to plunge wholeheartedly into all aspects of House activity. . . ."[14] Former Speaker Sam Rayburn once advised new members "to get along, go along, and that a man is never defeated by a speech he didn't make."[15] Donald Matthews, in his classic work *U.S. Senators & Their World*, addressed the folkways of the Senate, which has always been the more formal of the two houses in rules, dress, and behavior.[16] Folkways are the customs and traditions that operate in Congress and that have evolved over the years. They are the unwritten rules in the operation of each house. For example, seniority long governed the selection of committee and subcommittee chairs. The member of the majority party who had served on the committee longest normally became its chair. Another governing tradition is the collegiality members normally exhibit when they address one another from the floor. This was evident in the behavior of members during the impeachment hearings and trial.

Congressional folkways began to weaken in the 1960s, when Congress and the president became locked in a battle over the Vietnam war and television became a significant political instrument. Just as the president came to circumvent the traditional media, so members of Congress used the media to evade institutional folkways. However, this development eventually limited Congress's ability to act collectively.

At the same time that they were using the media, however, beginning in the 1980s and through the 1994 election, the Republican Party used polls indicating the public's dissatisfaction with the mass media. Many politicians played to this sentiment and ran against the mainstream media to exploit the public's hostility, even as they hypocritically used the media themselves.

While many members broke with congressional traditions, no one used the media more effectively than Newt Gingrich. Since his first election to Congress in 1978, the Georgia Republican had used the media to circumvent the House's traditions. He paid little attention to his committee assignments or to short-term legislative achievements. He focused instead on the broad picture, and instructed Republican leaders to avoid accommodations with Democrats.[17] "Gingrich may well have loved to blast the news media for what he called a 'disinformation' campaign against him," writes Matthews. "But only Richard Nixon could rival Gingrich in being simultaneously a creation of the news media and its harshest critic."[18]

Gingrich's success in gaining a majority in the House was in part associated with his communications strategy. Hedrick Smith, in *The Power Game*, quotes Gingrich as having stated, "Be splashy; be original; be outrageous; be strident; even be inflammatory."[19] When Gingrich became Minority Leader in the House in 1989, his use of the media to carry the message of the conservatives in Congress became increasingly important to the broader strategy of electing more conservatives to Congress. With the introduction of television cameras in the House of Representatives in 1979 and the Senate in 1986, the dynamics of Congress changed. Members would make impassioned speeches in the chambers of an empty House and Senate, although the viewers did not know the chambers were empty because the cameras were fixed in place. It was C-SPAN that brought these images into the homes of America. The free television was particularly beneficial to Republican members of the House because it gave them a television audience, albeit small, for their attacks on the Democratic majority. Gingrich first won national attention through his late-night tirades on C-SPAN, needling then-House Speaker Tip O'Neill and painting the Democrats as "corrupt thugs." Ironically, it was Speaker O'Neill, a Democrat, who championed the initiative to have cameras in the House and the Republicans were the beneficiaries of his initiative.

Since news broadcasts are always looking for the dramatic, sensational, and brash, it is not surprising that members of Congress quickly adopted the aggressive individualism this new technology allowed. This new behavior is also reflected in the time and money allocated to media relations by individual members of Congress. Dwight Morris of the *Los Angeles Times* found that $69 million was spent on congressional television and radio ads in 1994 and that this represented a 60 percent increase from 1990.[20] Media expense caused former Senator Bill Bradley to observe, "You simply transfer money from contributors to television stations."[21] Media costs are part of the drive for campaign finance reform. The most recognizable members spend more time on image building, sound bites, and visual bites than on the complexities of the legislative process.

There are many examples of representatives who have high media profiles as a result of press conferences, appearances on television and radio talk shows, and a large presence in the print media. Newt Gingrich came to the attention of many through his use of the media. His aggressive style helped propel him into the national media spotlight and aided his rise within his party. Building on their successful media attacks and the perception the Democrats had controlled Congress too long, Gingrich and the Republican Party recaptured the majority in the congressional elections of 1994, and Gingrich became the Speaker of the House.

The Republican Party introduced its Contract with America in a staged media event in which Republican members of Congress signed a document that proclaimed a new Republican majority would immediately pass eight major reforms. These ranged from requiring all laws that applied to other Americans to apply to Congress to limiting the terms of those chairing committees and banning the practice of proxy voting. According to the contract, these reforms aimed at "restoring the faith and trust of the American people in government."[22]

The effects of the contract on the election were mixed. The contract gave Republican candidates the opportunity to campaign on national issues, rather than the localism that would benefit incumbent Democrats. It also provided a means of mobilizing the party. The Republicans challenged voters to throw them out if they broke the contract. Most important, the contract gave the media a shorthand angle for covering the election. However, post-election surveys found that 80 percent of voters had not heard of the contract and few had read it.

Following the election, Gingrich was elected Speaker of the House and was hailed as the architect of a new Republican revolution. He became the most media-oriented speaker in history, and was frequently quoted in the media. But this had unexpected consequences. When Gingrich made an off-the-cuff suggestion that he had allowed the government to close down during the budget impasse with the White House in 1996 to pay back President Clinton, who had not invited him to exit from the front of Air Force One on returning from the funeral of Israel's Prime Minister Rabin, the public quickly blamed the Republicans for the budget problems.

Gingrich's subsequent low popularity became an issue in the 1996 and 1998 elections. In 1996 CNN's Judy Woodruff referred to him as "too extreme" and "too scary."[23] In 1998 the Republicans barely held on to their majorities in both houses and began to question his leadership. While a number of issues contributed to the members' displeasure, Gingrich's last-minute decision to run ads, primarily in the South, that focused on the scandals surrounding President Clinton, backfired. The ads motivated Democratic voters and suppressed Republican turnout, which led to Democratic gains in the off-year election. After the Republicans' poor performance, Gingrich resigned from Congress. The case of Newt Gingrich shows how the media can perform both positive and negative roles for an individual, and how one can go from being their poster child to their foster child in a brief period.

Media coverage of congressional investigations

History has shown that politicians quickly adapt to each new medium. Today television is the most accepted and trusted form of political communication. Television's primary function is entertainment, which helps explain some of the difficulty Congress faces when it vies for media attention with the president. However, there have been times when Congress has upstaged the president and provided good theater in the process. Congressional hearings are the most effective way for Congress to capture the nation's attention. In the process, many relatively unknown politicians have become "showhorses," a term given to those who have high media visibility, as opposed to "workhorses," those who work to move the processes of government along.

Congressional hearings have performed important roles throughout the nation's history, but television introduced a new role. Television first had a major impact on the congressional process in May 1950, when the Senate Committee on Organized Crime investigated the link between organized crime and interstate commerce. Chairing the new committee was the junior Democratic senator from Tennessee, Estes Kefauver. The committee traveled to fourteen cities to take testimony exposing the links between organized crime and politics. These hearings were significant for two reasons. They were the first to be televised, and the subject, organized crime, provided drama. These hearings made not only Kefauver a household name, but also the names of organized crime figures. The televised hearings resulted in Kefauver's candidacy for the Democratic presidential nomination in 1952. However, local political machines—some with close ties to organized crime—denied him the nomination, and selected instead the highly regarded Illinois governor, Adlai Stevenson.

The 1950s also saw the rise of a previously unknown senator, Republican Joseph McCarthy of Wisconsin. After gaining the majority in the Senate, the Republicans gave the chairmanship of the committee investigating communist influence in government to McCarthy. McCarthy's televised committee hearings caused the nation to become obsessed with the "communist threat." McCarthy bullied and humiliated witnesses, and made unsubstantiated accusations against government officials and private citizens. The Senate ultimately censored his behavior, and the term "McCarthyism" is used today pejoratively to refer to someone who adopts extremely intolerant and self-righteous positions.

During the 1960s, Democratic Senator J. William Fulbright of Arkansas became well known when his Senate Foreign Relations Committee examined the conduct of the Vietnam War. When the first witness, Secretary of State Dean Rusk, appeared, CBS, the most profitable of the networks at the time, chose not to carry the hearings, instead opting for an *I Love Lucy* rerun while ABC and NBC carried the hearings. The resulting criticism led to the resignation of the president of CBS News. Senator Fulbright was among the first to question and oppose American involvement in Vietnam.

The highest drama in committee hearings in the modern media era was provided by the Watergate hearings in the 1970s. The drama was intense as members of the Nixon administration appeared before the Senate and House committees. The hearings produced daily drama that had viewers glued to their televisions. There were heroes, villains, and mystery persons (Deep Throat), all the elements needed for drama. However, the stakes were real, the nation's stability tested, and history made as the first sitting president resigned from office. Some have argued that this was the point when American journalism began to deviate from its established norms. *Washington Post* reporters Bob Woodward and Carl Bernstein were credited with exposing President Nixon's misdeeds and their resulting fame inspired other young journalists to aggressively investigate other public officials at the national, state, and local levels. Others, however, have argued that the media should not receive credit for exposing Watergate because governmental agencies were already uncovering the scandal.[24] Regardless of the correct interpretation, a new ethos between the media and public offices began as the media became more skeptical of the public statements of all officials. The Watergate hearings became a kind of model for congressional investigations, and similar subsequent hearings have generally been televised.

During the 1980s and 1990s, Congress turned to televised hearings to address such issues as the handling of the Iran hostage crisis, Clarence Thomas's confirmation for the Supreme Court, the Waco siege, Whitewater, campaign finance reform, and the impeachment and trial of President Clinton. Clearly the media, and television in particular, have become a major part of the congressional investigative process.

As a new generation of lawmakers and voters have grown up in a media-rich environment, the connection between the media and the political process has become stronger than at any other time in history. The result is a tendency to seek individual visibility at the expense of legislative achievement. The folkways of the past have been abandoned and new ways of legislating are evolving, with the media as the channels of power.

congress on television

As mentioned above, in 1979 television cameras were first allowed to broadcast House proceedings. The House had held out against television in the chamber since the 1950s, when television was the newest medium of communication. The Watergate hearings had made television celebrities out of many members of Congress. The mid-1970s brought such changes as the introduction of *The MacNeil-Lehrer Report* on public television and *Good Morning America* on ABC.

As a result of these changes, Michael Robinson noted, "younger members and maverick members [had] more political visibility—and hence greater power—than ever before."[25] A generation that had grown up with television found it a natural part of campaigning. The class of 1974, which included such young Democrats as Timothy Wirth of Colorado, Thomas Downey and Stephen Solarz of New York, Tom Harkin of Iowa, Robert Edgar of Pennsylvania, and Chris Dodd and Toby Moffett of Connecticut, has been credited with changing the temperament of the Congress. Its members were independent voices, irreverent about the congressional establishment and folkways. They used television to take the lead on issues away from the party establishment. Four years later a large class of Republicans was elected who shared the same orientation toward the medium of television. Thus, in the post-Watergate years, the media were more attentive to politics and those seeking and holding office used this opportunity to achieve increased media exposure.

The placing of cameras in the House and Senate and the government's sponsorship of C-SPAN as a means to provide extensive coverage would seem to have "opened the process" to more citizens. However, since 1979 Congress has restricted the public's ability to view its deliberations by limiting what the cameras can show and cutting back the distribution of C-SPAN telecasts. Government technicians produce congressional television, and strict rules govern the pictures provided from the two chambers. In 1992, Congress passed the Cable Television Consumer Protection and Competition Act, which provided programming produced by federal licensed broadcast stations the first right of access to local cable systems, and thus priority over C-SPAN or any other cable network. The direct effect on C-SPAN was to eliminate nearly 10 percent of its customer base. In 1995, C-SPAN, along with the other major networks, sent letters to Speaker Newt Gingrich and Senate Majority Leader Bob Dole asking them to allow live broadcasts from the chambers. Senator Dole said he "would take a serious look at anything that increases public access."[26] However, Congress has still not expanded media coverage of its deliberations.

congressional impeachment and the media

The impeachment and trial of President Clinton provoked another clash between Senate traditions and contemporary public demands for openness in government. One issue involved the proposal to open the trial to cameras. CNN asked Chief Justice William Rehnquist to open all the proceedings, arguing that to do otherwise violated the First Amendment. Part of the argument was the change in society. Senator Kay Bailey Hutchison, Republican of

Texas, noted, "Our society in 1868—and more significantly still, our law in 1868—was far different than it is today. The First Amendment jurisprudence as we know it—as it governs and binds the Senate—is essentially a creature of the 20th century. That jurisprudence assures public scrutiny, not public ignorance."[27] Senate Republicans defeated the proposal, contending that it would break the rules and traditions of the Senate.

A second issue concerned televising the actual vote on guilt. As Senator Hutchison stated, "People have come to expect more knowledge of their government's decision-making process."[28] She noted that a plan to open the Senate for the vote would not overturn Senate precedent but return it to the tradition of open trials that began with Samuel Chase's trial in 1805 and ended with President Andrew Johnson's proceedings sixty-four years later. How-ever, other senators argued that the prying eye of the camera and the outside world would affect the debate. Ultimately the senators decided cameras would violate the Senate's customs and traditions.

The Republican-led House of Representatives became part of American history when it voted the Articles of Impeachment against President Clinton in December 1998, making Bill Clinton only the second president in history to be impeached.[29] The media attention, particularly television, had a direct effect on the behavior of House members. Prior to the beginning of the hearings, Robert Wexler, Democrat of Florida, told an interviewer, "I'm not going to reply to the gentleman from Georgia because the two of us are going to appear on the TV show *Crossfire* tonight, and I'll reply to him then. I don't want to spoil the show."[30] Christopher Cannon, Republican of Utah, admitted he had left his seat to go outside in the hall and see how the hearings "looked" on television. Others, like Congressman Howard Coble, Republican of North Carolina, acknowledged that the spirited orations were intensified by television: "Actually, we get along pretty well together when the TV lights are extinguished."[31]

These comments illustrate two points. First, members of Congress have become increasingly adroit at using the media. Second, the media affect the legislative process by altering the behavior of legislators. Today more politicians "play for the media" through the use of sound and video bites that make the national news. The media have personalized congressional behavior to a degree unprecedented in American history. This personalization transcends political parties, and makes members captive to those who have high media profiles.

The media's role in the process included not simply how members of Congress reacted to the coverage, but also how the media reacted to the historical event. The coverage of the impeachment process exposed changes in the media's beliefs about "newsworthiness" and "objectivity." Tabloid personalities like Larry Flynt and Matt Drudge were frequently interviewed, thereby becoming associated with the mainstream media. However, the driving force behind the obsession to report the lurid, the sensational, and the provocative was technological developments in the media. The insatiable appetite of all-news television channels and Web sites, for example, requires a constant infusion of new material. These demands caused leaks and unsubstantiated material to be accepted and disseminated too quickly, complicating an already complex story and leaving the public turned off by both the politicians and the media.

The general public eventually perceived the impeachment hearings and subsequent trial as a mixture of serious charges, partisanship, and showmanship. For this and other reasons, the public's perception of the Republican leadership in Congress from 1997 through the end of 1998 remained low. According to Louis Harris polls during the period, only 36 percent of the public rated Republicans as doing an "excellent/pretty good job" and 59 percent viewed their performance as "only fair/poor."

Impeachment did drive up viewing levels for virtually every television news outlet that covered it, but not to the extent of some other major news events of recent years, including the death of Princes Diana and the O.J. Simpson trial. CBS, which was obligated to cover the New York Jets/Buffalo Bills football game, drew higher ratings than did channels covering the impeachment vote. The football game drew 12 million viewers at its peak, more than doubling the viewership for ABC and NBC coverage of the impeachment vote. As Table 9.1 shows, the public did not follow the impeachment vote very closely. In fact, it did not fall within the top ten stories in terms of public attention.

Doris Graber and Brian White studied the media's coverage of the Senate vote that ended the trial of President Clinton.[32] They sampled a cross section of media—newspapers, local and national television news programs, newsmagazines, and the Internet—and drew several conclusions. They found that the coverage was prominent and ample, suggesting that the vote was indeed a significant event. The media stressed the likely consequences of the vote more than the story's background. The exception to this was the Internet, where numerous links to past and present impeachment stories were available. Most stories were framed to deal with speculation and interpretation—what did the vote really mean? With few exceptions, coverage characteristics, including framing, were quite similar across all media, laying the basis for a unified collective memory. Finally, the overwhelming majority of sources represented Republican viewpoints, generally divided between members of the House and Senate. These findings suggest that news coverage, with the exception of the Internet, lacked diversity.

congress under media siege

Congress has long been a target of media criticism. However, changes in the media brought about by mergers, increased competition, and an increasingly apathetic public have led to an unfavorable portrayal of the institution and its members. That portrayal has in turn created an increasingly

Table 9.1
Public Attention to Top Stories of 1998

STORY	PERCENT FOLLOWING VERY CLOSELY
Jonesboro, Ark., shooting	49
Oregon high school shooting	46
U.S. Capitol shooting	45
Military strikes against Iraq	44
Military strikes in Sudan and Afghanistan	44
Outcome of 1998 elections	42
Unseasonable weather	39
Nationwide heat wave	38
Conflict between Iraq and UN weapons inspectors	36
Clinton/Lewinsky investigation	36
House impeachment vote	*34*

Source: The Pew Research Center for the People & the Press press release, "Turned Off Public Tuned Out Impeachment," December 24, 1998.

negative public perception of the institution. In 1996, when individuals were asked, "When there are major disagreements between President Clinton and Congress, who do you tend to support, the President or Congress?" over half responded the president and one third the Congress. Those seeking seats in Congress have sought to use that negative perception to their own benefit. Challengers frequently attack Congress for its inability to act swiftly or to represent citizens' interests, and structure their campaigns to appeal to the generally negative attitudes toward Congress.

Washington Post reporter David Broder in a 1991 column laid the responsibility of the public's contempt for Congress at the feet of his own profession—the media. Many journalists, he wrote, had practiced a form of prejudice "that makes it impossible for people even to recognize individual differences within the reviled group."[33] He identified some of the members of Congress who were contributing in a positive manner and concluded, "Somehow, their efforts go largely uncelebrated in the press. It's easy to get on the best seller's list by writing of Congress as a 'Parliament of Whores' or to jump aboard the term limits bandwagon, feeding popular prejudice in the process. It takes more courage and independence to challenge the notion that everyone in Congress is crooked or incompetent or both. . . .Where is the journalism that reminds people that it's just as wrong to say that politicians are all the crooks as to pretend they are all saints?"[34]

Sensationalism has increasingly driven the media's reporting on Congress, focusing on transgressions of varying degrees of seriousness. Congress, the largest federal institution, provides many opportunities for transgressions. In the early 1990s, 269 House members were found to have overdrawn their house bank accounts, and twenty-four had committed serious abuses of the bank.[35] The Senate had the Keating Five, five senators who were accused of pressuring federal banking regulators on behalf of campaign contributor Charles Keating, head of the former Lincoln Savings and Loan. The ethics problems of House Speakers Jim Wright and Newt Gingrich and the sexual preferences of several House members all received prominent coverage. A sexual transgression led to the resignation of Speaker-elect Robert Livingston in 1998. Furthermore, after he left office in 1998, it was learned that Newt Gingrich had had an affair with a House aide that began in 1993. His involvement was particularly ironic when viewed against his strong criticisms of President Clinton's behavior. Airtime that could be used to inform the public about issues is instead used to create doubt, increase confusion, and diminish support for Congress.

The Media and Congressional Scandals

The movement away from "party-centered" and toward "candidate-centered" campaigns has given added weight to rumors, allegations, and innuendo. The media have reported instances of corruption and misbehavior with increasing frequency in recent years.[36] Campaigns have become increasingly personalized as candidates focus on their opponents' moral character, personal finances, daily habits, use of perquisites, and related matters. Susan Welch and John Hibbing examined the effects of charges of corruption on congressional voting between 1982 and 1992. They found that incumbents rarely lost in the primaries, but in the general elections corruption charges were associated with a 25 percent rate of defeat (nine times more than usual) and a decrease in voter turnout of 10 percent.[37] While the authors found a relationship between corruption and voter behavior, the question remains: why is the relationship so weak in a media-rich environment?

Daniel Shea provided one explanation when he focused on the local media's tendency to bolster an incumbent's positive image or provide a negative image.[38] Using data from the 1992 congressional check-kiting scandal, which revealed that many members of Congress had written checks when they had inadequate funds to cover them, he tested two hypotheses. The first was that the more local news coverage of an elected official's scandalous act, the more likely he or she would be defeated at the polls. The second was that the more negative the local media coverage or spin, the more likely the official would be defeated at the polls. Shea did not find support for the first hypothesis but did for the second. This finding suggests that local media are the key to whether members of Congress with scandals in their past escape or are punished at the polls.

Why the Negative Reporting?

Many studies have speculated about the reasons for the increasingly negative reporting of Congress. One partial explanation found by most studies is the changing nature of the media's reporting. Thomas Dye and Harman Zeigler have pointed to "a post-Watergate code of ethics" in which journalists seek out scandal and delve into the personal lives of public figures and other areas than were once considered off limits. Congressional scholar Norman Ornstein has also noted a new generation of investigative reporters, inspired by Watergate reporters Bob Woodward and Carl Bernstein, who have focused on scandal.[39] A second explanation is the tediousness of the legislative process. Former Senator Alan Simpson once described it as "the very driest of human endeavors."[40] Former White House speechwriter William Safire explained in a 1973 article that editors instruct reporters to avoid "MEGOs": stories that make "make eyes glaze over."[41] Third, complex stories about policy take longer to research and develop and do not arouse as many readers, viewers, or listeners as stories of transgressions. Finally, the competition for audiences drives the media to produce stories more quickly and to include the dramatic and sensational. Woodward and Bernstein noted in the 1970s that it was not unusual for a story to be delayed several weeks so reporters could authenticate it. This is a practice that is not available in today's media market.

summary

The media's coverage of Congress is considerably less extensive than its coverage of the president. The most important reason is that the president, unlike members of Congress, is seen as the "voice" of the American people. Congress, in contrast, consists of 535 members who represent smaller, more discrete constituencies. Yet there are similarities in the way the two institutions are covered. For example, the media are more interested in the legislative game—who's winning and who's losing—than in understanding policies and their implications. Also Congress, like the president, is portrayed in more negative than positive terms. In addition, congressional members are becoming more adroit at using the media to their advantage by producing sound bites and video bites to enhance their appeal both nationally and with their home constituents.

The changing media and political landscapes, which have moved the political process from one that was "party-centered" to one that is "candidate-centered," have resulted in the weakening of institutional folkways. The changes began in the 1950s, when television was first used by congressional investigative committees and made familiar the names of those involved. The impact of the media on the congressional process is changing as well. The impeachment of President Clinton shows that television's effect on the general public has changed. The public is not as dependent on television and does not view television news as regularly as it did in earlier decades. The media did, however, alter the behavior of some of the members involved in the political process.

Finally, changes in the media and in politics have brought the institution of Congress under greater scrutiny as the media seek out evidence of official and personal misconduct. This increased inspection of members' lives and the increasingly large amounts of money members feel they must spend on the media in their campaigns demonstrate the growing impact of the media on the political system.

ENDNOTES

[1]Doris A. Graber, *Mass Media and American Politics*, 5th ed. (Washington, D.C.: Congressional Quarterly Press, 1997), 289–293.

[2]*Ibid.*

[3]Rich Cohen, "Covering Congress," *National Journal*, 15(November 12, 1983):2376.

[4]Mark Rozell, "Press Coverage of Congress, 1946–1992," in Thomas E. Mann and Norman J. Ornstein, eds., *Congress, the Press, and the Public* (Washington, D.C: American Enterprise Institute and The Brooking Institute, 1994), 109.

[5]*Ibid.*, 108.

[6]Charles Tidmarch and John J. Pitney, "Covering Congress," *Polity*, 17(1985):482.

[7]Robert Lichter and Daniel Amundson, "Less News Is Worse News: Television News Coverage of Congress 1972–1992," in Thomas E. Mann and Norman J. Ornstein, eds., *Congress, the Press, and the Public* (Washington, D.C.: American Enterprise Institute and The Brookings Institute, 1994), 134.

[8]Kimberly Coursen Parker, "How the Press Views Congress," in Thomas E. Mann and Norman J. Ornstein, eds., *Congress, the Press, and the Public* (Washington, D.C.: American Enterprise Institute and The Brookings Institute, 1994), 160.

[9]John R. Hibbing and Elizabeth Theiss-Moore, "The Media's Role in Public Negativity Toward Congress: Distinguishing Emotional Reactions and Cognitive Evaluations," *American Journal of Political Science*, 42(April 1988):475–498.

[10]Abraham Tesser and G. Clary, "Affect Control: Process Constraints versus Catharsis," *Cognitive Therapy and Research*, 2(1978):265–274; Murray Millar and Abraham Tesser, "The Effects of Affective-Cognitive Consistency and Thought on the Attitude-Behavior Relationship," *Journal of Experimental Social Psychology*, 25(1989):189–202; and Timothy Wilson, Dana S. Dunn, Dolores Kraft, and Douglas J. Lisle, "Introspection, Attitude Change, and Attitude-

Behavior Consistency: The Disruptive Effects of Explaining Why We Feel the Way We Do," *Advances in Experimental Social Psychology*, 22(1989):287–343.

[11]Hibbing and Theiss-Morse, *op. cit.*, 494.

[12]Richard Fenno, *Home Style: House Members in Their Districts* (Boston: Little, Brown, 1978).

[13]Douglas Arnold, *The Logic of Congressional Action* (New Haven, Conn.: Yale University Press, 1990).

[14]Charles L. Clapp, *The Congressman* (Garden City, N.J.: Doubleday and Company, Inc., 1964), 12.

[15]*Ibid.*

[16]Donald Matthews, *U.S. Senators & Their World* (New York: Vintage Books, 1960), Chapter 5.

[17]Timothy E. Cook, "Evolution and Revolution," *Media Studies Journal*, 10(Winter 1996):17.

[18]*Ibid.*, 16.

[19]Hedrick Smith, *The Power Game: How Washington Works* (New York: Random House, 1988).

[20]Common Cause news release, "Channeling Influence: The Critical Role of Television in Political Campaigns," April 2, 1997.

[21]*Ibid.*

[22]*Republican Contract with America.*

[23] "The Janet Cooke Award," *MediaWatch*, January 1, 1996:2.

[24]Gladys Engle Lang and Kurt Lang, *The Battle for Public Opinion: The President, the Press, and the Polls During Watergate* (New York: Columbia University Press, 1983).

[25]Michael J. Robinson, "Three Faces of Congressional Media," in Thomas Mann and Norman Ornstein, eds., *The New Congress* (Washington, D.C.: American Enterprise Institute for Public Policy Research, 1981), 98.

[26]Cited in Brian Lamb, "Getting the Whole Truth," *Media Studies Journal*, 10(Winter 1996):76.

[27]Eric Smith, "Support Grows to Deliberate in Public View," *New York Times*, February 4, 1999:A19.

[28]*Ibid.*

[29]Andrew Johnson was impeached on February 24, 1868.

[30]Blackie Sherrod, "Cynicism Is No Longer the Exclusive Domain of Journalists," *Dallas Morning News*, December 17, 1998:39A.

[31]*Ibid.*

[32]Doris Graber and Brian White, "The Many Faces of News: From Mainstream Media to Cybermedia," paper presented at the 1999 Annual Meeting of the American Political Science Association, Atlanta, Ga., September 2–5, 1999. The study did not include radio.

[33]David Broder, "Yes, There Are Good People in Congress," *Washington Post*, November 6, 1991:A23.

[34]*Ibid.*

[35]David Johnston, "Investigators Find Evidence of Crime in House Banking Issue," *New York Times*, December 17, 1992:1A.

[36]Suzanne Garment, *Scandal: The Crisis of Mistrust in American Politics* (New York: Times Books, 1991).

[37]Susan Welch and John R. Hibbing, "The Effects of Charges of Corruption on Voting Behavior in Congressional Elections 1982–1990, *Journal of Politics*, 59(February 1997):226–239.

[38]Daniel M. Shea, "All Scandals Politics Is Local: Ethical Lapses, the Media, and Congressional Elections," *Press/Politics*, 4(Spring 1999):45–62.

[39]Thomas Dye and Harmon Zeigler, *American Politics in the Media Age*, 2nd ed. (Monterey, Calif.: Brooks/Cole, 1986; Norman J. Ornstein, "The Open Congress Meets the President," in Anthony King, ed., *Both Ends of the Avenue: The Presidency, the Executive Branch, and Congress in the 1980s* (Washington, D.C.: American Enterprise Institute, 1983), 201.

[40]Greg Schneiders, "The 90-Second Handicap: Why TV Coverage of Legislation Falls Short," *Washington Journalism Review*, 14(June 1985):44.

[41]William Safire, "The MEGO News Era," *Washington Star*, September 6, 1973:A15.

CHAPTER 10   The courts and the media

Through the years the courts have enjoyed the highest level of public support and confidence of the three branches of government. This has been attributed in large part to their low media visibility, as well as their structure and role in the political system. The lack of media exposure serves to shield the public from the complexities of the legal process, the often personal decision making, and the judges' very human personalities. However, in recent years, as the public has become increasingly concerned about crime, its frustration has been reflected in national surveys concerning the courts. In Harris surveys between 1995 and 1997, less than one third of those responding had "a great deal of confidence" in the U.S. Supreme Court, while over half indicated that they had "only some" confidence and 15 percent had "no confidence."[1] Another contributing cause to the public's decreasing confidence could be the media's coverage of the courts, which has been described by Philip Kurland as inept and abominable.[2] The public has a poor understanding of the fundamental process through which court proceedings become news, particularly at the trial level. Surveys indicate that most Americans cannot name the judges of the United States Supreme Court, and only a small percentage can identify the chief justice.

A look at how the media cover the Supreme Court is instructive. Except when landmark decisions are being handed down, about fifty reporters regularly cover the Court, primarily representatives of the major wire services, national newspapers, and broadcast networks. One reason for the sparse coverage is that the Court does not regularly produce the dramatic or sensationalistic stories the media normally feature.

Unlike their counterparts covering Congress, court reporters cover a relatively small and complex branch of government. Their task is to develop a basic understanding of the Court's latest rulings. A 1988 survey of court reporters found that, of the twenty-four who regularly covered the Supreme

Court, nine were lawyers.[3] Anthony Lewis claimed that, while covering the Court, he heard or looked at every *certiorari* petition, attempted to discuss the case with "informed lawyers," and attended all oral arguments.[4] In a period of rapid communication and competition, it is unlikely that most reporters prepare as thoroughly as Lewis, but most court reporters spend hours reading and analyzing decisions.

Charles Press and Kenneth VerBurg provide a portrait of the court journalist: "Reporters sit in a basement room waiting to be presented a complicated legal document that they quickly have to puzzle out for themselves. They cannot interview the major sources of the story to ask them what they meant . . . Meanwhile they know that . . . editors do not regard most judicial decisions as very important or newsworthy. . . . An ambitious reporter, already making a name in bylines, is likely to consider the Court a dead end."[5]

Unlike other reporters, court reporters show little evidence that they see themselves as watchdogs.[6] They face the difficult task of making judicial stories both understandable and accurate at a time when the media have become increasingly dependent on drama and sensationalism. Oversimplification, a common method in reporting political and social stories, is not an option in reporting court decisions because their significance is typically found in their subtleties.

Another distinction is that court reporters function in a less participatory environment than colleagues covering other institutions. Judges, for example, rarely give interviews or elaborate on their decisions. Unlike elected officials, they are not accountable to the electorate on a regular basis and therefore are not as concerned with the latest opinion poll or economic or foreign crisis. Court reporters generally have a deep respect for the courts, and rarely attack the judicial reasoning behind court decisions.

Court reporters have relatively short tenures. One reason is the demands of the job, outlined above. In addition, professional journalists need exposure to develop a reputation (and the larger salary that commands) and the Court does not provide much exposure. Reporters covering the Supreme Court increasingly compete for time, and often for stories, with those covering other branches of government, and they generally lose in the competition for exposure. Unusually visible cases are exceptions. For example, the issue of prior restraint was again revisited in the Pentagon Papers case, which revolved around the unauthorized publication of classified Vietnam War documents. The United States Supreme Court refused to grant the Nixon administration's request to stop publication. In Senate hearings on controversial Supreme Court nominations, court reporters' work often receives great exposure. This was the case in the highly partisan and contentious hearings on Judge Robert Bork, who failed to receive Senate approval, and Clarence Thomas, who was ultimately confirmed.

crime and the reporting on the courts

The link between crime and the courts is obvious, and is important to understanding the justice system in America. The emphasis the national news networks place on crime stories can be seen in Figure 10.1. Between 1990 and 1997 the three major networks averaged 1,335.5 crime stories a year. At the local level the emphasis on crime is even greater. Studies have found that crime stories comprise between 20 and 30 percent of local television news content,[7] and Doris Graber found that 20 to 28 percent of newspaper stories involved crime.[8] The emphasis on violent crime is particularly pronounced. Graber found that over 64 percent of crime stories in the *Chicago Tribune* in 1994 dealt with murders, while murders accounted for only .3 percent of crimes in Chicago for the year.[9]

In his book *Victims in the News*, Steven Chermak content analyzed six print and three electronic news organizations in an attempt to ascertain how crime was presented to the public through the media.[10] He found that newspapers covered an average of nine crime stories a day and television stations four.[11] Rarely did the stories examine the causes of crime, the motives for particular crimes, or the effectiveness of the criminal justice system. Chermak quoted a news director for a television station: "Newspapers have to sell newspapers, sell ad space. They are not public utilities. They are businesses. We are a business, and I believe that you do what you have to do, legally, ethically, to get folks to watch your show. . . . We are owned by people that want

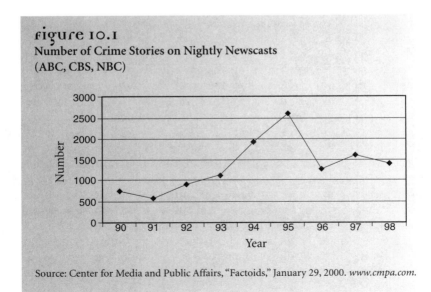

figure 10.1
**Number of Crime Stories on Nightly Newscasts
(ABC, CBS, NBC)**

Source: Center for Media and Public Affairs, "Factoids," January 29, 2000. *www.cmpa.com.*

to make money: they really don't care if I lead with a murder or not; they just want to know if anybody was watching."[12]

The coverage of crime is similar to other beats—the need for sensationalism is a primary criterion. However, to blame the media entirely would be incorrect. While the public complains about the emphasis on crime and violence on television, it is drawn to crime stories. The coverage of the O.J. Simpson cases shows the media and public fixation with the sensational. Other crimes that have had extensive coverage include the Jon Benet Ramsey murder and the Columbine High School shootings. The public is driven by its concern about public safety and its desire for excitement. Crime stories have helped local television news eclipse the national news in the battle for larger audiences.

conflicting rights: The first and sixth Amendments

When we think of the Constitution, our thoughts usually turn to individual rights and liberties. Yet most individual rights are protected not in the Articles of the Constitution, but in the amendments. The lack of such individual protections was a major criticism of those who opposed ratification of the Constitution. The resulting debates led to the passage of the first ten amendments, the Bill of Rights, in 1791. The First Amendment protects against actions by the federal government abridging freedom of the press, and that protection is further supported by the Fourteenth Amendment. In 1925 the Supreme Court ruled that freedom of the press was "among the fundamental personal rights and liberties protected by the due process clause of the Fourteenth Amendment from impairment by the states."[13]

However, the Sixth Amendment provides for fair trials. Conflicts can occur between the freedom of the press and defendants' constitutional rights to a fair trial, both guaranteed in the Constitution. A fair trial is not always possible in cases that are accompanied by undue media attention. One scholar has stated, "One reason the venerable free press–fair trial conflict is particularly perplexing is that it is not one between right and wrong, but rather between right and right."[14] Additional complexity occurs when the protection of free speech is considered. Supreme Court Justice Hugo Black addressed this problem in his opinion in *Maryland* v. *Baltimore Radio Show, Inc.*: "For free speech and fair trial are two of the most cherished policies of our civilization, and it would be a trying task to choose between them."[15] One purpose of a free press was to ensure fair trials through public access to accurate information about the events. Ensuring a fair and open process is normally in the interest of both parties in a case, as well as in the interest of the public and the press. The problem occurs when there is a conflict, perceived or real, between the exercise of press freedom and a fair trial.

The Sixth Amendment's guarantee of a "public" trial and "an impartial jury" for the accused in criminal cases is no less important to a democracy than the First Amendment's guarantee of a "free press." The apparent conflicts between these two amendments raise important questions regarding the media and courts. For instance, who has the right—in addition to the accused—to claim access to a courtroom based on the public trial guarantee? Does public access apply to the press? Does it apply to the public?

The Supreme Court Addresses the Conflict

The Supreme Court addressed the question of the public's right to access in *Gannett Co., Inc. v. DePasquale* in 1979.[16] The case arose from a pretrial hearing to suppress evidence (a confession and some physical evidence) in a murder prosecution in Rochester, New York. The trial judge granted a motion to exclude the press and public on the grounds that the inevitable publicity would prevent the defendant from receiving a fair trial. Justice Potter Stewart, writing the majority opinion, held that "members of the public have no constitutional right under the Sixth and Fourteenth Amendments to attend criminal trials." The Court ruled that the public interest in the trial was adequately preserved by the public availability of the transcript and the right of the press to report about the trial itself. However, in a concurring opinion, Justice Powell opened the way to further litigation. He argued that, while the purpose of a public trial was to ensure that the defendant received a fair trial, a reporter's interest in the judicial system, as an agent of the public, was protected by the First Amendment. Justice Rehnquist, in his dissenting opinion, argued, "The Constitution does no more than assure the public and the press equal access once government has opened its door."[17] The case produced uncertainty about whether the decision had resolved or simply reserved for another case the issue of whether the First Amendment guaranteed press access.

The Supreme Court was soon confronted with that precise question when in 1980 it heard *Richmond Newspapers* v. *Commonwealth of Virginia*.[18] The case involved a fourth trial of a second-degree murder case. The defendant moved that the trial be closed so prospective witnesses could not be informed about what had transpired in the courtroom. The owners of the papers appealed to the Virginia Supreme Court, which upheld the judge's decision. The case was then appealed to the United States Supreme Court. In writing the majority opinion, Chief Justice Warren Burger traced the long history of public trials in England and the United States: "At the time when our organic laws were adopted, criminal trials both here and in England had long been presumptively open. This is no quirk of history; rather, it has long been recognized as an indispensable attribute of an Anglo-American trial ....The critical prophylactic aspects of the administration of justice cannot function in the dark; no community catharsis can occur if justice is done in a corner [or] in any covert manner. People in an open society do not demand infallibility from their institutions, but it is difficult for them to accept what they are prohibited from observing."[19] The Court further stated that a trial is a public event and what transpires in the courtroom is public property. Writing for the Court, Chief Justice Burger wrote, "We hold that the right to attend criminal trials is implicit in the guarantees of the First Amendment; without the freedoms to attend such trials, which people have exercised for centuries, important aspects of freedom of speech and of the press could be eviscerated."[20] The Court's decision upheld Justice William O. Douglas's position in 1947 that "a trial is a public event. What transpires in the courtroom is public property. . . . Those who see and hear what transpires can report it with impunity. There is no special prerequisite of the judiciary which enables it, as distinguished from other institutions of democratic government, to suppress, edit, or censor events which transpire in proceeding before it."[21]

Legal Awareness of the Problem

Through the years the Supreme Court has ruled that the right to access is not absolute, but that limitations on access must be justified and weighed, and in the process the Court has provided a rather narrow interpretation for exclusion of the media. To ensure a balance between the First and Sixth Amendments, the courts have historically relied on four methods of legal control over the media's involvement in the judicial process. First, the *doctrine of constructive contempt* permitted judicial sanctions against newspapers that interfered with the administration of justice. While this Anglo-American concept has fallen in disuse over the last few decades, it has been applied about one hundred times through the years. Since the eighteenth century, British judges have used this concept to punish those who hindered the administration of justice. The American legal system first adopted this form of restriction on the press in 1831. Statutes have sanctioned misbehavior in the presence of the Court as an obstruction of justice. The use of the constructive contempt power against the press has been sporadic and usually, when appealed, unsuccessful. The Supreme Court has applied the "clear and present danger" test to some constructive contempt cases to bar convictions of newspapers, generally finding that the free discussion of the case did not impede the defendant's right to a fair trial.

Second, *bench and bar rules* prescribed certain kinds of press practices in the courts. As technology advanced and radio, film, and television became part of the daily lives of Americans, new sanctions have been added by the courts and the legal profession itself. Following the Lindbergh kidnapping trial in 1937, the American Bar Association adopted Canon 35 of the Code of Judicial Ethics, which called for "fitting dignity and decorum" in the court, barred taking photographs in the courtroom during sessions and recesses, and forbade the broadcasting of court procedures. The only exception to the canon was court-supervised ceremonial naturalization proceedings, in which immigrants choose to become American citizens and which are symbolically important to democracy.

The canon became entrenched in the law after *Estes* v. *Texas* in 1965.[22] In that case a well-known Texan, Billie Sol Estes, was indicted for swindling large sums of money by inducing farmers to buy nonexistent fertilizer tanks. At the time Texas was one of two states that allowed television cameras in the courtroom. After an unruly two-day pretrial hearing on the defendant's motion to ban television cameras, the motion failed and the trial continued with cameras (hidden to avoid distracting from the proceedings) broadcasting live coverage. Estes was convicted and appealed first to the Texas appeals court, which upheld the lower court's conviction. He then appealed to the United States Supreme Court, which in a 5–4 decision ruled that even limited broadcasting violated the defendant's Fourteenth Amendment guarantee to due process of the law because it deprived him of a fair trial. The court stated, "Prejudices of television may be so subtle that it escapes the ordinary methods of proof, but it would gradually erode our fundamental conception of trial."[23] One consequence of the Estes decision was that in 1972 the American Bar Association adopted Canon 3A(7) of its Code of Judicial Conduct, which replaced Canon 35 of the Code of Judicial Ethics and confirmed the ban on television in court. However, in 1978 the Conference of State Chief Justices adopted a resolution "advocating state experimentation with camera coverage." In 1982 the canon was amended to include television. Presently only Mississippi, South Dakota, and the District of Columbia forbid cameras in the courtroom.

Third, such *judicial procedures* as continuance, change of venue, *voir dire*, and specific instructions have been used to reduce the influence of the media on trials. While these do not apply only to the media, they have been used when the possibility of a fair trial is thought to be jeopardized by media access. Both continuances and changes of venue are used to reduce the potentially adverse effects of publicity. Continuances involve rescheduling trials for a later date to allow the influence of the media and the public's reaction time to subside. Changing the venue, or moving a trial to another location, is commonly done when the court believes a case has received inordinate media attention. The trial may be moved to a location where the case has received less attention in the hope that jurors can be found who have not been influenced by media accounts. Nowhere is the sophistication of the legal system more evident today than in the selection of juries. The *voir dire* process is perhaps the most important single step in the judicial process. Determining who sits in judgment has become a full-time industry for "jury consultants," whose job it is to develop "psychological profiles" of favorable juries for particular cases. In the jury selection process, lawyers attempt to ascertain the effects of the media on individuals' knowledge of the case. In his instructions to the jury, the judge has the latitude to instruct the jury before, during, and prior to deliberations in a trial on a wide range of matters, including media access.

Finally, a conviction can be *reversed* when the filtering procedures fail to prevent prejudice at the trial. In essence, American law does not guarantee that it will always be possible to find an impartial jury. In fact, such a goal may be unattainable. However, the law aspires to ensure that no defendant's conviction will be upheld if the jury was not impartial. Where the media have contaminated the court proceedings, the courts have reversed the conviction rather than punish the media, as in the case of *Sheppard* v. *Florida.*

Pretrial publicity does not always lead to conviction, or even to prejudice. There are instances in which media reports have actually become critical factors (exculpatory or incriminating) at the later trial. These reports may provide the public with information that the subsequent jury is not supposed to consider. Famous examples include the televised killing of President Kennedy's assassin, Lee Harvey Oswald, by Jack Ruby, Rodney King's beating by Los Angeles policemen, and the live broadcast of the pursuit of O.J. Simpson's Bronco. Reversals have become less common as the courts have adjusted to the media's presence and taken precautions to avoid grounds for overturning decisions. The courts today routinely set guidelines for the media prior to trials.

How well is the supreme court covered?

A major measure of the media's coverage of the courts is how well they report on the nation's highest court—the Supreme Court. It is small, but its decisions have lasting national significance. There are three difficulties for reporters who cover the Supreme Court. First, the Court, unlike Congress or the president, conducts its daily business in private and without media intrusion. This presents a structural barrier for court reporters unlike those faced by their colleagues who cover other government institutions. Second, there are barriers erected by reporters' employers. A case that has little audience appeal is unlikely to be covered in detail. Finally, court reporters, unlike their colleagues, must prepare by reading lengthy and complex legal documents, and unlike reporters covering the Congress or president, they cannot ask the justices to explain the details. However, when the Court makes its decisions public, there is one overriding question—are the decisions reported in a manner that will increase the public's understanding of the decisions and the Court?

Chester Newland studied the coverage of two highly visible Court decisions in sixty-three metropolitan newspapers.[24] In *Engel* v. *Vitale* (1962) the Court struck down a nondenominational prayer written by the New York Board of Regents for public school recitation on the grounds that it was improper for public officials to write or sanction official prayers. In *Barker* v. *Carr* (1962) the Court ruled that federal courts have jurisdiction over lawsuits challenging the apportionment of legislative districts on the grounds that malapportioned districts violated the equal protection clause of the Fourteenth Amendment. Newland found that stories about the two cases featured misleading headlines and sketchy and uninformative coverage, and contained serious errors.[25] Justice Tom Clark, a participant in the *Engel* v. *Vitale* case, complained that inadequate reporting led to misunderstanding and lack of compliance by the public.

Many important decisions are completely ignored by the media because their emphasis on conflict leads them to pay more attention to cases involving such issues as abortion, civil rights, or school prayer. One study found that during one typical Supreme Court term, the *New York Times* failed to mention 25 percent of all written opinions. In stories about the remaining 122 opinions, 29 lacked essential information.[26] The figure was higher for the *Detroit Free Press*, which failed to mention 70 percent of written opinions.[27] The cases the media choose to focus on are usually covered extensively and well.

Recently Elliot Slotnick and Jennifer Segal addressed television's coverage of the United States Supreme Court.[28] Through the use of content analysis, they examined television news coverage at two levels. At what they called the "micro level," they isolated two prominent cases and traced their coverage in the nightly news from the time the first stories appeared through the Court's decisions and well into the next year of the Court's term. The first case, *Regents of the University of California* v. *Bakke*, involved a white male medical student who claimed that the University of California at Davis had discriminated against him in its use of the university's affirmative action policy. He claimed that he was denied admission while students who had lower qualifications were admitted based on their minority status. The second case, *Webster* v. *Reproductive Health Services*, involved the constitutionality of a Missouri law that regulated and restricted the right of a woman to have an abortion. The authors also examined the media's coverage of the Supreme Court at the "macro level" by comparing the total network news coverage of the Court in 1989 to that in 1994. Presumably in a media-enriched environment, the coverage of the Court would be reflected in network news programs.

Slotnick and Segal studied at what point during the legal process television news programs reported on the cases and how they framed the reporting. They divided the process into three periods: from the time the first story appeared to the Court's granting *certiorari*, through the oral arguments and the decision vigil, and the decision and its aftermath. As Figure 10.2 indicates, the two cases were reported differently. In the Bakke case the networks divided their reporting equally between the preargument stage (38.3 percent) and the decision and its aftermath (38.3 percent). The period of oral arguments and waiting for the Court's decision received less coverage. The authors contend that this pattern of coverage may have reflected the broader concern at the time with the issue of affirmative action. Unlike abortion, affirmative action did not have a long legal history, so the Bakke case drew more media attention prior to oral arguments. In the Webster case, developments after the Court's decision received the most coverage, perhaps because abortion had been litigated for over two decades and the public was familiar with the arguments surrounding the issue.

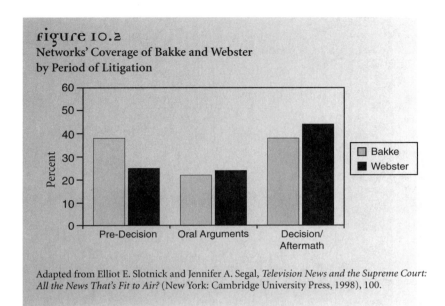

ꜰɪgυꞅε 10.2
Networks' Coverage of Bakke and Webster
by Period of Litigation

Adapted from Elliot E. Slotnick and Jennifer A. Segal, *Television News and the Supreme Court: All the News That's Fit to Air?* (New York: Cambridge University Press, 1998), 100.

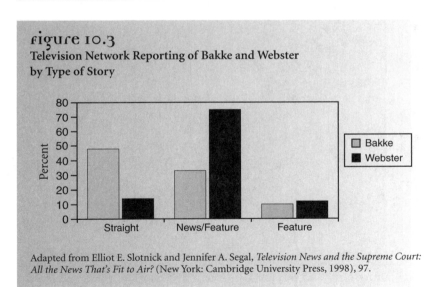

ꜰɪgυꞅε 10.3
Television Network Reporting of Bakke and Webster
by Type of Story

Adapted from Elliot E. Slotnick and Jennifer A. Segal, *Television News and the Supreme Court: All the News That's Fit to Air?* (New York: Cambridge University Press, 1998), 97.

The authors then analyzed how the stories involving the two cases were presented in newscasts. They developed three categories of stories: straight news, news reports with an elaboration on some element of the case in a combined news/feature format, and features, stories that did not report any newsworthy event. As Figure 10.3 show, the Bakke case was

Table 10.1
Content Analysis of the Networks' Coverage of the Supreme Court's 1989 and 1994 Terms

	1989 COURT TERM STORIES	1994 COURT TERM STORIES
Case facts		
Yes	106 (61.6)	77 (92.8)
No	66 (38.4)	6 (7.2)
Interest groups noted		
Yes	87 (48.6)	48 (51.6)
No	92 (51.4)	45 (48.4)
Interest groups quoted		
Yes	84 (46.9)	48 (51.2)
No	95 (53.1)	45 (48.4)
Case vote		
Yes	45 (54.2)	2 (5.9)
No	38 (45.8)	32 (94.1)
Ideological division		
Yes	5 (6.3)	0 (0)
No	75 (93.8)	33 (100)
Division of justices		
Yes	10 (12.7)	0 (0)
No	69 (87.3)	33 (100)
Concurrent writer identified		
Yes	2 (2.5)	2 (6.1)
No	79 (97.5)	31 (93.9)

reported primarily as straight news, with 48 percent of the stories falling in this category. An additional 33.3 percent were stories of news with elaboration and 10 percent were features. In the Webster case two thirds of the stories involved news with elaboration. Only 13 percent were straight news and 11 percent features. Again, the dissimilarities in the reporting of the two cases may reflect the public's different levels of understanding on the two issues.

To place how the Supreme Court is reported in a larger context, the authors content analyzed network coverage of two Court terms. They

Table 10.1 (continued)
Content Analysis of the Networks' Coverage of the Supreme Court's 1989 and 1994 Terms

	1989 COURT TERM STORIES	1994 COURT TERM STORIES
Dissenting writer identified		
Yes	25 (32.5)	10 (30.2)
No	52 (67.5)	23 (69.7)
Dissenting opinion quoted		
Yes	23 (29.5)	10 (30.3)
No	55 (70.5)	23 (67.5)
Majority writer identified		
Yes	30 (36.6)	18 (54.5)
No	52 (64.5)	15 (45.5)
Majority opinion quoted		
Yes	29 (35.4)	18 (54.5)
No	53 (64.6)	15 (45.5)
Case history		
Yes	33 (19.2)	5 (6.4)
No	139 (80.8)	73 (93.6)
Amicus briefs filed		
Yes	5 (2.9)	0 (0)
No	167 (97.1)	33 (100)

Note: Unit of analysis is Court-related story. Total number of stories in each cell represents docket-related stories for which each variable was applicable.

Adapted from Elliot Slotnick and Jennifer Segal, *Television News and the Supreme Court: All the News That's Fit to Air?* (New York: Cambridge University Press, 1998), Table 5.6, p. 183.

addressed two major questions: what stories did the networks report and how did they report them?

What is reported shapes the public's understanding of the Court, the legal process, and the entire legal system. As shown in Table 10.1, the networks paid very little attention to the history of the cases, and thus provided little context for viewers to assess the Court's decisions. They did a better job at presenting the case facts, particularly in the 1994 term. The reporting did not tell viewers about the division of the justices, how many voted for the decision, which is an important element in all Supreme Court decisions. The networks were more interested in the groups that were affected by the decisions. The picture that emerges from Table 10.1 is rather weak coverage of information on the Court, the cases, and their impact.

On the second question the authors concluded, "Generally, the data continue to illustrate that the opportunities for television viewers to learn about the Court are somewhat restricted, and that the networks have treated the courts as less newsworthy over time."[29] The time variable is particularly important in reporting on the Court because of the complex nature of the law and the judicial process, as well as the lack of public understanding of and sophistication about the Court. It has been noted that longer stories do a better job than shorter stories for they can provide the detail viewers need to comprehend the complexities.[30] As discussed earlier, television reporting is constrained by both time and the need to be competitive. The authors' findings may have been altered by the growth of cable and the development of channels devoted to courts like Court TV and programs like *Burden of Proof.*

The authors applied four standard indicators to address the issue of network coverage: the length of the story, its placement, who reported it, and its format. Table 10.2 provides an answer to the questions noted above as they relate to the 1989 and 1994 Court terms.

Slotnick and Segal's study had several significant findings. First, nearly 70 percent of all stories reported for the entire study occurred in the 1989 term. Second, over one half of reports on the 1989 term were less than 30 seconds in duration, while the 1994 term had fewer short stories and more two minutes long or longer. The placement of a story in the newscast has long been associated with its perceived importance, with the most important news coming at the beginning of newscasts.[31] Table 10.2 shows that the percentage of lead stories on the Court was larger in 1989 than in 1994, but only 35.5 percent of Court stories in 1989 appeared prior to the first commercial break, compared with over half (53.5 percent) of the 1994 term stories.[32] The general pattern of placement of Court-related stories for the two terms indicates that "viewers of network news programs had a greater chance of exposure to and, presumably, comprehension of the Court and what it had done during the 1989 term than they did in 1994."[33]

The actual reporting did not vary. Television news anchors combined with correspondents to present the majority of stories in each session. Finally, the majority of stories were in a news/feature, rather than straight news, format. Anchors tend to report straight news, while correspondents present features. During the 1989 term nearly 60 percent of the stories concerning the Court were feature stories. The 1994 term, in contrast, provided significantly fewer featured reports on the Court. These data led the investigators to conclude that "the three network news programs do not routinely

Table 10.2
Content Analysis of the Networks' Structural Coverage of the 1989 and 1994 Supreme Court Terms

	1989 COURT TERM	1994 COURT TERM
Number of cases	245	111
Story length		
Shorter than 30 seconds	125 (51.0)	43 (38.7)
Longer than 2 minutes	68 (27.8)	40 (36.0)
Placement		
Lead story	37 (15.1)	13 (11.7)
Before 1st break	87 (35.5)	59 (53.2)*
Reporters		
Anchor only	100 (40.8)	49 (44.1)
Anchor and correspondent	145 (59.2)	62 (55.9)
Story format		
News only	99 (40.4)	51 (45.9)
News plus feature	145 (59.2)	55 (49.5)

*Number of stories broadcast during the first ten minutes of the program.

Percentages will not necessarily equal 100% because some categories were not included.

Source: Elliot E. Slotnick and Jennifer A. Segal, *Television News and the Supreme Court: All The News That's Fit to Air?* (New York: Cambridge University Press, 1998), 177.

provide for their viewers news reports about the Court that are structured in such a way as to increase attention to and promote the comprehension of information about the Court."[34] The authors noted the general decline in news coverage of the Court in the 1994 term.

The first general conclusion that can be drawn is that Supreme Court stories appear to be subjected to the same criteria as other news stories. Sensationalism and human interest help guide the reporting. For instance, in reporting the 1989 term, the national networks covered four stories with four or more minutes of coverage. These included a case that dealt with abortion, one that involved the evangelist Jimmy Swaggart, a case involving the right to die, and longest of all, Justice Brennan's retirement from the bench. Second, while the courts work in an atmosphere removed from the media, what is reported is driven not by the need to inform, but by the need to sell. Former Court reporter Carl Stern noted that when he was covering the Court, "I generally had something in the range of six sentences to convey what the Court did. Most cases can't really be done justice in six sentences."[35] The public is not going to be well informed about legal matters through the traditional channels of communication—the media.

cameras in the courtroom

An estimated 20,000 curiosity seekers camped inside and outside the packed courtroom. To accommodate the demands of the large press contingent, a communication system unprecedented in sophistication and size was set up near the courthouse. This trial did not take place a few years ago in Los Angeles, but in 1935 in a small town in New Jersey. As mentioned above, following the sensational Lindbergh kidnapping trial, the American Bar Association passed Canon 35 and banned cameras in the courtroom. However, the media continued to be drawn to high-profile cases such as those of Billie Sol Estes and Dr. Sam Sheppard.[36] In 1965 Canon 35 was explicitly applied to television cameras in an attempt to stave off excessive and intrusive coverage.

The question of whether court proceedings should be televised raises additional questions about the role of the media in the judicial system. Those who argue that court proceedings ought to be televised claim that the founding fathers intended for all government decisions to be open to the public because it makes officials more accountable and informs the public. Those who oppose cameras in the courtroom argue that they detract from the seriousness of the institution and the case and change the behavior of lawyers and judges. Michael J. Epstein has argued that media claims about the public's right to know are suspect. He and others have pointed out that if the media's concern is to inform the public, proceedings should not be interrupted by commercials. Some local television stations place commercials as frequently as every six to eight minutes.[37]

During the early years of television, the equipment, lighting, and cables needed for live broadcasts were intrusive in the courtroom. However, modern technological advances have changed and with them came a renewed call for media access to the courtroom. The major case in the renewed effort to have television in the courtroom was a 1977 Florida case in which lawyers for the *Post-Newsweek*-owned television station in Miami sought a ruling from the Florida Supreme Court allowing "presumptive access" for electronic media.[38] In their argument, they noted that compact cameras, low lighting, and video equipment were less intrusive than sketch artists with easels and chalk. Making the argument for the station was Talbor D'Alemberte, a prominent Florida lawyer who would later become president of the ABA and Florida State University. The Florida court ordered a hearing to demonstrate the new technologies. After the hearing, it ordered a one-year trial experiment followed by a survey of judges and participants to evaluate the experiment. The court eventually issued a "presumptive access" rule, which was later adopted by several other states.

The Florida law was appealed to the United States Supreme Court in 1981 in the case of *Chandler* v. *Florida*, which involved a burglary carried out by policemen.[39] The key witness was an amateur radio operator who had overheard and recorded the policemen's conversations over their walkie-talkies during the burglary. The defendants objected to television in the courtroom. However, the trial judge claimed that he was operating under the experimental rule permitting television and ordered that the prosecution's key witness and the closing arguments be televised, but not the defense's case. The defendants were convicted and appealed to the United States Supreme Court. The Court noted Judge Brandeis's comment in 1932 that the rights of states to experiment in social and economic areas are "one of the happy incidents of the federal system." It went on to note that the Supreme Court "must be ever on our guard, lest we erect our prejudices into legal principle," and it deferred to the Florida Supreme Court, which had earlier upheld the judge's decision. This case allowed the Supreme Court to modify and clarify rules regarding television in the courtroom that had been in existence since *Estes* v. *Texas*. The resulting federal guideline was that television might be permitted in courts so long as there was no specific evidence of actual prejudice as a result.

The *Chandler* decision marked a change in the Court's view of cameras in the courtroom. As mentioned earlier, forty-eight states permit some type of audiovisual coverage of court proceedings. No state has repealed a decision once made to allow camera coverage in the courtroom. Only Mississippi and South Dakota do not permit cameras in the courtroom under any circumstances. However, under law, television coverage of federal proceedings at both the trial and appellate level is currently banned, and television coverage of federal civil proceedings is severely restricted. The federal courts are able to circumvent the federal law by claiming local jurisdiction, thereby allowing cameras in federal courtrooms.

Court TV

New technology led to another innovation in the media-court relationship. In 1990 cable networks began to become an important alternative source of information and entertainment. One of the first individuals to use the new cable technology was Steven Brill, a Yale-trained attorney and journalist on legal matters, who became the chief executive of the Courtroom Television Network. Court TV is a twenty-four-hours-a-day, seven-days-a-week cable channel that reports on legal and judicial developments in the United States and other nations. It has aired gavel-to-gavel coverage of some of the nation's most publicized trials, including those of Bernard Goetz, Jeffrey Dahmer,

Lorena Bobbitt, William Kennedy Smith, Rodney King, the Menendez brothers, and O.J. Simpson. By the middle of 1996 Court TV was in 100 million homes and had 26 million subscribers. The ability to see coverage of a variety of legal issues on a daily basis has made Court TV to the courts what CNN is to news, C-SPAN is to Congress, and MTV is to music—it has become the network of the courts.

The Federal Experiment

Federal trial courts in Indiana, Massachusetts, Michigan, New York, Pennsylvania, and Washington and the appellate courts in the Second and Ninth Circuits volunteered to experiment with cameras in the courtroom from July 1991 to the end of 1994. Controlled by the judge and subject to specific guidelines, the courts approved 82 percent of media requests during the period. Overseeing the experiment for the Federal Judicial Conference was the Federal Judicial Center, which was established in 1967 "to further development and adoption of judicial administration." By 1997 its budget was $17.5 million and it had a permanent staff of 139. At the conclusion of the period, the center provided anecdotal evidence that the experiment had been positive. The experiment had found the judges to be neutral toward the parties in the cases and the judges regarded the experiment favorably. Neither the judges nor the lawyers perceived any procedural effects caused by the television cameras. They observed little or no effect of the camera on the trial participants and reported "minimal or no detrimental effects on jurors or witnesses."[40]

Questions remained, however. Did cameras motivate people to tell the truth? Did their presence violate the privacy of the witnesses and make them unwilling to testify? Did they make those involved more attentive and responsive? Were attorneys better prepared, more theatrical, or more courteous? Were judges more attentive and courteous and less controversial? Finally, did the cameras provide an educational experience for those watching?

In an attempt to answer these questions, the center surveyed participating judges, attorneys, media representatives, and court staff involved in twenty-seven pretrial hearings, four bankruptcy cases, twenty-four appeals, and even a judge's swearing-in. The data gathered from this survey and data that had been collected by states involved in the experiment led the center to recommend that trial and appellate courts be equipped with television cameras. As noted above, the federal judiciary has still not endorsed cameras in the courtroom, but in recent years there has been some softening of its position.

The first instance occurred in 1996, in a civil case before a federal court in New York City.[41] In a class action case against the Child Welfare Administration, the plaintiffs argued that it was in the public's interest to know what was going on in the agency. Court TV asked permission to televise the complete oral arguments by the lawyers. The plaintiffs agreed, but the defense opposed the motion. The argument against televising the case was that the public might not comprehend the procedural aspects or the legal nuances of the case. Lawyers for Court TV pointed out that district courts have their own intramural regulations regarding cameras in the courts. The judge in the case ruled in favor of televised proceedings, stating, "The public interest would be served." The significance of the case was that the judge acted under local rule and did not consult the Judicial Conference before he ruled. Currently federal district courts employ the local rule when they wish and appellate courts are left to their own discretion. The Supreme Court of the United States remains committed to no cameras in its proceedings.

The media's coverage of the courts is influenced by the history and evolution of both institutions. As means of communication become faster and less intrusive, the courts' early reservations are less and less likely to prevail. State and federal district courts currently are open to televised proceedings, and the public's interest in the sensational, coupled with the media's need to sell a story, provides great incentives for future media coverage. However, studies thus far indicate that this does not translate into a better understanding of the judicial system. Instead, the marketplace pressure seems to override the need to inform.

summary

The judicial system is the least covered of the three branches of government. Two factors contribute to the media's overall low attention to this branch of government. First, the institution is complex and has low public visibility, and its members do not seek public attention (at least at the federal level) since they do not participate in the electoral process. Second, because the courts lack the visibility of Congress or the presidency, it is not an assignment most reporters seek to further their careers. Additionally, those who cover the courts need a special interest in the institution or a legal background, and preferably both.

The stories that are covered tend to misrepresent the judicial process. The media are drawn to crime stories. They dominate local news and play an important role in the national news. Stories about crime appear in far greater numbers in the media than in reality. The media have a long history of using expanded coverage of "high-profile" cases to increase their audiences.

The relationship between the media and courts draws attention to the tension between the First Amendment of the Constitution, the right to a free press, and the Sixth Amendment, the right to a fair trial. The courts have shown an increased awareness of this conflict and have in recent years attempted to address it.

Studies have shown that the media do not cover the activities of the federal courts as well as they do the president or Congress, causing the public to have a disturbingly poor understanding of the legal system. Evidence suggests that how well a particular Supreme Court case is covered is associated with the current importance of the underlying issue in society.

As technologies have made live coverage of court proceedings possible, some argue that it is desirable to have cameras in the courtroom. While experiments with cameras in federal courts have found no discernible effect on the process, the federal courts currently ban them. Federal district courts can circumvent this by adopting the rules of the state, and many do. Alternative media outlets—cable television primarily—have developed programming targeted specifically toward the courts. However, this coverage of the courts, like that of the president and Congress, depends on drama and sensationalism.

ENDNOTES

[1] Louis Harris national opinion polls, 1995–1997.

[2] Philip B. Kurland, "On Misunderstanding the Supreme Court," *University of Chicago Law School Record*, 7(1960):31.

[3] Rosie Sherman, "Media and the Law," *National Law Journal*, 20(June 6, 1988):32–36.

[4] Anthony Lewis, "Problems of a Washington Correspondent," *Connecticut Bar Journal*, 33(1959):363–371.

[5] Charles Press and Kenneth VerBurg, *American Politicians and Journalists* (Glenview, Ill.: Scott, Foresman and Co., 1988), 253.

[6] David Grey, *The Supreme Court and the News Media* (Evanston, Illinois: Northwestern University Press, 1968).

[7] Kaiser Family Foundation and the Center for Media and Public Affairs, "Crime the Most Common Story on Local Television News," Kaiser Foundation press release, March 3, 1998, http:/www.kff.org, and Paul Klite, Robert A. Bardwell, and Jason Salzman, "Local TV News: Getting Away with Murder," *Press/Politics*, 2(Spring 1997):102–112.

[8] Doris Graber, *Crime and the News and the Public* (New York: Praeger, 1980), 24–25.

[9] Doris Graber, *The Mass Media and American Politics*, 5th ed. (Washington, D.C.: Congressional Quarterly Press, 1997), 311.

[10] Steven M. Chermak, *Victims in the News: Crime and the American News Media* (Boulder, Colo.: Westview Press, 1995).

[11] *Ibid.*, 13.

[12] *Ibid.*, 22.

[13] *Gitlow* v. *U.S.*, 268 U.S. 652 (1925).

[14] Ronald L. Goldfarb, *TV or Not TV: Television, Justice, and the Courts* (New York: New York University Press, 1998), 18.

[15] *Maryland v. Baltimore Radio Show Inc.*, 338 U.S. 912 (1950).

[16] *Gannett Co., Inc.* v. *DePasquale*, 433 U.S. 368 (1979).

[17] *Ibid.*

[18] *Richmond Newspapers, Inc.* v. *Commonwealth of Virginia*, 488 U.S. 554 (1980).

[19] *Ibid.*

[20] *Ibid.*

[21] *Craig* v. *Harney*, 331 U.S. 367 (1947).

[22] *Estes* v. *Texas*, 381 U.S. 532, 538 (1965).

[23] *Ibid.*

[24] Chester A. Newland, "Press Coverage of the United States Supreme Court," *Western Political Quarterly*, 17(1964):15–36.

[25] *Ibid.*

[26] David Ericson, "Newspaper Coverage of the Supreme Court: A Case Study," *Journalism Quarterly*, 54(Autumn 1977):605–607.

[27] *Ibid.*

[28] Elliot E. Slotnick and Jennifer A. Segal, *Television News and the Supreme Court* (New York: Cambridge University Press, 1998).

[29] *Ibid.*, 177.

[30] John P. Robinson and Mark R. Levy, *The Main Source: Learning from Television News*, 2nd ed. (Beverly Hills, Calif.: Sage, 1986).

[31] Herbert Gans, *Deciding What's News: A Study of CBS Evening News, NBC Nightly News, Newsweek, and Time* (New York: Pantheon Books, 1979).

[32] Slotnick and Segal, *op. cit.*, 180.

[33] *Ibid.*

[34] *Ibid.*, 181.

[35] Slotnick and Segal, *op. cit.*, 179.

[36] *Estes* v. *Texas*, 381 U.S. 532 (1965), and *Sheppard* v. *Maxwell*, 384 U.S. 333 (1966).

[37] Michael J. Epstein, "The Case for Trials on Television: What's the Verdict?" *Television Quarterly*, 28(1997):60–70.

[38] *In re Petition of Post-Newsweek Stations, Florida*, 347 Southern 2d. 404 (1977).

[39] *Chandler* v. *State of Florida*, 449 U.S. 560 (1981).

[40] Goldfarb, *op. cit.*, 85.

[41] *Marisol* v. *Giuliani*, 95 Civ 10533, 929 F.Supp 660, 662 (1996).

CHAPTER 11

The Media and Military Involvement: A New Era

The media's role in foreign policy changed drastically with the conclusion of the Cold War. For generations capitalism and communism had offered distinctly different world views, helped define the United States' national interest, and determined the nation's foreign policy, including its use of military force. The Cold War also provided journalists with the elements to develop a story that would be readily understood by the public and acceptable to editors: tension and conflict, immediacy, and hard facts (budget figures, numbers of missiles, tanks, troops, etc.). In the post–Cold War years, following the breakup of the Eastern European bloc in 1989–1990 and the collapse of the Soviet Union in 1991, these elements were less significant and reporting became more difficult.

The effect of television on American foreign policy and public opinion has been widely debated, and the debate intensified with the unrest that followed the collapse of communism in Eastern Europe. Such events as the Chinese students' uprising in Tiananmen Square, the Persian Gulf War, coup attempts in Moscow and around the world, and conflicts in Kosovo, Bosnia, and Somalia not only required a new approach to foreign policy, but also altered the role of the mass media in covering foreign policy.

The Cold War had helped create a market for foreign policy news. Foreign policy makers in the post–Cold War era worried that the public might lose interest in foreign affairs in the absence of rivalry with the Soviet Union. In fact, the attention of most Americans appears to have shifted more toward domestic issues. Furthermore, the post–Cold War period has thus far failed to provide a new consensus on how to define and carry out foreign policy.

In the absence of a clearly defined foreign policy, the impact of the mass media on foreign affairs has increased to an unprecedented level. The media serve as the world's communications network. Governments communicate through the news media. The media turn their cameras on whatever areas provide vivid and dramatic stories, such as floods, famines, epidemics, and civil wars and insurrections. They instantly transmit information about foreign events that affect both the public's reactions and our foreign policy. For example, when Saddam Hussein renewed his repression of the Kurds following the Gulf War, television cameras showed cold, hungry, sick, and dying refugees, thus framing the issue. When President Bush announced the establishment of a safe zone for Kurds in northern Iraq at a news conference, Walter Goodman noted that CNN divided the screen: "To the lower right was the President; upper left was a larger picture of the refugees. Visually the president appeared to be responding to the pressures from above."[1] More recently the images of refugees fleeing Kosovo provided similar visuals.

Post–Cold War foreign policy has been chiefly concerned with the United States' interventions in a host of smaller, less powerful nations. With the dissolution of the Soviet Union, a new set of objectives governing the United States' interventions has developed. The first is to safeguard the global order and establish global standards for acceptable governmental behavior and human rights. The second is to destroy weapons of mass destruction in the hands of smaller, less sophisticated, and less predictable nations. The third is to intervene when humanitarian needs are at stake. International organizations, like the United Nations, and nongovernmental organizations (NGOs), such as Amnesty International, have performed increasingly important roles in the development of new global standards.

Media coverage of foreign policy and international conflicts

One way of viewing the media's coverage of foreign affairs is through the "indexing" hypothesis, which holds that the "mass media professionals . . . tend to 'index' the range of voices and viewpoints in both news and editorials according to the range of views expressed in mainstream government debate about a given topic."[2] According to other views, the media's reporting on foreign affairs is closely linked to the media elites' support for that policy, and in most cases the media do reinforce the current administration in foreign affairs.[3] For instance, Robert Entman and Benjamin Page, in a study of news coverage just before the Gulf War, conclude: "It appears that the media calibrate news judgments rather precisely to the clout of the powerful actors whose remarks or actions are covered: the higher their power to share newsworthy events, the more attention they receive. The lower the power, the less attention, even if the substantive information offered might be of great value to a deliberating citizen."[4] William Dorman and Steven Livingston, in a study of media coverage after the United States and its allies invaded Iraq in 1991, found little dissent among the elite from the administration's interpretation of events. They contend that the elite media, like the *New York Times* and the *Washington Post*, "fell short of helping to create a robust culture of debate."[5] There is increasing concern among many observers that as the media become more concentrated, elitists' viewpoints will become even more dominant.[6]

Relations with foreign governments, whether economic, social, or political, involve foreign policy, but the media cover foreign policy most intensely when there is conflict between nations, so this will be our focus.

The CNN Effect

Some analysts have discerned what they term a "CNN effect" in the reporting of foreign affairs in recent years. They believe that television in general, but primarily Cable News Network (CNN) because of its international scope, plays a new and central role in foreign affairs. Steven Livingston suggests that the media perform at least three conceptually different and analytically distinct functions in the foreign policy arena that arise from the CNN effect.[7] The first is as an *accelerant*. The media accelerate or shorten decision makers' response time. The second is as an *impediment* to foreign policy. The media can impede foreign policy by undermining the public's support for a policy or by jeopardizing operational security. Finally, the media can become *agenda-setting agents* through their coverage of such emotional situations such as mass starvation, atrocities, and other humanitarian crises, which may reorder foreign policy makers' priorities. Livingston points out that "these possible effects may be evident over time—sometimes a very short time—on a single policy issue."[8] For example, the media may draw attention to a problem (set the agenda), shorten the time for policy makers' decision making (accelerate), and cover traumatic events that alter the development and implementation of policy (impede).

The existence of the CNN effect is debatable, especially in the case of foreign interventions, but that does not diminish the critical role of the mass media in foreign policy. Policy makers must increasingly take the media into account in their strategy planning.

In the years immediately following the end of the Cold War, American foreign policy makers have been increasingly faced with choosing between political and humanitarian considerations in decision making. Until policy makers develop a clearer set of policies, their decisions will be influenced disproportionately by media coverage of humanitarian concerns. The problem with relying on the media for information is that they oversimplify complex issues and focus on the sensational and dramatic and rarely on underlying causes. In addition, they have very short attention spans. As new stories break, they cover them at the expense of earlier stories. Public policy requires a continual monitoring of events. Decision makers have long relied on "images" to sell, defend, and explain their positions. In a world where images are so powerful, presidents and their advisors have become increasingly fearful of the impact of negative news about foreign interventions. Hence, they are increasingly reluctant to intervene, even if conditions warrant such action.

Media Reporting of Military Involvement: Two Models

Discussions of the media and military involvement frequently focus on the media's impact on specific policy objectives and particularly on military engagement or disengagement. Consequently, the media have been criticized for leading the nation into unwise and unwanted international situations. Since the Vietnam War, there have been lingering questions about the media's role in the foreign policy process. Foreign policy includes such diverse areas as international trade, treaties, regional alliances, and all other relations the United States enters into with other nations. However, it becomes most visible to the public and the media when the United States becomes militarily involved. As the nature of foreign involvement with other countries changes, for example, from military to peacekeeping and humanitarian operations, the role of the media in reporting these events also changes.

While some argue that new technologies have altered the nature of reporting and the impact of the media in foreign affairs, others disagree.[9] Ever since the Spanish-American War (1898), the daily newspapers have focused on emotional aspects of foreign situations and called for governmental officials to "do something" about them. Warren Strobel argues CNN plays on emotions today much the same way the nation's press did over one hundred years ago. In both cases, he argues, the appeal to the masses is based on a "simplistic portrayal of events in emotive images." Circulation battles between competing "yellow press" newspapers were a major factor in the buildup to the Spanish-American War. Similarly, live televised images of the Gulf War provided CNN both legitimacy and profit. The role of the media is enhanced when there is no clear foreign policy or when the media can present instant images to the world.

Two models have been developed to depict the media's coverage of foreign affairs over the years, particularly when American military forces have been deployed.[10] The *pull model* dominated media-government relations from 1914 to roughly 1965. Several factors affected the reporting of military involvement in this model. These included institutional leadership support for military actions; public support for the action; a defined mission and known enemy; domestic stability or the absence of widespread social, political, or economic unrest; media reports based almost exclusively on official government sources; and censorship, either government-imposed or self-imposed. Under these conditions, the media's reporting is passive and constrained. The media follow the government line and offer little analysis or criticism. When one or more of the above factors are absent or weak, the media become more assertive.

In the *push model*, other factors dominate. Military forces are frequently not involved in combat; rather, they are often used as a conduit of supplies and a source of nonmilitary expertise. The media frequently "spotlight" the crisis through their reporting and operate without censorship. International organizations, including NGOs, are often involved. There is sparse knowledge of the crisis in the United States, and the distinction between "good" and "bad" is unclear. This model produces conditions that foster a more "aggressive" media, which often leads the government to act. In the post–Cold War era the push model has become more important for two obvious reasons. The absence of another superpower frees the United States from past constraints imposed by the Soviet Union, and military operations do not involve a high risk of casualties to U.S. military forces.

The spanish-american war

The Spanish-American War marked the beginning of the nation's role as a world power. Previously the United States had been an insular nation with little international presence. It also represented the adoption by the media of an active role in foreign affairs. In the nation's first major conflict beyond its borders, newspapers became the chief means of communicating events.[11] In the late 1800s the national media used sensation-loving "yellow journalism" as a way to sell papers. As a consequence, Spain's mistreatment of Cubans was reported at length in the daily newspapers. The newspapers focused on emotional stories, portrayed events in simplistic terms, and spurred the public's demand for some government response. They stepped into a gap left by a lack of presidential and institutional leadership. One of the day's most notable "yellow journalists," William Randolph Hearst, declared, "The force of the newspaper is the greatest force in civilization. Under republican government, newspapers form and express public opinion. They suggest and control legislation. They declare wars."[12]

The Spanish-American War demonstrates the action of the push model as a result of the absence or weakness of a primary element of the pull model—in this case the lack of presidential leadership in foreign policy. When conditions produce unsettled or inconsistent foreign policy messages, the role of the media is heightened. H. Wayne Morgan addressed this issue in *America's Road to Empire*,[13] arguing that "newspaper pressure of the day helped cause the war by keeping diplomacy unsettled"[14] at a time when public opinion was mounting and congressional calls for action were increasing.

world war I

World Wars I and II commanded all the elements essential to the "pull model" of media coverage—strong presidential leadership, a high consensus among the public that supported the government's actions, and a defined mission and known enemy. The result was the creation of a new relationship between the media and foreign policy makers, the reverse of that which occurred during the Spanish-American War.

World War I (1914–1918), the nation's first "total war," occurred at a time journalism was just becoming a profession. Unlike the case with the Spanish-American War, journalists accepted governmental officials as their primary sources of information. The media also identified with the goals of the war. Initially President Wilson was reluctant to engage in the conflict and the public was divided, but once the nation was committed, the media were among the most valuable allies of the government by helping to send a unified message to the public. Severe sanctions were placed on the media before the war, and some remained after the United States entered the war. World War I sent conflicting messages to the media. The government wanted the media's assistance to build public support. At the same time this period saw "a hysterical war hatred of all that seemed not to conform,"[15] and this included critical journalists.

In response to the war, Congress passed some of the nation's most restrictive legislation, including the Espionage Act of 1917, the Trading with the Enemy Act of 1917, and the Sedition Act of 1918. All had a profound impact on the media, but the Sedition Act of 1918 was the most restrictive. It stated:

> Whoever, when the United States is at war, shall wilfully make or convey false reports or false statements with the intent to interfere with the operation or success of the military or naval forces of the United States . . . [or] wilfully utter, print, write, or publish any disloyal, profane, scurrilous, or abusive language about the form of government of the United States, or the Constitution of the United States . . . shall be punished by a fine of not more than $10,000 or imprisonment for not more than twenty years, or both.

These acts had prolonged consequences for the relationship between the media and the government in the area of foreign affairs. Two important precedents were established during this period. First, the government became involved with the media on two fronts—the "home front" and the "war front"—and attempted to protect both. Second, to achieve access to the war's front, journalists had to submit their material for review prior to publication.

world war ii

World War II marked the era of greatest cooperation between the media and the government, which stemmed from outrage over the Japanese attack on Pearl Harbor and Germany's declaration of war on the United States. The usual tension between the media and the government was muffled by the broad consensus over the goals of the war effort. Censorship was imposed on the media both by the government and the media themselves. The nature of the relationship between the media and government can be seen in a memorandum from the Allied High Command in April 1944 that stated that a "minimum amount of information will be withheld consistent with security." While disputes occurred, both the military and the government saw the role of the media as maintaining support for the war effort at home. The pull model fits World War II well, for all the essential elements were in place: leadership, consensus, and a defined mission and known enemy. Consequently, independent reporting was reduced, to a large degree because of self-imposed censorship.

The media's coverage of World War II raised questions of what should be reported and how it might affect public support. Some have argued that the media's portrayal of casualties in terms of both numbers and graphic images diminished the public's support for the war effort, while others have argued that such coverage did not produce a decline in the support for American policy and the troops.[16] The debate returned in the 1960s with the Vietnam War.

The Korean War

The first test of the pull model outside of a declared war occurred when the United States entered into a "limited" war in Korea. The Korean War was also the first war covered by television reporters, the first armed conflict between communist and noncommunist forces, and the first conflict to be sanctioned by the United Nations. But there were also similarities to earlier wars. Even though the relationship between the media and the military was largely cordial, the Army's Eighth Headquarters formally censored all reports.

The media's role in the coverage of the conflict began with President Truman's using the new medium of television to announce the administration's decision to seek the United Nations' support to stop the invasion of South Korea by North Korea. As in previous wars, the components of the pull model contributed to the nature and scope of the media's coverage. In many respects the Korean War marked a "bridge" in military conflict coverage. While the relationship between the media and the military remained essentially the same as during World War II, the coverage represented a shift away from the passive role of the pull model. Two factors were primarily responsible: the nature of the conflict—an undeclared war—and the role of the United Nations.

This conflict reaffirmed the importance of a public consensus for a successful foreign policy. When President Truman first sent troops to Korea, 77 percent of the public supported his decision, but that support soon declined. Several factors contributed to this decrease, including the entrance of Chinese forces into the conflict, internal conflict among policy makers (highlighted by General MacArthur's eventual dismissal), and the increasing realization that the war was not "winnable." By the end of 1951 support had dropped to only 39 percent.

The vietnam war and its Aftermath

The media's reporting of the Vietnam War has been the subject of great debate. Many critics believed the media's coverage of military operations, particularly television coverage, undermined public support for the war and eroded troop morale. They termed this phenomenon the "Vietnam syndrome." These critics argued that the media's active, aggressive reporting altered the traditional foreign policy decision-making process. There is little evidence to support the contention that the media's reporting of the war was a major contributor to its unsuccessful conclusion. However, the media's coverage did represent a departure from the pull model of reporting that had prevailed up to that point in the twentieth century.

There were many parallels between the Korean and Vietnam wars. Both were "limited" wars, and both evoked similar patterns of public support and remarkably similar electoral patterns. But there were differences as well. The domestic environment was tranquil during the Korean conflict, in contrast to the tumult of the Vietnam War years, and the Vietnam War was televised while the Korean War was not.

Many factors contributed to the changing media coverage. One important factor was the media's unprecedented freedom in their coverage. While a natural tension always exists between the military and the media, in no other modern war were members of the media allowed such open and uncensored reporting. In addition, the new medium of television was widely accessible to the American public.

It is also important to view the Vietnam War in the context of the social unrest that was occurring at the time. The 1960s, when the United States became increasingly committed to the defense of South Vietnam from the communist North Vietnamese and Viet Cong, was also a period of domestic tumult. The nation witnessed urban riots, civil rights demonstrations, college campus unrest starting with the Berkeley free speech movement, and the assassinations of a president, a presidential candidate, and civil rights leaders, as well as assaults on antiwar protesters. These events contributed to a decline in public trust in all institutions and their leaders—from the government to the church. This was followed by a decade that saw even more cynicism and distrust in both public and private institutions as a vice-president and then a president resigned their offices.

At the same time an important structural change was occurring in television news. In 1963, CBS and NBC expanded their nightly newscasts from fifteen minutes to thirty minutes, followed two years later by ABC. The reason for this increased time was that the news divisions of the networks were very profitable. Increased news time translated into increased revenues and more reporters, and aided network affiliates.

Some have argued that "operational procedures" shaped the way the war was presented to the public. Michael Mandelbraum notes:

> The special case of Tet aside, the operational procedures of television news did shape the way the war was presented to the public. These arose from the needs of the news organizations themselves, not from the political views of those who worked for them . . . . The producers of the news programs encouraged their Saigon correspondents to shoot film of combat, especially before 1968. Combat scenes tended to be more dramatic, more exciting, and therefore—and this was the primary consideration—more likely to attract viewers than other kinds of coverage. Because there was little interest in showing Vietnamese, the subjects of the combat footage produced were invariably Americans, who were usually engaged in unspecified, but seemingly successful military activity.[17]

Support for the idea that combat footage was more important than other stories about the war is found in Edward Jay Epstein's *News From Nowhere*.[18] In detailing how the networks operated during the war, he notes that combat stories had a higher rate of acceptance and that many journalists were paid on the basis of aired stories, which drove them to submit more combat footage.[19]

The evidence relating for a precise impact of the media on the Vietnam War is mixed. However, all agree that the war received enormous attention in the press through daily television reports from the battlefields. Rarely did a night pass without the networks' reporting on official government proclamations of war aims, together with charts and graphs of troop movements, casualties, bombings, etc. Beginning in the mid-1960s, the networks increasingly featured more on-the-spot pictures and clips of American troops in combat, sometimes showing the deaths of Viet Cong and American soldiers. The reality of the war was brought into the homes of millions of Americans on a nightly basis. The protracted nature of the conflict, plus the many domestic issues, eroded the public's support for the war.

In a content analysis of network broadcasts from August 20, 1965 (the height of public support for the war), to the ceasefire of January 27, 1973, David Hallin addressed the question of whether the media changed their role in reporting the war, as is often argued.[20] Breaking the coverage down into three categories, the pre-Tet offensive, the Tet offensive (1968), and the post-Tet period, Hallin examined the sources of the news contained in the broadcasts in an effort to delineate differences in coverage. Was there a change in television's coverage of the war from predominantly favorable prior to Tet to predominantly critical after Tet? As Figure 11.1 indicates, the media's sources for stories did change after Tet: officers and GIs declined as news sources while critics of the war increased. Hallin argued that this shift reflected the public's general orientation toward the war. Early in the war the media focused on the troops and their actions, but after Tet the focus

figure 11.1

The Sources of Television News Stories on the Vietnam War

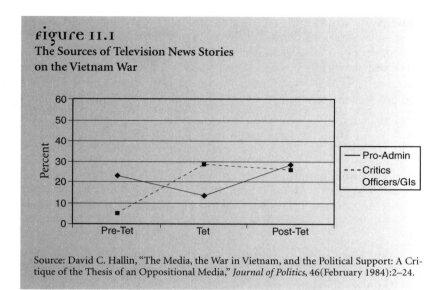

Source: David C. Hallin, "The Media, the War in Vietnam, and the Political Support: A Critique of the Thesis of an Oppositional Media," *Journal of Politics*, 46(February 1984):2–24.

shifted to reactions at home, such as antiwar demonstrations. Thus, Hallin concluded that television merely mirrored the public's disillusionment. He argued the media were passive in the initial stages of the intervention and did not question the government's policies, but instead focused on "unity and clarity."[21] However, as opposing factions became more abundant and vocal, the media shifted their attention to the domestic debate.

While the sources of information about the Vietnam War were altered somewhat by the Tet offensive in 1968, an exhaustive study of American media's coverage of this pivotal point in the war indicates that the public received a distorted picture of the event. The Tet offensive was generally portrayed as a military defeat for the United States when, from a military perspective, it was a greater setback for the North Vietnamese and the National Liberation Front. They suffered enormous losses and did not trigger the expected "uprising" across Vietnam.[22]

The impact of television on Vietnam was due in large part to the popularity of the nightly news anchors, like Walter Cronkite, David Brinkley, Chet Huntley, John Chancellor, and Frank Reynolds. When Walter Cronkite returned from a visit to Vietnam in 1968, he presented a special report to the nation that had a significant impact on the public's support for the war. During the broadcast he stated, "It is increasingly clear to this reporter that the only rational way out . . . will be to negotiate, not as visitors, but as honorable people who lived up to their pledge to defend democracy, and did the best they could."[23] Cronkite's assessment had a dual impact. First, a person whom the American public held in high regard had presented a picture of the war that was different from those making policy decisions. Second, the report came at a time when the American public's support for the conflict was already eroding.

The impact of television on the war and U.S. foreign policy is evident in the comments of President Johnson the day after he announced that he would not seek reelection:

> As I sat in my office last evening, waiting to speak, I thought of the many times each week when television brings the war into the American home. No one can say exactly what effect those vivid scenes have on American opinion. Historians must only guess at the effect that television would have had during the earlier conflicts on the future of this Nation: during the Korean War, for example, at that time when our forces were pushed back to Pusan; or World War II, the Battle of the Bulge, or when our men were slugging it out in Europe or when most of our Air Force was shot down that day in June 1942 off Australia.[24]

It is clear from these remarks that the president believed the role of television in the Vietnam War was critical. The Vietnam War represented a shift from the passive, pull model of reporting to a new and more active, push model. Many factors contributed to this change: social unrest, the inability to win the war in a conventional sense, confusion over the war's objectives, and the public's loss of commitment to the effort. America's involvement in foreign countries was deeply changed by the events in Vietnam. Today many believe that a protracted war is nearly impossible in an era of live media coverage.

The first United States military action after the Vietnam War occurred in the small Caribbean island of Grenada in 1983. Since gaining independence in 1974, the island had lacked political stability. In 1983 a socialist and black power advocate was elected prime minister, and the Reagan administration subsequently reported that the Soviet Union was preparing to use the island as a launching base for Communist expansion. On October 23, 1983, the administration sent military forces to install a new government and hold new elections. Remembering the Vietnam experience, the military and the administration *excluded* the press from the initial operations. When the press complained, the administration allowed a small, rotating group of reporters to cover military operations, accompanied by military personnel in the initial stages.

Six years later, the concept of "pooled" reporting was tested when the United States designed a mission to depose Panamanian President Manuel Noriega. The experiment failed. The fourteen reporters assigned to the pool arrived hours after the operation began. In addition, their movements were restricted to tours provided by the military, and there was a high level of censorship. The Vietnam mindset that the media were no friend of the military and administration policy persisted.

Neither of these conflicts falls within the models discussed. The public was not well informed, there were no declarations of war, even on a limited basis, nor was there an international crisis. The United States copied the

British model of operations used in the Falkland Islands, which imposed a news blackout during the operations.

The persian gulf war

The Gulf War broke out *on* television, or at least that is how television viewers in many parts of the world remember it. In the United States on Wednesday January 16, 1991, the Gulf War erupted on prime-time evening news. The ABC network was the first to break the story on its program, *World News Tonight*, with a live telephone interview with its reporter in Baghdad, Gary Shepphard. But it was CNN that gave the world most of the video feeds of the war, and it was CNN that became the conduit of information from both sides during the war. Television's extensive role in the conflict resulted in the Gulf War's being called the "television war."

However, the media's role in the crisis started well before the actual military conflict. The United States had sent mixed signals to Iraq's Saddam Hussein prior to his invasion of Kuwait. Iraq had been the beneficiary of a western support, both military and economic, in an effort to counterbalance Iran and to bring stability to the region. Immediately after Iraq's invasion of Kuwait, the Bush administration did not perceive a "crisis." At an early morning meeting on August 2 "the prevailing attitude among the group, according to one participant, was, 'Hey, too bad about Kuwait, but it's just a gas station, and who cares whether the sign says Sinclair or Exxon?'"[25]

The nature of the relationship between Iraq and the United States was also evident in the method of coverage of the early events. Timothy Cook content analyzed the sources of news stories surrounding Iraq's invasion of Kuwait.[26] As shown in Figure 12.2, although the Gulf War was international from the start, the news during the first two months of the crisis was reported more by domestic reporters than foreign. Cook contends that the media have choices of where to allocate their personnel and which reporters to feature most heavily in a developing a story. By selecting domestic reporters, the media were giving information from the administration the highest priority. As a result, the conflict was portrayed as a White House policy problem, not a complex international crisis.

Through the autumn and winter of 1990, Philip Taylor notes, CNN defined itself "as an instant electronic interlocutor between Baghdad and Washington and it became clear that television would play a particularly prominent role in any conflict."[27] The 10-year-old CNN frequently carried exchanges between Saddam Hussein and George Bush, breaking the tradition of diplomatic secrecy in such negotiations. The two leaders were engaging, instead, in televised diplomacy, which affected how the war would ultimately be perceived by the world.

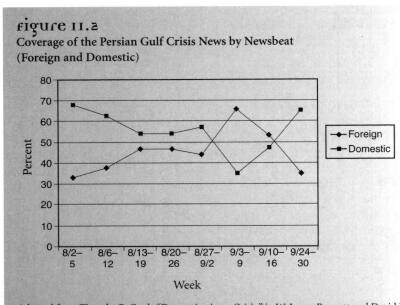

fiɣure II.2
Coverage of the Persian Gulf Crisis News by Newsbeat
(Foreign and Domestic)

Adapted from Timothy E. Cook, "Domesticating a Crisis," in W. Lance Bennett and David L. Paletz, eds., *Taken by Storm* (Chicago: The University of Chicago Press, 1994), 113–114, Tables 1a and 1b.

The Gulf War illustrates the relationship between the media and political institutions as well as any domestic issue we have discussed. There is a mutual need for each other in foreign events just as there is in political campaigns, and the Gulf War was a political campaign waged primarily through the medium of television. The Bush administration adroitly used the media to present its message, to portray Saddam Hussein's Iraq as a danger to national security. Once the war broke out, the military employed censorship to control information.

The Gulf War was fought on a wide variety of fronts—economic, diplomatic, psychological, political, and military. But it was the military front that television favored because it lent itself to visual coverage and provided the military with important information, and its coverage tended to create a simplistic impression of a complex war, as well as an illusion of open coverage.[28] Television's need for pictures has been described as a "pathology," and during the Gulf War it resulted in endless pictures of what the allied commanders allowed to be filmed. Former Reagan aide Michael Deaver said at the time, "The Department of Defense has done an excellent job of managing the news in an almost classic way. There's plenty of access to some things, and at least one visual a day. If you were going to hire a public relations firm to do the media relations for an international event, it couldn't be done any better than this."[29]

There is evidence that television coverage of the conflict in the Persian Gulf significantly affected Americans' evaluation of President Bush. Prior to the crisis, Americans were preoccupied with economic problems and crime, and these issues determined their feelings toward the president.[30] Following the invasion of Kuwait, the Gulf crisis became the public's paramount concern and the president was evaluated in terms of foreign policy. From November through February, the Gulf War was the number one concern of the public and President Bush's approval ratings reached record highs. However, as soon as the war ended, the public's focus returned to economic concerns and the president's approval ratings plummeted.

Another effect of the Gulf War was a by-product of communications technology. The speed of communications lessened the reflection, interpretation, and sifting of the news that had been present in reporting on earlier conflicts. The televised coverage of the Gulf War had three major themes. First, it presented the war as a contest between good and evil, with President Bush representing the good and Saddam Hussein the evil. Second, the coverage focused heavily on the skill, character, "toughness and stamina" of the American soldier. Finally, the machines were as important to the drama as the soldiers in this war.

The Gulf War is the most recent example of the pull model and demonstrates successful control of the media by the policy makers and the military. The technology that was so successful in bringing the war into the homes of America profoundly altered the relationship between the media and government. During the six weeks of the Gulf War, more people watched more hours of television a day than in any other time in history. The era of televised foreign affairs had arrived.

The Intervention in Somalia

The United States involvement in Somalia was the first commitment of United States troops overseas after the Gulf War. Three types of television images from the United States' involvement in Somalia are most frequently remembered. The first are images of famine, disease, and death. The second are American Marines landing on the beaches in the glare of bright television lights. The third are shots of a dead American soldier being dragged through the streets of Mogadishu. As a result, some have charged that the media directed America's policy in this crisis. It was widely believed that television's images of famine directed the nation's attention toward Somalia and not other countries in the region that were also in the midst of mass starvation. The images of the Marines landing without resistance seemed to build support for intervention. Finally, the image of a soldier being dragged through the streets was thought to be responsible for the withdrawal of U.S. troops. What was the media's role in Somalia?

figure 11.3
Number of Network Evening News Stories Mentioning Somalia, 1992 (ABC, CBS, NBC)

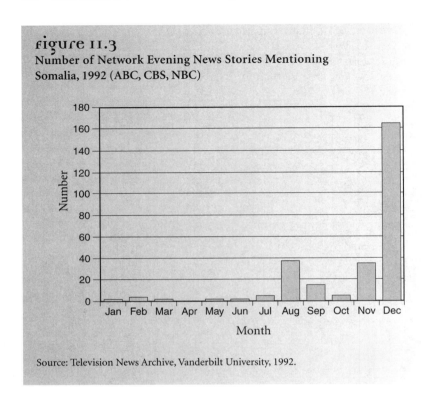

Source: Television News Archive, Vanderbilt University, 1992.

Somalia represents the complexities associated with nontraditional military operations, in which there are frequently no clear enemy, no clear-cut victories or defeats, and no clearly delineated sides in the conflict. Such operations often change as events force new approaches and place demands on the intervening nations. In Somalia the United States changed its stated objectives as tribal hostilities increased and drew in nations that were attempting to aid a nation in distress.

There is evidence that the images of starving children on television had a personal impact on President Bush and members of his administration.[31] However, what was not reported was that the United States had provided 12,000 tons of food to Somalia *prior* to the news media's reporting of the crisis in 1991. The media's spotlight on conditions in Somalia did raise public awareness, which helped policy makers assist in humanitarian efforts, but there is also evidence that the government used the media to promote its policy.[32]

Figure 11.3 shows the number of stories on Somalia aired by the three major networks and suggests the media were not that important in the determination of policy. If the media pushed American policy makers into greater activity in Somalia, then media coverage of Somalia should have been significant *prior* to August 14, when President Bush announced Operation

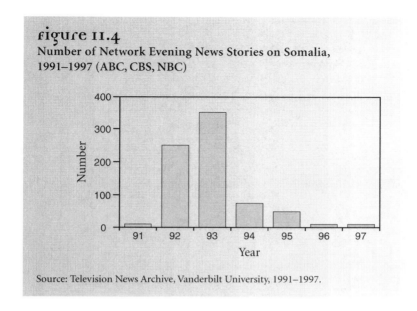

figure 11.4
Number of Network Evening News Stories on Somalia,
1991–1997 (ABC, CBS, NBC)

Source: Television News Archive, Vanderbilt University, 1991–1997.

Provide Relief. However, only 15 of 257 stories (or 6 percent) involving Somalia aired prior to President Bush's announcement. In this case the media
followed the administration's lead. In August, when the president announced
the humanitarian effort, the media more than doubled their coverage compared to the previous seven months. In addition, the data clearly indicate
that the media coverage in 1992 was strongly associated with direct military
involvement. Nearly two thirds of all stories on Somalia were aired during
December, when American troops entered the country. As Figure 11.4 shows,
the network's coverage of Somalia from 1991 through 1997 was clearly associated with the presence of U.S. troops in the country. In 1993 there were
340 stories on Somalia and one fifth of those occurred when U.S. troops
were withdrawing from the country.

These data suggest the images broadcast by the networks were far less
important than is widely assumed. Rather than pushing military involvement, the media were pulled by the actions of the United States government.
The media focused on the conflict and on the dramatic, but not on the causes or consequences of the problems in the country.

The Bosnian Conflict

In the early 1990s Yugoslavia began to slowly unravel as first Slovenia and
then Croatia sought and won their independence. The independence movement within Yugoslavia became an international crisis when Bosnia

figure 11.5
**Trends in Americans' Attention to Bosnia
(Variation from the Mean*)**

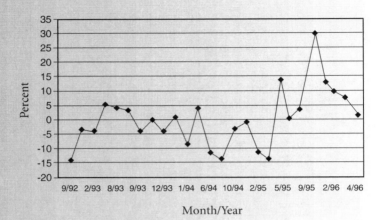

Month/Year

*The mean represents "very close" and "fairly close" responses to the question of attention paid to news stories about the situation in Bosnia.

Source: Adapted from Stephen E. Bennett, Richard S. Flickinger, and Staci L. Rhine, "American Public Opinion and the Civil War in Bosnia: Attention, Knowledge, and the Media," *Press/Politics,* Vol. 2 (Fall 1997), Table 1: 91. Data Source: *Times/Mirror*/Pew Research Center for The People and The Press Polls.

attempted to become independent. Unlike Slovenia and Croatia, which were each dominated by one religion, Bosnia had large Muslim, Orthodox, and Catholic populations, which had long-standing animosities. For four years the American government received little guidance from its NATO allies in the region about the nature of the Bosnian conflict. As a consequence, the United States' policy was shifting and unclear. For instance, President Clinton referred to the conflict at various times as a war of aggression, a threat to U.S. values, and a three-sided civil war. This allowed the media to define the conflict in their own way.

What role did the media play in providing information on this crisis and how receptive was the public to the information? Stephen Bennett and his colleagues addressed these questions by examining Bosnia coverage in the *New York Times* and on the three networks.[33] Using public opinion data from the *Times-Mirror*/Pew surveys and content analysis of the *Times* and the network news, they compared the attentiveness of those who said they had followed the coverage of Bosnia "very closely" and "fairly closely" to the actual coverage.

Figure 11.5 shows the public's attentiveness to Bosnia was directly related to possible or actual military action. Eleven of the twenty-six polls

figure 11.6
Number of Network Evening News Stories on Bosnia,
1990–1998 (ABC, CBS, NBC)

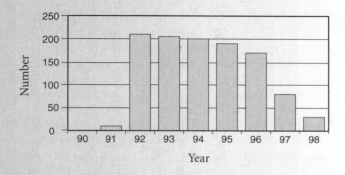

Source: Television News Archive, Vanderbilt University, 1990–1998.

included in the study showed public attentiveness to Bosnia above the mean. However, nine of these eleven (80 percent) polls were taken between September 1995 and July 1996—a period that coincided with increased military action by the United States and NATO and the downing and rescue of American pilot Captain O'Grady. The authors concluded that overall the media's coverage exceeded the public's interest. Kohut and Toth have argued that "the media failed to engage the public's attention in Bosnia. . . . Moreover, the level of public interest in Bosnia over the course of the conflict has shown no correlation to the amount of media coverage."[34]

As Figure 11.6 indicates, the network coverage of Bosnia peaked in 1992, when the three major networks ran 211 stories. In 1995 the network coverage decreased slightly, with the networks airing 185 stories, and in 1997 and 1998 there was a greater decline as the networks aired 85 and 24 stories, respectively.

The conflict in Bosnia was characterized as a one-sided, brutal war of aggression carried out by Bosnian Serbs against the Muslim-led government in Sarajevo. Warren Strobel has charged the U.S. media with "lacking any historical understanding of the Balkans and simplistically dredged up memories of Nazi concentration camps, reducing the war to a one-dimensional struggle of good (Muslim) and bad (Serb)."[35] The coverage in Bosnia was similar to the coverage of national politics. It was simplistic and distorted, lacked substance, and was characterized by "pack journalism." Having said this, there is little doubt that the media performed a vital role in focusing attention on this conflict.

Intervention in Haiti

The United States' intervention in Haiti in 1994 was another example of post–Cold War era American foreign policy. There were similarities as well as differences with the media's role in Somalia. Each situation had a low media profile until the possibility arose of committing American troops. Both presented tests of the "CNN effect" or the push model of the media in foreign relations. Finally, in each case the media's role was a significant factor, focusing attention on problems in the countries. The major dissimilarity was the reason for the United States' intervention. In Somalia the justification was humanitarian, while the Haitian situation was creating an immigration problem for the United States. The problem began in 1991 with the overthrow by a military coup of the popular president, Jean-Bertrand Aristede. As political unrest and dire economic conditions increased in Haiti in 1994, illegal immigration to the United States sharply increased.

As Figure 11.7 indicates, the network news coverage of Haiti slowly but steadily increased between 1990 and 1993. In 1993 two thirds of all network stories dealt with the refugees. The political impasse caused by the coup in 1991 was seldom covered in the 142 stories aired. The American public and policy makers were more concerned with the potential economic impact of waves of refugees. The United States government refused to allow the refugees to enter, and this policy was upheld by the Supreme Court. However, as economic and political conditions worsened, African-American

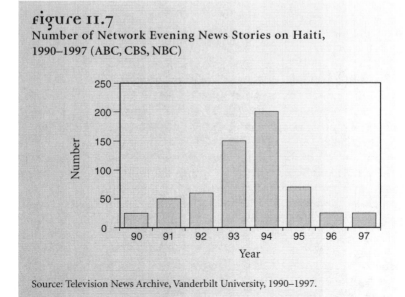

figure 11.7
Number of Network Evening News Stories on Haiti,
1990–1997 (ABC, CBS, NBC)

Source: Television News Archive, Vanderbilt University, 1990–1997.

communities in the United States and the Congressional Black Caucus increased pressure to restore order to the island.

In 1994 the United States embarked on a new course of action—to return Aristede to office, by force if necessary. The media's coverage of the Haitian problem focused on three major events: the United States' efforts to restore the elected president; efforts by special envoys former President Carter, General Colin Powell, and Senator Sam Nunn to negotiate a peaceful removal; and the military buildup and preparations to invade Haiti. Lessons learned in Somalia were applied to the media in Haiti. To avoid negative public reaction to the coverage, as in Somalia, the military went to unprecedented lengths to accommodate the media. For instance, some journalists were provided with detailed classified operation orders for the invasion. Provisions were made to have journalists fly aboard the military's command and operations plane for the first time in history. However, positive diplomatic efforts made military action unnecessary.

Because the public had little advance warning of the problems in Haiti, there was no "CNN effect." Coverage was driven by the implications of the country's internal problems for America—immigration problems and the possible need for military force to restore an elected president. There was in this situation, unlike in Bosnia, a perception that the national interest, albeit narrow and ill defined, was involved.

The Kosovo Conflict

On March 22, 1999, the United States joined by its NATO allies, authorized air strikes against Serbian forces in Kosovo, a region in Yugoslavia with large Serbian and ethnic Albanian populations. The Rambouillet peace talks between the Kosovar Serbs and ethnic Albanians had failed to bring a diplomatic resolution to many years of civil strife in the region. Once the air strikes began, armed forces loyal to Serbian President Slobodan Milosevic began implementing a policy of "ethnic cleansing," mass killings and forced deportations of ethnic Albanians into neighboring Albania, Montenegro, and Macedonia. The media focused on the human tragedies in both Kosovo and Serbia resulting from the civil strife and the air attacks.

The Kosovo coverage raises two important questions concerning the media and foreign policy. Did the media push the American government to react to the atrocities in Kosovo, and once NATO action began, what was the media's role in the conflict?

Warren Strobel's earlier observations concerning the media's coverage of Bosnia also apply to Kosovo. Here, too, the lack of historical understanding of the Balkans led to simplistic stories about the actions of the Serbian police and army and reduced the conflict to a one-dimensional struggle between good and evil. The Clinton administration played into this characterization of the situation in Kosovo by depicting President Milosevic as the new Hitler.

When President Clinton first proposed active American military involvement in Kosovo, few Americans knew of the region, the issues, or the reason America should become involved. However, poll data indicated that once pictures of the refugees began to appear on television, public support for the president's handling of the situation and NATO involvement increased.

Such interventions are often controversial, but Kosovo was particularly so because it occurred in the wake of long and bitterly fought impeachment proceedings, which hardened the resistance of some Republican members of Congress and the public to anything associated with the president. Furthermore, the presidential campaign for 2000 was unfolding and potential candidates had mixed reactions to U.S. policy. The Republican Party was particularly polarized, with candidate Pat Buchanan strongly arguing that the United States had no national interest in the region and that the conflict was a civil matter within a sovereign nation, while unannounced candidate Arizona Senator John McCain supported the president's policy.

Modern means of communication were particularly pronounced in Kosovo, as both sides waged war through the mass media, satellites, cell phones, and the Internet. These modern communication technologies were used more extensively than in other conflicts. Both NATO and the Serbian government quickly established Web sites, and used them to weigh and try to secure national and international support.

To address the first question, we reviewed the television news coverage of Kosovo from 1990 through April 9, 1999. If the media had a "CNN effect," then there should have been an increasing number of Kosovo stories leading up to the NATO bombing on March 24, 1999. The networks aired 241 Kosovo stories prior to the beginning of NATO's air strikes on March 24, 1999, and only thirteen of those stories, all except one by CBS, appeared before 1998. Only 14 percent of all stories broadcast on the three networks appeared prior to the commencement of air strikes. Clearly Kosovo was not a major news story until 1998.

Figure 11.8 shows the distribution of Kosovo stories from January 1998 through April 1999 and reveals several noteworthy patterns. First, during 1998 there were an average of sixteen network stories on Kosovo per month. Second, in four months (the last in November) there were no network news stories about Kosovo. Finally, nearly two thirds of the stories (63 percent) occurred in two months, June (22 percent) and October (41 percent), and only 2 percent appeared in December 1998. These data suggest that, in the case of Kosovo, the media were pulled into coverage by the actions of the United States and its NATO allies. Once the United States and NATO began the seventy-nine days of bombing, network coverage shifted dramatically. Figure 11.9 shows that after the first two weeks of the conflict, the media's attention began to decline. By the second week, as reporters began operating in the area, they were able to provide dramatic images of fleeing refugees. As the bombing continued into the third and fourth weeks, the networks reduced their coverage.

fiʒure 11.8
Number of Network Evening News Stories on Kosovo (ABC, CBS, NBC)

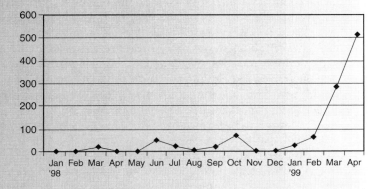

Source: Center for Media and Public Affairs, "Tracking the Crisis in Kosovo," *Factoids*, October 28, 1999, *http://www.cmpa.com.*

fiʒure 11.9
Number of Network Evening News Stories on Kosovo from April 1 Through May 24 (ABC, CBS, NBC)

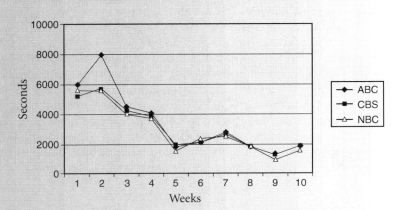

Source: Center for Media and Public Affairs, "Tracking the Crisis in Kosovo," *Factoids*, January 15, 1999, *http://www.cmpa.com.*

To understand the fluctuations in coverage, it is useful to recall the major events that attracted the media's attention. For instance, during the second week, when the most airtime was given to coverage of Kosovo, two events dominated that coverage. The first was the mass influx of refugees into neighboring countries, which strained the ability of those countries and humanitarian organizations to provide adequate shelter and food. The second was the Serbian army's capture of three American servicemen. From week two through week six there was a steady decline in network coverage, followed by an increase in weeks seven and eight. During week seven the Rev. Jesse Jackson arrived in Belgrade and secured the release of the three American servicemen. The following week the Chinese embassy was mistakenly bombed, adding another international dimension.

There are four lessons to be learned from the network coverage of Kosovo. First, it was not media-driven but event-driven. Second, the military conflict and the humanitarian situation (particularly the refugee situation) were the media's focus. Third, as the bombing continued, the media coverage declined. Finally, the latest communication technologies were used by both sides to an unprecedented degree.

some conclusions on conflicts

Overall, the role of the media as it relates to international interventions seems to be increasing. The media helped Americans understand the national interest in the Gulf War, but in Somalia the media's images of dead soldiers hastened the withdrawal of military forces. In Bosnia the media failed to accurately depict the complex issues involved, which resulted in a low level of tolerance for direct involvement. In Haiti the media coverage focused on concern about immigration and its impact on the United States, and later on military intervention to restore the president.

James F. Hoge, writing in *Foreign Affairs*, addressed the new role of the media in foreign affairs: "Television images usually have a short shelf life, and their emotional effects can be tempered by reason. But that requires political leadership that constructs supportable policy, explains it and knows when to stand fast behind it."[36] The irony in the post–Cold War era is that the use of force is more likely in the absence of a strong counterforce. The external constraints have been removed, but at the same time there is a lack of consensus on the proper role of the United States in the world today. In the vacuum created by these events, the media have emerged as agenda setters and determinants of foreign policy.

summary

The end of the Cold War brought numerous changes in United States military activities and the media's reporting of these events. One of the most discussed and controversial of these changes involves situations when media coverage leads the nation into military action, a phenomenon commonly referred to as the "CNN effect."

To understand how the media have reported military involvement, we reviewed the media's involvement in major military actions beginning with the Spanish-American War. Through the years two models of media reporting have emerged. In the pull model, the media are constrained in their reporting by both the government and self-imposed censorship. This model was dominant through the early years of the Vietnam War, but the push model dominated later in the conflict. In the push model, the media are more aggressive and assertive in their coverage of foreign events, and in the process often push the government into action or reaction. Somalia represents the push model.

The Vietnam experience taught important lessons about the military and the media. The media were excluded from covering the initial phases of the Reagan administration's invasion of Grenada, leading to media complaints of a "news blackout." A new policy was then developed that allowed reporters selected from a "pool" to observe the actions and then report their observations back to their fellow journalists. This was used during the United States invasion of Panama to arrest General Noriega. However, the pool reporters did not arrive until well after the military operations had begun. During the Gulf War, the media's coverage was based primarily on military press releases and on CNN reports live from inside Iraq. In subsequent military actions the media's coverage has been a mixture of models, with little evidence that it pushed the government into action.

Modern technology allows the media to be more assertive in their coverage of foreign events. The advent of CNN and the Internet may lead to more active reporting of foreign news. However, our examination of the military's involvement in the Persian Gulf War, Somalia, Haiti, Bosnia, and Kosovo found that the media generally reacted to events, rather than pushing the government to act. The findings indicate that while the manner in which the media covered each event differed, there is no evidence of the "CNN effect." In fact, examination of the three major networks' coverage reveals little evidence that it prompted the dispatching of troops. On the contrary, the media generally focused on the area at the time of or slightly before the military involvement; they did not spur these events, but rather reacted to them.

Endnotes

[1] Walter Goodman, "The Images That Haunt Washington," *New York Times*, May 5, 1991:H33.

[2] W. Lance Bennett, "Toward a Theory of Press-State Relations in the United States," *Journal of Communication*, 40(1990):106.

[3] Robert Entman and Benjamin I. Page, "The News Before the Storm: The Iraq War Debate and the Limits to Media Independence," in W. Lance Bennett and David L. Paletz, eds., *Taken*

by Storm: The Media, Public Opinion, and U.S. Foreign Policy in the Gulf War (Chicago: University of Chicago Press, 1994), 82–101; Daniel C. Hallin, *We Keep America on Top of the World: Television Journalism and the Public Sphere* (London: Routledge, 1994).

[4]Entman and Page, *op. cit.*, 97.

[5]William A. Dorman and Steven Livingston, "News and Historical Content," in Bennett and Paletz, *op. cit.*, 76.

[6]*Ibid.*, 63–81.

[7]Steven Livingston, "Beyond the 'CNN Effect': The Media-Foreign Policy Dynamic," in Pippa Norris, ed., *Politics and the Press: The News Media and Their Influences* (Boulder, Colo.: Lynne Rienner Publishers, 1997), 291–318.

[8]*Ibid.*, 293.

[9]Warren P. Strobel, *Late-Breaking Foreign Policy: The News Media's Influence on Peace Operations* (Washington, D.C.: United States Institute of Peace Press, 1997).

[10]These "models" are derived from Warren P. Strobel, *Late-Breaking Foreign Policy: The News Media's Influence on Peace Operations* (Washington. D.C.: United States Institute for Peace, 1997).

[11]The first armed conflict was the Mexican War (1846–1848), which resulted from the United States' annexation of Texas in 1845.

[12]Douglas Johnson II, *The Impact of the Media on National Security Policy Decision-Making* (Carlisle Barracks, Penn.: U.S. Army War College, Strategic Studies Institute, 1994), 1.

[13]H. Wayne Morgan, *America's Road to Empire: The War With Spain and Overseas Expansion* (New York: Alfred A. Knopf, 1965).

[14]*Ibid.*, 14.

[15]T. Harry Williams, Richard Current, and Frank Freidel, *A History of the United States Since 1865* (New York: Alfred A. Knopf, 1959), 397.

[16]David C. Hallin, "The Media, the War in Vietnam, and Political Support: A Critique of the Thesis of an Oppositional Media," *Journal of Politics*, 34(February 1984):2–24.

[17]Michael Mandelbraum, "Vietnam: The Television War," reprinted by permission of *Daedalus: Journal of the American Academy of Arts and Sciences*, from the issue entitled "Print Culture and Video Culture," 111(4)(Fall 1982):159.

[18]Edward Jay Epstein, *News From Nowhere: Television and the News* (New York: Vintage Books, 1973), 183.

[19]*Ibid.*, 184.

[20]Hallin, *op. cit.*

[21]David C. Hallin. *The Uncensored War: The Media and Vietnam* (New York: Oxford University Press, 1986).

[22]Peter Braestrup, *Big Story: How the American Press and Television Reported and Interpreted the Crisis of Tet 1968 in Vietnam and Washington* (Boulder, Colo.: Westview Press, 1977).

[23]Robert Metz, *CBS: Reflections in a Bloodshot Eye* (New York: Signet Books, 1975), 352.

[24]"Remarks in Chicago Before the National Association of Broadcasters," in Lyndon B. Johnson, *The Public Papers of the President of the United States, 1968* (Washington, D.C.: U.S. Government Printing Office, 1969), 484.

[25]J.C. Smith, *George Bush's War* (New York: Henry Holt, 1992), 17.

[26]Timothy Cook, "Domesticating a Crisis: Washington Newsbeats and Network News After the Iraq Invasion of Kuwait," in Bennett and Paletz , *op. cit.*, 105–130.

[27]Philip M. Taylor, *War and the Media: Propaganda and the Persian Gulf War* (Manchester, England: Manchester University Press, 1992).

[28]*Ibid.*, 17–18.

[29]Micheal Deaver, quoted in Alex S. Jones, "War in the Gulf: The Press; The Process of News Reporting on Display," *New York Times*, February 15, 1991:A9.

[30]Shanto Iyengar and Alan Simon, "New Coverage of the Gulf Crisis and Public Opinion," in Bennett and Paltez, *op. cit.*, 167–185.

[31]Strobel, *op. cit.*, 32.

[32]*Ibid.*

[33]Stephen E. Bennett, Richard S. Flickinger, and Staci L. Rhine, "American Public Opinion and the Civil War in Bosnia: Attention, Knowledge, and the Media," *Press/Politics*, 2(Fall 1997):71–86.

[34]Andrew Kohut and Robert Toth, "Arms and the People," *Foreign Affairs*, 73(November/December 1994): 47–61.

[35]Strobel, *op. cit.*, 100.

[36]James F. Hoge, Jr., "Media Pervasiveness," *Foreign Affairs*, 73 (July/August 1994):136–144.

CHAPTER 12

The changing political landscape

We have examined the evolving relationship between the mass media and political institutions, and have found a political landscape in which the media have increasingly been the initiators of change. We have not argued, as some have, that the media are the sole cause of change, but rather that they provide what Walter Lippmann called a pseudo-environment—a world they have created. As the media have changed, so too has our view of the world.

This study has examined the media's impact on the political process and the institutions of government. We have seen that the media have become more responsible for political socialization than families, schools, or churches. Other agents of socialization, most notably the family, have also undergone profound change, but the media have done very little to explain those changes to the American public. The media focus on the difficulties families face (episodic reporting), neglecting the social and cultural factors that contribute to those difficulties. This results in Americans' focusing on the changing family and not on the factors that contributed to the changes.

There have been significant changes in every aspect of the relationship between the media and the world of politics, including how scholars study these changes. However, five areas of change are particularly significant, for they have altered the foundation upon which the political process rests. They are government regulation, the sources of political information, the content of that information, the standards imposed by the media, and technological advances.

Government Regulation

The concepts of freedom and regulation may seem in conflict, yet without regulation there can be no freedom. The regulation of the media was relatively simple and did not have much impact on political life until the advent of broadcasting. While issues of libel, slander, privacy, and privileged communication have long legal histories, they have not altered the political landscape of American politics as forcefully as have changes in how the broadcast media are regulated.

Originally broadcast owners sought government regulation, and the responsible agency since 1934 has been the Federal Communication Commission (FCC). One of its principle functions has been to oversee licensing, access, and ownership. In the 1980s two factors, new technology and deregulation, converged to drastically change the role of the FCC and the media's role in politics.

Under the Reagan administration six important changes occurred in regulation. The FCC was reduced from seven members to five. Station licenses were extended from three to five years. Radio and television stations were no longer required to maintain daily program logs. News organizations for the first time were allowed to organize political debates. The "fairness doctrine" was deleted from the FCC access requirements. Finally, rules were changed to allow the single ownership of increasing numbers of AM, FM, and television stations.

Deregulation continued during the Clinton administration, during which a record number of mergers in the communications industry occurred. In addition, the passage of the 1996 Telecommunications Act allowed telephone companies to transmit television programs through their lines. When the installation of fiberoptic lines is completed, these companies will be able to offer as many as 500 different television channels.

These changes have had a major impact on how political information is presented to the public for several reasons. First, in 1998 media mergers represented the second largest group of mergers in terms of both numbers and dollars. Second, as corporate America continued to buy and control the means of communication, the control and mission of news gathering were directly affected. Ben Bagdikian, a long-time scholar of the media and mergers, argues that these mergers will inevitably affect journalists' standards, despite CEOs' claims to the contrary: "There have been 100 that have cheapened their news for every one that promised it would not. The promises are made easily, but they are seldom kept."[1] Third, as the media have become less accountable to the public, the boundaries between news and entertainment have become increasingly blurred, if not abolished. Finally, there is increasing evidence that the entire process of gathering, transmitting, and analyzing political information has undergone an enormous transformation, one that could have dangerous consequences for democratic governance.

The sources of information

The print media were the dominant source of political information from the nation's inception to the 1920s. While the print era saw numerous changes in the coverage of politics, these were minor compared to those in the era of broadcasting. The introduction of the radio and television into American politics not only changed the manner in which the public received information, but changed who could succeed in politics, as well as who participated. Candidates, campaigns, and the style and ultimately the reporting of politics were transformed.

While the radio altered politics profoundly, its long-term effects were tempered by two factors. First, radio was the "new" communicator from only 1922 to the 1950s. Second, the public during this period still relied on newspapers as the major source of their political information. The changes brought about by television have been longer-lasting and the public's use of and confidence in newspapers has declined significantly, leaving television the most used and most trusted source of political information.

The programs people are using as information sources have changed as well. A 1997 Pew Center survey during the 1996 presidential election found that one quarter of respondents claimed they received their political information from Jay Leno or David Letterman.[2] This figure increased to 40 percent for those under 30 years old. In addition, 15 percent claimed that MTV was their primary source of political information.[3] The consequences of these changes for the electoral process and the health of democracy are considerable.

Moreover, changes within television have revolutionized the flow of political information. First, news programs have changed as networks have been merged with or taken over by large conglomerates like General Electric, Viacom, and Disney. Where once network news programming was a source of revenue, today these units have been reduced in size and importance because they no longer generate the revenues they did in earlier years. Furthermore, the relationship between owners and those in the news departments is more remote in today's conglomerate media structure. This has produced homogenized news reporting, with less diversity in reporting and increasingly blurred lines between news and entertainment. It has also produced what veteran journalist Daniel Schorr believes to be the fundamental problem today—that television is "a medium whose heart is really in Hollywood."[4]

In addition, where once national newscasters were revered and their programs relied on for accurate political information, today most Americans claim to receive most political information from local television. This development is troubling because the amount of local news time that is actually "news" is only twelve to sixteen minutes, compared with twenty-two minutes for the national broadcasts. Of those sixteen minutes, few if any cover politics, further reducing the amount and depth of political information. Additionally, the quality of news personnel varies widely across the country, and few have the resources to adequately and accurately provide political information at the local, state, or national level. Finally, reliance on local news increasingly fragments society, for what is perceived as important in one locality may not be so perceived in another.

In another development, the new medium of the Internet is reshaping the way Americans shop, entertain themselves, and obtain their political information. Although in its infancy, the Internet is bringing about another major transformation in political communication. The danger is that its entertainment use will overshadow its ability to provide instant political news.

The content of information

As the sources of political communication have changed, so too has the content. The transition from print to broadcast brought momentous changes, but the most profound and subtle occurred with the arrival of television. The way information is presented as well as its content are critical to the political process. At a minimum, these changes have affected the agenda-setting process.

A study conducted by the Committee of Concerned Journalists in 1997 reviewed the news content of television of network news programs, newspapers, newsmagazines, and television newsmagazines.[5] The committee used a random sampling of stories in the years 1977, 1987, and 1997 to ascertain if changes had occurred in the presentation of news and, if they had, to determine their nature. Their analysis resulted in three general findings. First, there was a shift toward lifestyle, celebrity, entertainment, and celebrity/scandal coverage and away from government and foreign affairs, but "infotainment" still did not dominate over traditional news. Second, there was an even more pervasive shift toward "featurized" news that focused on people rather than substantive issues. Finally, the news media were dividing into market-based niches, which meant that an individual's perception of society could vary greatly depending on his or her news source. For example, television newsmagazines, which have replaced documentaries on network television, have nearly abandoned traditional news topics like government, social welfare, education, and economics, and instead emphasize lifestyle stories. Print newsmagazines, once a primary source of political news, have moved heavily toward celebrity coverage. Newspapers continue to cover government, foreign policy, and domestic issues as their staple, and the network news programs have become a hybrid of the other media. Figure 12.1 shows the decline in straight news in newspapers, network news, and print newsmagazines from 1977 to 1997.

The shift of emphasis in the news can be seen in the reporting of presidential campaigns. In 1968 the average network news sound bite, or continuous speech segment, for presidential candidates was 42.3 seconds. In better than one in five instances networks permitted candidates to appear unedited for a minute or more. By 1988 the average candidate sound bite had shrunk to 9.8 seconds and all were under 60 seconds. By 1996 the average sound bite was only 8.4 seconds. As a consequence, candidates cannot convey much substance; instead, their words are heavily edited to advance the reporter's story.

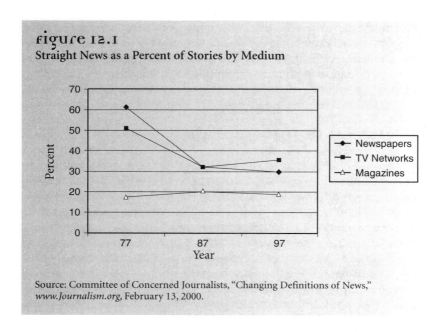

fiǥure 12.1
Straight News as a Percent of Stories by Medium

Source: Committee of Concerned Journalists, "Changing Definitions of News," *www.Journalism.org*, February 13, 2000.

The one constant we have seen in the media's reporting of the political process, whether in their coverage of campaigns, candidates, or institutions of government, is their increasing emphasis on the sensational and dramatic over substance. This led media expert Robert Lichter to comment, during the 1996 presidential campaign, "The real negative campaign this year is being waged by the media. The candidates are talking more about serious issues, but TV reporters spend more time kibbitzing and kvetching than covering what they say. When television tries to arbitrate an election instead of narrating, the voters end up losers."[6]

In an examination of the relationship between the media and voters' evaluations of the economy in 1992, Marc Hetherington found that "the more news voters consumed and the closer they followed the campaign through the media, the worse their retrospective assessments of the economy were."[7] He attributed this to the unchallenged importance of the economy during the campaign, the news media's almost exclusively negative accounts of the economy's performance, and Clinton's and Perot's constant focus on the issue. What was not covered, according to the author, was the recovery from the 1990–1991 recession, which had not been as pronounced as the 1984 recession.[8]

The changes in the content and method of reporting have led Jim Lehrer, among other members of the media, to attribute the media's low public approval ratings in 1998 to "the new blurring of the lines among straight reporting, analysis, and opinion."[9] These critics argue that as the media shift from straight news reporting to analysis of events and opinions, the public is faced with the increasingly difficult task of distinguishing hard news from analysis and opinion.

A second type of blurring, between news and entertainment, results from the scramble for ratings, and ultimately for money that can be charged to advertisers. This has forced news executives to place conflict and entertainment ahead of substance. Daniel Schorr observed that the media's blurring of the lines between fantasy and reality has had a negative effect on the way people view facts and truth.[10] Brit Hume, a former chief White House correspondent for ABC who moved to the FOX News Channel, observed that pieces for ABC's *World News Tonight* were trimmed to the point where "they cut all the context. When that happens, I'm not particularly happy that it's seen by a lot of people."[11]

Cable news networks, in contrast, distinguished themselves in their coverage of the impeachment and trial of President Clinton, for they covered the proceedings gavel to gavel, while most broadcast networks stayed with regularly scheduled daytime soaps. The 2000 presidential campaign was marked by the emergence of two all-news networks—MSNBC and FOX News Channels—that were not factors in the 1996 presidential campaign. MSNBC televised three straight nights of presidential primary debates, and FOX and CNN also carried debates. While the audiences were small by national network standards, the two new cable news channels more than doubled their normal audiences to an estimated 1.6 to 2 million viewers.[12]

The new network news has had a profound impact on the transmission of information, for it suggests that there is no line between entertainment and news. The changes in content and the blurring of the lines between news, entertainment, and analysis have caused many in the public to become skeptical of the media and its motives. For example, as mentioned earlier, ABC's Sunday news program, *This Week with Sam Donaldson and Cokie Roberts*, once concluded with a discussion of likely winners of the upcoming Academy Awards. When George Steinbrenner, the owner of the New York Yankees, appeared on *Seinfeld*, the local CBS affiliate ran this on its evening news. Such occurrences add to public skepticism about the news media.

Media standards

Closely related to content are the standards the media use to guide their judgments of what is newsworthy, as well as what is professional and socially responsible reporting. These standards have always been debated among professional journalists, the public, and those in political life. In 1890 Brandeis and Warren wrote, "Gossip is no longer the resource of the idle and of the vicious, but has become a trade, which is pursued with industry as well as effrontery. To satisfy a prurient taste the details of sexual relations are spread broadcast in the columns of the daily newspapers."[13] The

Lewinsky scandal and subsequent impeachment of President Clinton renewed the debate over what are private and public matters. In the months following the Senate's acquittal of the president, members of the media began to reexamine their coverage, particularly whether they maintained adequate skepticism about their sources.

A study conducted by the Committee of Concerned Journalists sought to ascertain what type of information the media actually provide to the American public, and how well this information is verified. The initial phase of the study, designed by the committee and conducted by the Princeton Research Associates, involved a detailed examination of 1,565 statements and allegations about the Lewinsky story. During the first five days of the story, the committee found, 41 percent of stories had no factual reporting, 40 percent were based on a single anonymous source, and only 1 percent were based on two or more named sources. The authors noted that "so much of the news media culture today involves commenting on the news rather than reporting it that in follow-up coverage, especially on television, the principle of keeping fact separate from suspicion and analysis separate from agenda setting is no longer clearly honored."[14] Another study found only 14 percent of the breaking stories were confirmed by two sources while 33 percent provided single attributions. The remaining 53 percent provided no authoritative attribution.[15]

Table 12.1 summarizes data on media news sources during the initial days of the Lewinsky story. It shows a heavy reliance on unidentified sources, with television and the tabloids being somewhat closer to one another in this regard than print. These data point to two problems in the coverage of the Lewinsky scandal. The media relied heavily on anonymous sources in breaking the story, and the mainstream media did not behave significantly differently from the tabloids in this regard. While the tabloid press was more likely to use named sources, only the evening news programs used more unnamed sources in their reporting. Table 12.1 shows that newspapers and the Associated Press were significantly less likely to offer opinions than the other media.

The committee's study did not consider the tone of the story's presentation. How the media reported the story did not diminish the actions of the president, but it does illustrate that the content of the "news" has significantly changed. These changes led Doris Lynch, political editor of CBS News, to state, "Almost everyone we are talking to [on this story] has an agenda, and I don't think we've been very straightforward with viewers and readers on where that information is coming from and how it might be tainted as a result."[16] The media's failure to report the sources of their information and to identify the bias of these sources, as well as their use of analysis and opinion, contribute to the public's perception of bias in the news.

The coverage of President Clinton's affair was only the most notable in a series of questionable performances by the media. In July 1998 CNN retracted a story that the U.S. military had dropped nerve gas on American defectors in Laos during the Vietnam War. The network's attorney, Fred Abrams,

Table 12.1
Sources and Attributions of the Lewinsky Story by the Media (March 5–6, 1998)

	NAMED	UNNAMED	OTHER MEDIA*	ANALYSIS/ OPINION
Newspapers	32	11	36	21
AP Wire	34	11	44	11
The News Hour	29	0	43	28
Morning news	23	7	42	28
Evening news	31	27	16	27
Print magazines	19	16	21	44
Tabloids	41	21	9	29

*Includes the leak of the Clinton deposition.

Source: Committee of Concerned Journalists, "The Clinton Crisis and the Press: A Second Look," *www.Journalism.org*, October 10, 1999.

reported that the central thesis of the story "could not be sustained."[17] Two of the show's producers were fired, the senior executive producer resigned, and senior correspondent Peter Arnett was reprimanded. *Time* magazine retracted a print version of the story, which it had run as part of a joint venture with CNN. Early in the same week, the *Cincinnati Enquirer* fired a reporter, renounced his series of stories on banana giant Chiquita Brands, and agreed to pay the company $10 million. The stories had alleged that Chiquita bribed foreign officials and used life-threatening pesticides on its fruit. An internal investigation of the series revealed that part of the stories were based on illegally obtained voicemail messages of Chiquita employees.

Finally, in June 1998 both the *New Republic* magazine and the *Boston Globe* newspaper fired writers caught fabricating characters and quotes. First the *New Republic* admitted that it had published more than a dozen stories by Associate Editor Stephen Glass that had been at least partially fabricated. Later in the month *Boston Globe* columnist Patricia Smith resigned after confessing that she had invented both people and quotes to enhance her columns. She had been a Pulitzer Prize nominee and had won the American Society of Newspaper Editors Distinguished Writing Award earlier in the year. All these cases illustrate the pressures to use sensationalism to attract and maintain an audience in today's media environment.

Technological Advances

America's political landscape has always been shaped by the means through which information is transmitted to the public as news. From the days of the early cylinder press through the telegraph, radio, television, and now the Internet, each innovation has helped change the means of mass communication and ultimately altered the political process. The vast changes that occurred as a result of television not only affected how people received their information, but also spawned a new profession—the media consultant. Both politicians and the media must continually readjust to the impact of these changes on American life.

Today's technologies allow information to be distributed to larger and larger areas. People increasingly rely on the newest technologies of the computer and the Internet for information and entertainment.[18] Users must independently evaluate the source, content, and validity of that information. The accessibility of public records, speeches, and specialized sites run by those with a political agenda present a new paradox in politics. There is more information than ever. Political candidates can send citizens direct messages via e-mail and Web sites that are open twenty-four hours a day every day of the week. But there are virtually no checks on that information, making it more difficult for citizens to distinguish between credible and noncredible information.

Just as radio and television altered politics in the 1920s and in the 1960s, the high-tech media of computers, faxes, and e-mails are presently changing the communication process, as well as political life in Washington. The first major change involves the form and method of political communications. As mentioned earlier, candidates and political parties are using telecommunications for money raising, issue advocacy, and political advertisements.

Second, high-tech industries are playing a more visible and aggressive role in Washington. The formation of the political action committee Technology Network (Technet) in 1997 marked a departure from earlier years when such industries kept their distance from Washington and politics. Their efforts have met with success, as they have seen an increase in the number of foreign immigration visas for high-tech workers, a moratorium on collecting sales taxes on the Internet, and passage of a bill that would cap the amount of money awarded in lawsuits resulting from the Y2K computer bug. These industries are also playing a new role in the financing of politics. As Figure 12.2 indicates, there has been a substantial increase in high-tech industry campaign funding since the mid-1990s. During the first nine months of 1999, this sector contributed more than $900,000 to political campaigns. It is evident that in the years ahead, the nature of politics, as well as the entire fabric of American life, is going to significantly be affected by high technology.

These changes have also revived old and persistent questions. One is the question of privacy. Should documents in the medium be protected? Is the

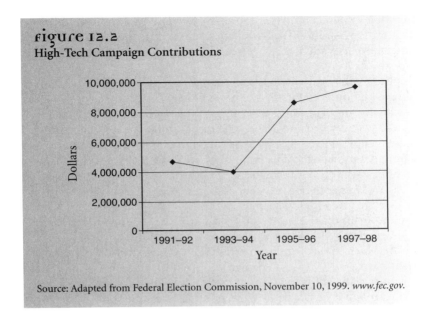

figure 12.2
High-Tech Campaign Contributions

Source: Adapted from Federal Election Commission, November 10, 1999. *www.fec.gov.*

Internet user entitled to privacy? Intel's introduction of the Pentium III microprocessor renewed the national debate about privacy and the use of the computer and the Internet. When the processor was first issued, each included a unique identifier. Privacy advocates feared this was a way for e-commerce sites, as well as anyone else, to obtain personal information about individual owners of computers. Intel later announced that users could determine whether their computers transmitted their identification number to others. All processors would be shipped with transmission in the "off" position; those who wished to have this feature would have to turn it on.

While technological changes have rapidly changed how we receive, process, and respond to political information, they also raise the oldest of questions, and these questions are sure to increase as more Americans adopt these new technologies.

The consequences of change

New methods of communication have been associated with changes in the political environment. As communications have changed, they have altered the message, style, and qualities needed for success as a candidate. The cylinder press and telegraph expanded the printed word, while the radio both increased the audience and altered the methods of campaigns.

Through television, candidates could reach ever larger numbers of people. Talk radio has reinvigorated many sectors of the political spectrum. The Internet has made it easy to research and answer the most obscure questions.

But there are negative aspects to change as well. While information is available in an unprecedented amount and variety, it lacks the cohesiveness and objectivity found in earlier reporting on the political process. The newspapers, radio, and television all provide recognizable formats, but the new media landscape consists of large conglomerates and diffuse sources of information that provide the illusion of diversity. However, the conglomerates have produced political information that is actually homogenized because programs are similar in both content and presentation, and drama and sensationalism are given high priority.

As new forms of communication, primarily the Internet, become more accessible, the citizen is faced with the daunting task of evaluating information that lacks checks and standards. Such information contributes to fragmentation and increases cynicism about politics, the media, and society in general. The ability to present information in a fast and frequently unchecked manner has decreased the public's attachment to the political process and trivialized the information process. Finally, these changes have resulted in a failure in "civic education." Politics is seen as faceless, untrustworthy, and irrelevant to the daily lives of increasingly large numbers of people.

summary

In this chapter we have discussed regulation, sources of information, content, media standards, and technology. It is the last that drives the others. Changes in the media continue at an unprecedented rate as new, more sophisticated forms of communication alter the relationship between citizens and their government. These new means of communications are redefining American politics and supplying new answers to questions that are at the core of the study of politics—who gets what, when, and how? This new information-rich environment will also place a greater burden on citizens, requiring them to be more sophisticated in discerning which information is correct and which is not—a task that will challenge our democracy.

endnotes

[1] Interview with Ben Bagdikian, "News Influenced by Investor's Demand for Profits," *Dallas Morning News*, January 30, 2000:J1.

[2] Pew Research Center Poll, 1996.

[3]MTV does provide news, although it is narrow in scope.

[4]Walt Duka, "Is TV Turning Politics into a Game?" *AARP Bulletin*, 41(February 2000):14.

[5]Committee of Concerned Journalists, "Changing Definitions of News," *www.Journalism.org/laststudy.html*, July 10, 1999.

[6]Center for Media and Policy Analysis, February 29, 1996.

[7]Marc J. Hetherington, "The Media's Role in Forming Voters' National Economic Evaluations in 1992," *American Journal of Political Science*, 40(May 1996):391.

[8]*Ibid.*

[9]Jim Lehrer, "Journalism on the Precipice," *Christian Science Monitor*, October 16, 1998:15.

[10]Duka, *op. cit.*

[11]Ed Bark, "Trading for Air Time, Action," *Dallas Morning News*, March 1, 1999:1C.

[12]Ed Bark, "Cable, Satellite TV Dishing Up Politics Aplenty," *Dallas Morning News*, January 7, 2000:15A.

[13]Louis D. Brandeis and Samuel D. Warren, "The Right to Privacy," *Harvard Law Review*, 4(1890):87–88.

[14]Committee of Concerned Journalists, "The Clinton/Lewinsky Story: How Accurate? How Fair?" *www.journalism.org/DCReport3.html*, January 19, 2000.

[15]Bill Kovack and Tom Rosensteil, *Warp Speed* (New York: The Century Foundation Press, 1999), 100.

[16]*Ibid.*, 2.

[17]United States Internet Council, Washington, D.C., 1999 (*www.usic.org*).

[18]The Pew Research Center for the People & the Press, "Internet Sapping Broadcast News," *www.People-Press.org*, June 6, 2000.

Index

MASS MEDIA AND THE POLITICS OF CHANGE
Edited by Diane Culhane
Production supervision by Kim Vander Steen
Designed by Jeanne Calabrese Design, River Forest, Illinois
Composition by Point West, Inc., Carol Stream, Illinois
Typefaces, Minion and Democratica
Paper, Finch Opaque
Printed and bound by The P. A. Hutchison Company, Mayfield, Pennsylvania